T0178911

Information Evaluation

Information
Evaluation

Edited by
Philippe Capet
Thomas Delavallade

Series Editor
Jean-Charles Pomerol

WILEY

First published 2014 in Great Britain and the United States by ISTE Ltd and John Wiley & Sons, Inc.

ISTE Ltd
27-37 St George's Road
London SW19 4EU
UK

www.iste.co.uk

John Wiley & Sons, Inc.
111 River Street
Hoboken, NJ 07030
USA

www.wiley.com

Library of Congress Control Number: 2013952601

British Library Cataloguing-in-Publication Data
A CIP record for this book is available from the British Library
ISBN 978-1-84821-659-4

Table of Contents

Foreword   xi
Alain JUILLET

Introduction   xvii
Philippe CAPET and Thomas DELAVALLADE

**Chapter 1. Information: Philosophical Analysis and Strategic
Applications**   1
Mouhamadou El Hady BA and Philippe CAPET

    1.1. Introduction   1
    1.2. State of the art in philosophy   2
        1.2.1. History   3
        1.2.2. Information at the crossroads between epistemology
    and philosophy of language   5
    1.3. Information warfare   15
        1.3.1. The role of falsehood and of intentions   17
        1.3.2. Deception, simulation and dissimulation   19
        1.3.3. Addressees of information or the art of communicating . . .   24
        1.3.4. Information warfare as a play on beliefs   25
        1.3.5. Disinformation and associated notions   26
    1.4. Conclusion. Comprehending information in order
    to evaluate it   31
    1.5. Bibliography   32

Chapter 2. Epistemic Trust   35
Gloria ORIGGI

    2.1. Introduction.   35
    2.2. What is social epistemology?   36
    2.3. History of the discipline   39
    2.4. Social epistemology and externalism.   40
    2.5. Realism and constructivism in social epistemology   41
    2.6. Believing other people   43
    2.7. Reductionism and antireductionism.   45
    2.8. Trust and communication.   49
    2.9. Conclusion   51
    2.10. Bibliography   52

Chapter 3. The Fundamentals of Intelligence   55
Philippe LEMERCIER

    3.1. Introduction.   55
    3.2. Information evaluation in the language of intelligence   56
        3.2.1. A context which is not clearly defined, open to multiple
        interpretations.   56
        3.2.2. An informational model historically based on the
        evaluation of information and of sources.   64
    3.3. Attempt to formalize generic models appropriate for
    the new issues facing the intelligence services.   76
        3.3.1. Functional analysis as a support for definition   76
        3.3.2. Paradigm shifts   77
        3.3.3. Attempt at a rigorous definition of intelligence   87
    3.4. Conclusion   99
    3.5. Bibliography   100

**Chapter 4. Information Evaluation in the Military Domain:
Doctrines, Practices and Shortcomings**   103
Philippe CAPET and Adrien REVAULT D'ALLONNES

    4.1. Introduction.   103
    4.2. Presentation of the existing situation   104
        4.2.1. Information evaluation in the intelligence cycle   105
        4.2.2. Reliability and credibility of information   108
    4.3. Illustrative scenario with multi-sourced information.   110

4.4. From an inaccurate definition to an attractive but
unusable concept   112
    4.4.1. Estimation of reliability   112
    4.4.2. Estimation of credibility   115
    4.4.3. Combining dimensions – what is the comparability
    of the ratings?   119
    4.4.4. Raw data, enriched intelligence – can information
    evaluation qualify everything?   121
4.5. A few suggested refinements to information
evaluation techniques   122
4.6. Conclusion and future prospects   124
4.7. Bibliography   125

**Chapter 5. Multidimensional Approach to Reliability Evaluation of
Information Sources**   129
Frédéric PICHON, Christophe LABREUCHE,
Bertrand DUQUEROIE and Thomas DELAVALLADE

5.1. Introduction   129
5.2. Multi-criteria aggregation by the Choquet integral:
application to the evaluation of the reliability of sources   132
    5.2.1. Multi-criteria decision support   133
    5.2.2. Multi-Attribute Utility Theory   134
    5.2.3. Concepts of measurement and construction of
    utility functions   135
    5.2.4. Aggregation function A: limitations of the
    weighted sum   137
    5.2.5. The Choquet integral   138
    5.2.6. Determination of the aggregation function A   139
    5.2.7. Multi-level preference models   140
    5.2.8. Estimation of a degree of reliability via the
    multi-criteria approach   141
5.3. Reliability of sources on Twitter   142
    5.3.1. Twitter   142
    5.3.2. Reliability of sources on Twitter: state of the art   143
5.4. Multi-criteria model for the reliability of Twitter accounts . . .   148
5.5. Conclusion   156
5.6. Bibliography   156

Chapter 6. Uncertainty of an Event and its Markers in Natural Language Processing   161
Mouhamadou El Hady BA, Stéphanie BRIZARD, Tanneguy DULONG
and Bénédicte GOUJON

    6.1. Introduction.   161
    6.2. State of the art   162
        6.2.1. Detection of named entities   162
        6.2.2. Detection of events   164
        6.2.3. Detection of uncertainty   164
    6.3. Model for representing the uncertainty of an event   168
        6.3.1. Named entity model   168
        6.3.2. Event model   168
        6.3.3. Uncertainty model   169
    6.4. Linguistic resources   172
        6.4.1. Technological context   172
        6.4.2. Development and test corpora   172
        6.4.3. Linguistic resources for named entity recognition.   173
        6.4.4. Linguistic resources for event extraction   174
        6.4.5. Linguistic resources for uncertainty extraction.   176
    6.5. Realization   181
    6.6. Conclusions and perspectives   182
    6.7. Bibliography   184

Chapter 7. Quantitative Information Evaluation: Modeling and Experimental Evaluation.   187
Marie-Jeanne LESOT, Frédéric PICHON and
Thomas DELAVALLADE

    7.1. Introduction.   187
    7.2. Formal framework used: possibility theory   190
        7.2.1. Reasons for using possibility theory   190
        7.2.2. Recap of possibility theory   192
        7.2.3. Aggregation operators for possibility distributions   194
        7.2.4. Application to information evaluation.   197
    7.3. Proposed architecture   198
        7.3.1. General principle   199
        7.3.2. Inputs to the process of information evaluation   200
        7.3.3. Evaluation of individual elements   206
        7.3.4. Fusion of individual ratings   209
    7.4. Experimental study   212
        7.4.1. Realistic generation of the uncertainty of a source   213
        7.4.2. Description of the experiments   217

7.4.3. Measures of quality   221
7.4.4. Results   222
7.5. Conclusions   226
7.6. Bibliography   228

Chapter 8. When Reported Information Is Second Hand   231
Laurence CHOLVY

8.1. Introduction   231
8.2. Domains involved and related works   234
  8.2.1. Document mining on the Web   234
  8.2.2. Military intelligence   234
  8.2.3. Analysis of press reports   235
  8.2.4. Modal logic, validity and completeness
  of information sources   236
  8.2.5. Modal logic and modeling of lying   238
8.3. A logical model to decide whether
reported information is credible   239
  8.3.1. Logical formalism   240
  8.3.2. One level of imbrication   241
  8.3.3. Two levels of imbrication   243
  8.3.4. Conclusion about the logical model   245
8.4. Taking account of uncertainty. A model for estimating
the degree of credibility of a reported piece of information   245
  8.4.1. The numerical model   246
  8.4.2. One level of imbrication   247
  8.4.3. Two levels of imbrication   249
  8.4.4. Conclusion about the numerical model   251
8.5. Use of the logical model to generate hypotheses about the
information sources   251
  8.5.1. Motivation   251
  8.5.2. An algorithm to generate responses   253
  8.5.3. Illustration   253
  8.5.4. Conclusion about the generation of hypotheses   254
8.6. Conclusion   255
8.7. Supplements   256
  8.7.1. Main notions of logic   256
  8.7.2. Main notions from the Theory of Evidence   258
8.8. Bibliography   259

**Chapter 9. An Architecture for the Evolution of Trust:
Definition and Impact of the Necessary Dimensions of
Opinion Making**   261
Adrien REVAULT D' ALLONNES

    9.1. Introduction.   261
    9.2. A perspective on trust.   262
    9.3. Dimensions of information evaluation   263
    9.4. General evaluation of the source: reliability.   269
        9.4.1. Evaluation of reliability in the original scenario   270
    9.5. Contextual evaluation of the source: competence   271
        9.5.1. Evaluation of competence in the original scenario   271
    9.6. General content evaluation: plausibility   272
        9.6.1. Evaluation of plausibility in the original scenario   273
    9.7. Contextual content evaluation: credibility   273
        9.7.1. Evaluation of credibility in the original scenario   275
    9.8. Global expression of trust   275
    9.9. Architecture of information evaluation: characteristics   276
        9.9.1. Order of integration of the dimensions   277
        9.9.2. Sequentiality of the information evaluation chain   279
    9.10. Architecture of information evaluation: a description   279
        9.10.1. Reminders about the evaluation of the dimensions   280
        9.10.2. Reliability of the source   280
        9.10.3. Competence and plausibility.   281
        9.10.4. Credibility   282
    9.11. Personalization of information evaluation: modeling levels
    of gullibility   283
        9.11.1. Reliability of the source   284
        9.11.2. Competence and plausibility.   285
        9.11.3. Credibility   287
        9.11.4. Discussion   288
    9.12. Conclusion.   290
    9.13. Bibliography   291

List of Authors   295

Index   297

Foreword

One of the distinguishing features of the 21st Century is the extraordinary expansion of information in all its forms. The possibilities that each and every one of us now has at our fingertips for acquiring knowledge and for keeping track of events would, only a few years ago, have been utterly unimaginable. Long gone are the days of Giovanni Pico della Mirandola, or of the humanist scholars at the University of Paris, who dazzled their contemporaries with the extent of their erudition. Today, with the help of the Internet and a few good technical practices, any student is capable of throwing up open sources of information which would enable him to adequately respond to nearly all the questions posed to those academic giants of yesteryear.

In France, the awareness of the advantage of having the maximum possible amount of data available in order to make the best possible decision has gradually progressed from the military to other spheres since the publication of the *Livre blanc de la défense et de la sécurité nationale* (White Paper on Defense and National Security). In numerous domains of activity, the reading of Sun Tzu's work and the methods and practices of competitive intelligence have revealed that which seemed obvious: mastery of the cycle of selection, acquisition and processing of knowledge useful to a decision-maker provides a defensible – and, above all, long-lasting – competitive advantage. From sporting intelligence to judicial, touristic or cultural intelligence, the provision of information, which has become a reliable fount of knowledge because of processing, opens up untold possibilities in the worldwide competition which has become our daily diet.

Therefore, the notion of information provision, and the way in which it is perceived by the general public, are undergoing major alterations, acquiring positive connotations and breaking out of the "ghetto" to which they have hitherto been confined by our cultural history and certain ideologies. However, this proliferation, which means all now have easy access to information which had previously been the preserve of a select few, carries with it a major risk: some of the information circulating around our various networks is false, incomplete or biased. Furthermore, certain players now have no hesitation in circulating untrue information, to give their side the upper hand in operations of influence, exploiting the faults in our system to their own advantage. For this reason, certain experts estimate that 20% of all information available is incorrect, be it deliberately or unwittingly.

It is undeniable that the mass presence of media in today's world has changed the role of journalists and other information providers. Forced to move fast so as not to be overtaken by his competitors in the publication of the scoop or comment, a journalist no longer has the time to check the reality of the information. He trusts the press agency which provided the initial information, which he supplements with a comment, which will then be added to with other successive comments. All together, these nuggets of information form a highly structured and very interesting multi-faceted whole, the only problem with which will be the lack of trustworthiness of the reality of the initial information. If that information is incorrect, the house of cards collapses. In this case, we have to wait for the completion of the lengthy tasks of investigative journalists, researchers, university students or judges before a clear idea of the initial reality comes to light.

That which has become acceptable in terms of communication, sometimes stemming from misleading of the consumer, is not only unethical; it is unusable for a professional when decisions need to be based on that information for warfare, international politics or business strategy. At that stage, the information needs to be crosschecked and verified, which takes time. Beyond identification of the sources, evaluation of those sources and traditional techniques for valuation drawn from military experience, a multi-dimensional approach is needed for the evaluation of the reliability of those sources. We need to integrate the level of uncertainty of the events into our thought process, and practice creative doubt in order to deal with the changes in level of trust or mistrust.

These procedures, which are necessary – if not absolutely imperative – cause a delay before transmission and diffusion, which puts professional intelligence collection at a disadvantage. Its credibility suffers because of the rapidity of diffusion of the media, whose influencing capacity will often lead a politician or CEO of a company to form a false idea. This may also lead the professional, when faced with the obligation to react quickly, to base his reasoning on erroneous or unconfirmed information. In a world which is constantly reducing reflection time in the interests of immediacy and direct action, analysts therefore have to develop procedures and find tools to help reduce his intervention time without renouncing his fundamental integrity.

Today, in addition to Clausewitz's factors of political and military conflict, economic conflict is a never-ceasing reality in the worldwide competition between the different poles which will structure the world of tomorrow. Faced with this ever more real situation, we are becoming aware of the importance of evaluating information. That is where the merit of this book lies – a book written by recognized experts which forces us to take note of the advantages, constraints and techniques relating to information evaluation. It is time to integrate into all of our organizations and services charged with reflection and preparation of the decision of those in power the requirement that the reliability of the information used be verified.

It is important to remember that information is forged from raw facts, which are untreated and therefore objective data. On the basis of these true or false data, the information is constructed which will circulate between interested parties. Yet it must not be forgotten, in view of the conditions and actions mentioned above, that that information needs to be crosschecked with other information, and it will be necessary to evaluate it in order to draw from it an affirmation, i.e. a credible, identified and evaluated piece of information which can then be used in our reasoning and our strategic and tactical constructs. To remain at the level of the raw information, against the advice of the fervent partisans of total transparency, opens us up to a multitude of errors, whose consequences may sometimes be disproportionately far-reaching.

For reasons probably relating to the individualism and Cartesianism of its citizens, France suffers from a lack of culture of information control, which means that the French are insufficiently inclined to doubt the information given to them. Trusting in their own intellectual capacity, they favor reasoning over information seeking. They have a tendency to take any information given to them as gospel, so long as it is consistent, logical or, worse still, if it supports their philosophical and political convictions. The recent examples of the Arab Spring and the dreadful errors in interpretation to which it gave rise serve as an unfortunate reminder of this.

This is the major difference between French culture and that of the English-speaking world, which includes a high degree of caution, constructed over centuries of practice, and a realism far removed from any sensitivity. It is unsurprising, therefore, that Americans, for instance, work on the different facets of the profession of an analyst to orientate, search for, select and then evaluate the pieces of information that are useful for a decision-maker's thought process. It is interesting to note that in Britain and in the United States, analytical works are very popular, whereas in France, the emphasis is placed on vigilance, playing down the importance of using perspective to define the boundaries of the search, and disregarding evaluation of the pieces of information to filter them by their value and their usefulness.

In the face of the burgeoning torrent of information, the problem is no longer one of finding information, but rather one of being selective about the information we use from the veritable ocean of data at our fingertips. We need to trust in the expertise of an analyst to break down this barrier by zeroing in on what is essential. A far cry from simple deduction, which usually involves extrapolation of the past, the task of an analyst is to use other logical forces based on a process of induction/deduction, broadening the field and the possibilities available to him. Drawing upon a perfect knowledge of the basic dossier created over time and constantly updated, an analyst is capable of interpreting weak signals and detecting changes and trends which facilitate the effective practice of anticipation. At this stage, cognitive software which mimics the behavior of the human brain, and the potential of cyberspace – of which we have only begun to scratch the surface – are extremely promising for the coming years.

The quality of the information selected is dependent on the perfect definition of the context for the search. The efficacy of the evaluation of that information is crucially important for the trust of the people that use it. The speed of transmission is often a determining factor in the successful construction and implementation of a winning strategy. All of this is founded on effective teamwork both in terms of the gathering of information and in terms of its exploitation and use. An analyst will be well aware of this, because his success depends on the availability of good information, the use of effective tools and above all, exchanges and confrontations with other analysts so as to prevent errors caused by his unique thought process and his inability to make a creative breakthrough.

In a world which is increasingly dominated by machines intended to replace human beings by working more quickly and more cheaply, it is comforting to see that in the field of intelligence, the analyst is still irreplaceable. Regardless of the qualities of the tools used, the analyst remains the keystone in the evaluation of the information, without which no serious work can be done. The strength of this book is that it brings that fact home to us, using a methodical and in-depth approach, making it impossible not to become aware of it.

Alain JUILLET

Former Senior Director of Competitive Intelligence
Orrick Rambaud Martel
December 2013

Introduction

I.1. An information society?

The "information society" to which we all now supposedly belong immerses us – or submerges us – in a constant and historically-unprecedented torrent of informational data, whose origins and topics are so different that they become incomprehensible, or at least impossible to organize, memorize, utilize… Nowadays, we spend our entire lives receiving and sending information by telephone, e-mail, Web consultation or SMS…

There is no need to labor the point, so let us now leave aside this type of consideration, and other trivialities that are poorly defined but are bandied about by so many of our thinkers. Assuming it is indeed true that today's society is an information society, then of which other form of society is it the successor? In terms of traditional chronologies, our predecessors lived in an *industrial* society, whose advent is often qualified as a revolution that took place in the 19th Century. If we greatly simplify the changes that were brought about, the revolutionizing factor in yesteryear appears mainly to be the simultaneous development of techniques stemming from scientific discoveries immediately preceding them: the steam boat, the

---

Introduction written by Philippe CAPET and Thomas DELAVALLADE.

locomotive, the electric light bulb, the telephone, the motor car, etc. Significant advances in medicine or agriculture can also be seen to coincide with these new technical means. These inventions, and a great many other scientific breakthroughs, caused considerable changes in demographics, transport, communication and public health services.

Yet, it is noteworthy that with these two sets of factors – technological innovations and practical results – we can systematically associate *measurements*. A steam boat is revolutionary because of the far shorter time it takes to cover a given distance than a sailboat. Similarly, a change in healthcare can be measured by the reduction in infant mortality, increased life expectancy or other quantifiable criteria. A light bulb provides better light over a longer period of time than a candle does (measured in light intensity and seconds), and the evolution in the demographic can be measured overall in terms of numbers of people per unit of time and space (density, population growth, etc.). Put differently, the new society was industrial because of factors which are all, to a greater or lesser extent, measurable.

What can now be said of the "information society", and what would we measure it by? The time each person spends glued to their telephone each day? The power of computers? The number of billion bytes exchanged per day? These measurements would offer absolutely no indication of the switch from one society to another: they still demonstrate a purely industrial evolution in what is called ICT (information and communication technology), and this is not what we mean by "information". The subtext, in fact, is entirely different: we have passed from being a society where material items predominated to another, where the immaterial has – if not overtaken the material – at the very least been shown to be on the rise. However, the question of how to *measure* that immaterial commodity is, *a priori*, unanswered, and therefore presents a challenge.

I.2. From raw information to its evaluation

Yet what is the advantage, and wherefore is there a need to obtain information? Moreover, what is the need to evaluate it?

To the first question, it appears legitimate and natural to respond that *everybody* needs information. In passive terms, *being informed* and *gathering* information is part of a vital necessity shared by all creatures, and could almost be called our seventh perceptory sense. In a very general sense, information is of crucial importance for understanding of the world and for survival within it. An animal is alerted to a danger, to a need to find food or to any situation where its survival is at stake. That alert is delivered to the animal by way of a certain piece of information (a predator in its field of view, a bodily indicator telling the animal of the needs which it has to rectify, etc.). In terms of an active pursuance of information, *seeking to be informed, going in search of* information, represents a precursor to the passive sense. This precursor is usually sufficient but not necessary: it is possible to be informed without wishing to be, i.e. without seeking out information.

Now to the second question, the answer seems even more obvious. In the broadest sense, evaluation seems to be indispensable: a piece of information which has not been evaluated, quite simply, holds next to no interest. When faced with a ferocious predator, the animal's reflex needs not to be identical to that experienced when faced with a seemingly harmless creature that might be a less dangerous potential predator or might even be potential prey. The hunger of which the animal is made aware may be slight or may be critical. In more general terms, the appropriate reaction to the information received stems from evaluation of that information.

Throughout this book, we shall restrict our discussion to the information transmitted and received by a *human being*. Although non-human elements can deliver information (the appearance of the sky informs us about the time of day, a radar informs us about the passage of a missile, the mewling of a cat informs us that it is lost, etc.), in such cases both the transmitter and the receiver will (except with conceptual consideration of the information and with exception made for military intelligence of non-human origin) belong to the species *Homo sapiens*. For this subset of the animal kingdom, information acquires a more special status because of the specific nature of communication, cognition and social life amongst humans.

The *exchange* of information between one individual and another occupies a particularly important place. In such circumstances, one is informed and seeks to be informed, but also informs those around him in return. He then looks for confirmation that the information given has been received and understood, and this to-ing and fro-ing, tacit or otherwise, creates knowledge or belief which is not only shared between the interlocutors, but is common to them.

However, this exchange of information does not always take place: it may be deliberately cut short. Understood in the typical sense rather than in Shannon's theoretical sense, and excluding some of the nuanced meanings of the word, information certainly engages at least two individuals. Information is created, obtained, sought, in the wake of a move to inform another, or to be informed. With regard to the first verb here – "to inform another", an active construct – a source, a transmitter, informs somebody else about something. The information thus created and possibly received therefore gives rise to an addressee who, if the attempt to inform is even partially successful, is in fact a receiver. Yet with the second verb – "to be informed", a passive construct – both the transmitter and the receiver already exist: the agent being informed seeks out a piece of information, and thereby becomes the receiver or seeks to be so, and this quest is accompanied by a search for transmitters who hold the piece of information in question. To read the daily newspaper is to inform oneself (to be informed) about the news or events which have happened, of which the journalists are the transmitters, in the same way as looking for the definition of a word in a dictionary is aimed – with a more specific intention – at informing oneself by consulting the compiler of that book. Thus, an agent who informs or who is informed is alternatingly a transmitter or a receiver – the informer or the informed. It is important to take account of this nuance in an age when the amount of transmitted and received information has undeniably burgeoned. It is for this reason that we can indeed speak of an information society, although this absolutely does not mean that the industrial society has been left behind – far from it, in fact: it is the unwavering persistence of the industrial society which has facilitated this increase.

As an example which is constantly but legitimately repeated, the development of the Internet – by way of personal or institutional Websites which it has become childsplay to create, its micro-blogging gateways and other associated social media – favors democratic diffusion and reception of information. Practically anyone can contribute equally – be it a government or an individual. The explosion of the Internet also amplifies the quantity of information, because the number involved in its promulgation is reaching similar levels to the population of the planet. In a military context, which is where this book primarily fits in, a subtle ploy by the exchange of falsified information becomes easier, and perhaps more tempting: not only in State-to-State conflicts – i.e. symmetrical or dissymmetrical conflicts – but also in confrontations between non-governmental entities (sometimes only one individual) and a State – i.e. conflicts which were originally asymmetrical (e.g. cyber-terrorism in support or indoctrination of physical terrorism) but which are becoming symmetrical because of the sudden equality between the competitors. By contrast with the biblical fable, David's defeat of Goliath would seem triflingly easy. However, this democratization of access to, and especially of creation, exchange and promulgation of information, however propitious for equality it may initially seem, presents the opposite of an in-differentiation of information sources: now nothing at all is certain *a priori*; we know neither the intention nor the aim pursued by a source in the field where a piece of information is expressed. Quite unlike that which might have been expected, the pieces of information received – because of the very way in which they are received and the amplification of their volume – inspire doubt rather than confidence. When information is received, the value of its sources as well as the quality of the information those sources are actually giving, are more or less unknown. Therefore, if an active or passive receiver wishes to make gainful use of that information, it has become a prerequisite to evaluate its quality in one way or another.

I.3. The precedence of the military world

Quite apart from its humorous aspect, the classic saying that military intelligence is "the second-oldest profession in the world" is most appropriate in terms of emphasizing the antediluvian nature of the practice, and its place in the history of the human race. It is even more crucial to obtain information about the enemy in the context of a conflict or a war than it is in more peaceful situations: the military capabilities of the enemy, their intentions, priorities and goals are factors, knowledge of which is invaluable and must be acquired as fully as possible if we want to win the battle. However, this set of information is of very little interest if it conveys only estimations tainted with inaccuracy. In particular, information fed to the person making decisions to direct the conflict needs to carry a certain *weight*, and to be comparable in some way with a different piece of information, which may contradict the first one. We shall see in this book that modern-day armies have attempted to circumscribe certain concepts associated with these necessities, related to the usage which must be made of the information. For a given piece of information, the terms *"reliability"* of the source and *"credibility"* of the content have, for several decades, been used as standard within the armed forces; the quantification of these notions is called *information evaluation*. It is important that the reader become familiar with this terminology now in the introduction to the book, as it will appear on nearly every page thereafter.

As follows from our opening discussion about the advent of the Internet, when any piece of information is received, it goes without saying that the question of its credibility and of the reliability of its source is posed, and there is nothing at all new about this attitude on the part of an information receiver, whatever the context may be. In the context of information-gathering with a strategic, diplomatic or military goal, this question is posed with far more acuity, and historical examples are plentiful. However, it is only very recently that a *degree of confidence* has been given as a result of that evaluation, based on a *scale* which needs to be determined at the outset. There is an almost explicit mention of this technique in a spy novel, an extract of which is given below. The protagonist has a stolen encoded diary from an individual involved in a vast geopolitical operation to spark off the First World War. Once he has decoded the diary, his observation is as follows:

"He stuck down his authorities, too, and had an odd trick of giving them all a numerical value and then striking a balance, which stood for the reliability of each stage in the yarn. The four names he had printed were authorities, and there was a man, Ducrosne, who got five out of a possible five; and another fellow, Ammersfoort, who got three."

The author himself employs the words "balance", "reliability" and "numerical value" – they are not terms of our invention. From this extract, we can see that the protagonist understands immediately from this single reading that these scores correspond to the *value* of the person in question – rather than, say, his importance within the network, which might (at first glance) appear more natural. It is as if the scale representing the reliability of a source were fully developed even at that time, and an astute observer were able at once, in spite of the scant indications, to see what it referred to.

However – and this is particularly surprising – the novel in question dates from… 1915. John Buchan is the author of *The Thirty-Nine Steps*, from which this extract is taken[1] – the novel which inspired the well-known Alfred Hitchcock movie of the same name. To our knowledge, this is the first historical reference – a century old – to such a scale for the reliability of a source. It is far from inconsequential that it is to be found in the context of military intelligence operations; more than the general world, the "world" of information evaluation historically regards intelligence-gathering as being *the single oldest* profession.

This historical antecedence and the necessities peculiar to the military domain lead to a conceptualization of information evaluation that is more advanced than in any other domain, and that inspires certain domains. For instance, competitive intelligence, which is extremely active and current, has undeniably borrowed from concepts and methods in the world of defense, from whence the main proponents of these new approaches in economic strategy also come. In line with the origin of information evaluation, this book may be considered to be "military-centered": the examples and solutions

---

1 BUCHAN J., The Thirty Nine Steps, House of Stratus, p. 35, 2001.

offered in its chapters refer mainly to a use context in defense. However, this is absolutely not to say that the reader needs to be familiar with a military context or come from a military background: it will be perfectly easy for him to simply transpose the discussion to his own areas of interest.

I.4. The French project CAHORS

CAHORS (*Cotation, Analyse, Hiérarchisation et Ontologies pour le Renseignement et la Sécurité* – Information Evaluation, Analysis, Hierarchization and Ontologies for Intelligence and Security) was a multidisciplinary project, funded by France's National Research Agency and run between 2009 and 2012. It was spearheaded by the two co-editors of this book, written immediately in the project's wake, with six partner entities from the spheres of industry, education and academic research.

Figure I.1. *Logo of the CAHORS project*

As suggested by the name, information evaluation constituted the origin and the heart of the project, oriented toward applications in defense and security. Although the dawn of information transfer and the new means, available to one and all, to play a part, largely justified the conception of such a project, these circumstances of our age were secondary, in the context of an attempt to resolve issues which predate these circumstances by millennia. A large portion of the project was, undeniably, rooted in the modern world, given the use of modern techniques, and neither the project's premises nor its results are supposed to be applicable to former times; nevertheless, the three keywords in its name (information-evaluation, defense and security) correspond to concerns that go back a very long way beyond modern times.

From the very outset, and throughout its progression, the project has always been *multi-* and *transdisciplinary*. As philosophy, logic and linguistics play a pivotal role therein, supplemented by ageless military and security considerations, one facet of the project does not relate closely to new practices or current techniques. The other facet is based on the development of computer technology, Natural Language Processing (NLP) and the military needs of the most recent decades, and in that sense it remains firmly anchored in contemporary society. One of the major challenges was to bring these two facets of the project together, and create harmony between disciplines and considerations that are not necessarily conflicting, but which ordinarily never come into contact with one another. In other words, with regard to the two facets mentioned here, CAHORS took a *logico-philosophical* direction to perform a sort of *artificial intelligence*, which here means semi-automation of the task of intelligence-gathering so as to relieve analysts from the field of tedious tasks.

I.5. A fictitious scenario to illustrate the chapters

I.5.1. *Function of the scenario*

For the purposes of this book, a fictitious scenario has been imagined, in which information plays a key role. The primary advantage to this scenario is that it establishes a guiding thread running through the book, for the benefit both of the writers and the readers: the illustrative or argumentative examples function on a common basis.

In addition, this scenario has been put in place in the interest of neutrality of the contexts mentioned. The scenario is devoid of any reality – although this does not reflect on the likelihood of such a scenario occurring – and through it, the chapters are more unified as a coherent whole than they would otherwise have been. The dates of the events and eras in the history fabricated here are left as indeterminate, which means the book has a perennial quality because it is timeless. Notwithstanding, the data in the scenario are easy to apply to a given situation in the present or the past in many corners of the world. The source of inspiration has been adjusted – amongst other reasons so as to allow the use of contemporary means of emission and transmission of information, particularly *via* the *Web*. This basic scenario was communicated to the chapter authors at the very beginning of the writing of the book, although of course, they were given the full freedom to preserve it exactly as it was, to enrich it as need be depending on the subject and needs of the chapters, or to ignore it entirely if no use needed to be made of it.

I.5.2. *Presentation of the scenario*

Located in the Middle East, Ektimostan is a small, secular State, with the city of Dagbas being its capital. The country comprises a veritable mosaic of small, overlapping regions holding antagonistic religious convictions. The governmental regime has been able to subdue these previously violent blind conflicts, but beneath the surface they are still boiling – all the more so because neighboring countries ostensibly provide support to some of these religious factions, often leading to the ramping up of the religious conflicts. Therefore, for decades, there have been very real tensions setting Ektimostan against some of its neighbors – sometimes for religious reasons, but usually for political and strategic ones.

Of apparently benign capacities on a global scale, and apart from the aforementioned border micro-tensions, Ektimostan is the subject of sustained attention from foreign countries: its geographical position directly between areas dominated by major powers, and the diplomatic and geopolitical adroitness of its leaders have lent the country a crucial place on the global chessboard. Thus, it is strategically allied with certain large powers, and closely watched with mistrust by others. In economic terms, Ektimostan is rich in crude oil and natural gas reserves, but its industry is still dependent on other countries – particularly its defense industry.

Having held power for a great many years, Colonel al-Adel governs the country with an iron fist. His Minister of the Interior and chief of the secret police, Balldar, has become the Number Two of the regime. However, in the spring, the whole of the surrounding region experienced a violent and contagious period, with the incumbent leaders being challenged by demonstrations and then uprisings, and eventually being overthrown. Ektimostan, which was not originally affected by movements of this sort, is in turn beginning to experience instability: accusing him of authoritarianism, opponents of al-Adel sporadically stage revolts for various reasons. The situation is worsening, as other States offer their support – either openly or covertly – to one or other of the camps (the legitimate government or the factious fighters).

As these conflicts grow in magnitude, certain regions of Ektimostan begin to fall under control of the insurgents. In parallel, a mysterious group supporting this revolt emerges in a foreign capital. This group, under the direction of a man named Usbek – a dissident who left the country over ten years ago, claims to be a neutral pacifier of the insurrection, and creates a press agency, the *Ektimostan Free Press* (EFP), which soon becomes an authoritative source of information for certain countries: its communiqués are taken up in foreign fields without the local media appearing overly concerned about checking the reliability of the event that triggered their transmission. Usbek is suspected, by the Ektimostan regime, of being the true initiator of the revolts, and his neutrality is regularly called into question.

In Ektimostan itself, Captain Ixil is the leader of the heteroclite opposition coalition, called the *Free Resistance of Dagbas* (FRD), which is the opposition force tacitly recognized by Usbek and his EFP, and by several leaders of foreign powers. In addition to his role as leader, Ixil also acts as the spokesperson for his movement, and claims responsibility for its actions in video recordings on online filesharing sites, whose origin is masked. Ixil is also responsible for a sort of belligerent propaganda on the same Websites. According to Ektimostan's official press and al-Adel's discourse, the guerilla force is supported by Usbek and his group, who supply it with arms, ammunition, money and possibly military personnel providing training and tactical support. Usbek, *via* his press agency, has always denied these accusations.

In terms of the media and technology, there is no real freedom of the press in Ektimostan, while Usbek's group claims to represent a diverse range of opinions and to be neutral in the internal conflict, the

Press Ektimo-Agency (PEA) is the official press agency in Ektimostan, and Usbek's *Ektimostan Free Press* (EFP) frequently contradicts the information diffused by the PEA. The activities of internet users are heavily monitored in Ektimostan by Minister Balldar's teams, and certain dissident bloggers have already been arrested.

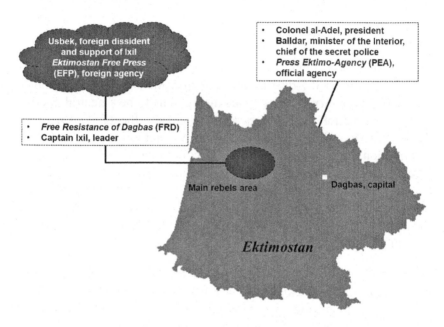

Figure I.3. *Geography and political situation of Ektimostan*

On 31 May, there is a bomb attack in the capital Dagbas, not far from the Ministry of the Interior, killing 26. Responsibility for the attack has not been claimed. For once, the FRD forces have not published a triumphant communiqué on the Web. Could this have been staged, with al-Adel himself being behind the operation? Is it possible that motives other than the political revolts are to blame for the attack, such as the settling of personal grievances? Is there a different group of opposition fighters – a splinter group from the FRD or a group newly created to carry out more radical actions? Could the bombing be the work of a counter-regime Ektimostanian terrorist movement that is not related to the uprising? There may be a very great many potentially-viable hypotheses, but al-Adel's regime officially holds only one: the FRD is guilty, and therefore so too, indirectly, is Usbek.

On this reinvented planet, on a different continent, the news in another country seizes our attention at this point, precisely because it has nothing to do with the troubles in Ektimostan. The Republic of Realleo is constantly experiencing round after round of military *coups d'état*. General San-Gerio and General Quieto replace one another time and again depending on which military junta is in power. whenever one is in power, the other wages a guerilla war from the forests of the country to take it back. Terrorist actions are regularly carried out by both factions against one another. These keywords – *attack* and *terrorism* – which are common to the situations in two geographically distant areas, are not at all likely to lead a human observer reading his newspaper to error; is the same true, though, for natural language processing tools?

From an informational point of view, with regard to the attack in Dagbas, various reports are emitted, in chronological order, by diverse sources and through various forms of media:

– on 31 May, just after the attack, Minister Balldar, chief of the secret police, declares that "the so-called *Free Resistance of Dagbas* could be involved in this morning's attack";

– on 1 June, Captain Ixil, head of the rebels in the field, asserts that "the *Free Resistance of Dagbas* is not responsible for the attack in Dagbas on 31 May";

– on 2 June, Colonel al-Adel affirms that "the terrorists from the western regions of our country are responsible for the attack in Dagbas on 31 May";

– on 3 June, al-Adel makes a provisional assessment of the result and vigorously states that "no fewer than 26 people were killed in the cowardly attack in Dagbas on 31 May";

– elsewhere, on 5 October of the same year, General San-Gerio, engaged in a guerilla war against General Quieto who is then in power in Realleo, declares "I claim full responsibility, and do so a hundred times over, for the attack in the capital of our country on 10 September against the tyrant."

I.5.3. *A scenario adaptable to each chapter, and a guiding thread for the book*

As we can easily see, the different elements of information are emitted with a greater or lesser degree of certainty: we may find adverbs or verbal moods which may be more or less categorical depending on the speaker or the date of a given speech act. The emitters of the information are far from neutral: a chief of secret police, an authoritarian leader and a renegade are liable to be suspected of partiality, or to use tricks of influence, disinformation, propaganda, etc. In addition, this news is, for the most part, not communicated directly to the populace: an intermediary channel is needed, such as a press agency, a newspaper, a more or less reliable Website or a television program to transmit the news, and these intermediaries are not necessarily neutral either: they may be in the pocket of power, as is the *Press Ektimo-Agency*, or possibly freer or even vigorously opposed to the regime. Other protagonists may come into play by other means, *via* social media or weblogs which may be more or less closely monitored by the regime in place. Thus, there are so-called *open* sources of information, meaning that they transmit public information that is accessible to one and all, but also *covert* sources such that espionage can use them, and they produce information intended for a specific receiver and (in theory) no-one else.

As we can see, the situations may be extremely varied, and involve any number of diverse agents, objectives and maneuvers. The "remodeling" that is therefore possible, and the enrichment of the basic scenario, mean examples can be constructed for any of the chapters as per the needs of the particular subject.

In all the cases used, whose basis we have just described, evaluation of the reliability of the source and the credibility of the information enter into the equation, in that when seeking to gain a genuine idea of the true culprit behind the 31 May attack, the origin and originator of the information, its taking up and relaying, its likelihood, the aims that it suggests, the patterns and ploys which may underlie it are all factors which could help in the formation of an opinion. Because of its diverse facets, the guiding scenario serves to illustrate how the information can be evaluated on the basis of these and other factors.

I.6. Division of the book

The book is divided into two main sections: firstly a theoretical part ("concepts and requirements"), and secondly a more practical and prospective part ("methods and perspectives"). The combination of these two viewpoints – which do not obviously appear to be mutually complementary – is achieved by cross-referencing between the chapters and shared bibliographical sources.

The book as a whole can be read in a variety of ways. To begin with, it presents a progression in the distribution of the chapters: the book moves from concepts regarding information to the need to evaluate it, before going on to discuss the methods by which we propose to serve that need; the whole therefore represents a set of perspectives, not only to fine-tune the methods discussed herein and to extend evaluation to other domains, but also to touch on other potential information processing techniques to be applied once it has been evaluated. In that respect, the book can be read with a certain degree of continuity. On the other hand, though, each chapter is largely intended and able to stand alone within the book: the reader may perfectly well choose to focus on chapters in those domains with which he is familiar first of all, or – on the contrary – by curiosity or *a priori* interest, choose those whose subjects are unfamiliar or totally unknown to him. Given that we have attempted to cater for both a specialized readership and a broader cultivated audience, the chapters should be read in whatever order the reader deems appropriate. However, in spite of this autonomy of the chapters, nearly all of them refer to other chapters in the book for an in-depth discussion of a topic which is deliberately only briefly touched upon. In that respect, we hope, the book escapes from any strict division, and acquires a certain harmony, which the fictitious example outlined above is only one means of achieving among others.

I.6.1. *Concepts and requirements*

The opening chapter deals with the initial question of information, as viewed by philosophers. Strange as it may seem, this concept was not subject to any philosophical reflection until the latter half of the 20th Century, in the wake of Shannon's work. The chapter retraces this timeline, and explains the various positions adopted at different times, and contemporary developments. Then, information viewed as a weapon in a real or a virtual war is examined in the light of these earlier philosophical musings.

The second chapter stays with the area of philosophy, focusing this time on the notion of trust – in this case epistemic trust, i.e. trust relating to knowledge. The trust lent to an individual is very closely linked to the estimation of reliability attached to that individual, and the two terms could almost be considered to be synonymous. The chapter concentrates on the relationship between trust and information, between belief and knowledge. A secondary discussion highlights the patterns which can be used to award, if not a score, at least a place to the reliability of a source, based on the extent of the trust afforded to that source.

In Chapter 3, the focus turns to information evaluation from the professional point of view of intelligence. Contemplating the landscape of this profession where information evaluation alone only lies in a few points, the chapter outlines a model of intelligence in all the senses attached to it by military doctrines. Information evaluation is one stage in a phase of processing and exploitation of the information to render it usable in intelligence. Here it forms one of the various starting points for the development of the model.

Chapter 4 deals with a similar area, but focuses on information evaluation as part of a cycle of intelligence activities. Doctrines – both French ones and those stemming from NATO's conceptual work – that are devoted to information evaluation certainly enrich reflection on the subject, but quickly become frustrating for an attentive reader because of the insufficiencies or even contradictions (so as not to say absurdities) they contain. The aim here is to establish a cogently-argued list to open the way to a more-or-less coherent definition of information evaluation and the methods it involves.

I.6.2. *Methods and perspectives*

In Chapter 5, we focus on how to measure the reliability of information sources. There is an abundance of academic literature on this subject, if we look at it from a formal perspective. The chapter proposes a different method: aggregation by the Choquet integral of dimensions which give a reading of reliability, borrowing from applied work in a number of fields; here, the originality lies in the taking into account of multiple factors and analyst preferences when estimating reliability. One application of the method could be an examination of Twitter accounts, which is the example used here.

The sixth chapter answers some of the theoretical and technical questions surrounding the quantification of the semantic uncertainty expressed in a sentence, a paragraph, a text, attempting to establish this by semi-automated means. Natural Language Processing (NLP) has become a recognized discipline in its own right, which offers methods by which to overcome the difficulties introduced by languages, not to a person but to a machine designed to learn how to detect and process the underlying uncertainty in a vernacular text. A tool which combines computer science and linguistics is presented by way of example.

The seventh chapter discusses the fundamental results of the original project. The formal stages are described with a view to segmenting the process of information evaluation, with the aim being to provide a response other than a binary (yes/no) one to the question "Did a particular event take place?" by supplementing the response with a degree of confidence. Overall, the chapter gives a discussion of the theory employed in the project – possibility theory – and the reasons why this theory was chosen. An experimental evaluation of the model is also presented, using a new protocol. The whole of the process constructed may have applications other than in defense and security, and may be enriched and experimented with by specialists in the potential domains.

Next, Chapter 8 deals with a crucial issue in a world where reported speech occupies a very important place: the term *media* is not without implication – there is indeed a *medium* which is intercalated generally between an initial source of information and us as receivers. The reliability of the man who has heard the man who heard the source of the information cannot be reduced to the combination of the reliability scores of the intermediaries. Here we need to study the levels of reliability which stem from these intermediary relations.

The ninth and final chapter looks at the formalization of the process of building confidence, and then its evolution. In response to Chapter 4, and to resolve the problems manifesting themselves in the most clearly established military doctrines of all domains of application, the chapter discusses how we can trust a piece of information, and the way in which we form an opinion of it, irrespective of the truth of the fact which it reports. A model for the construction and evolution of trust is therefore put forward.

I.7. Acknowledgments

First and foremost, we extend our thanks to those French state organisms which helped us to bring the CAHORS project to fruition. Next, the writing of several chapters by authors who were not involved in the project has enriched the book, enabling it to provide a broader view of the issue of information evaluation, not only facilitating the exploration of multidisciplinary avenues, but particularly extending the range of domains which still remain to be explored. We are very grateful to these collaborators.

We owe heartfelt thanks to Jean-Charles Pomerol for accepting this book into the ISTE–Wiley collection. We also wish to thank Ben Engel, who translated each of the chapters - which cover a wide range of fields with specific vocabulary - quickly and efficiently.

Finally it must be made clear that those people mentioned above should not be held responsible if ever the reader, in disappointment, gives this book a poor score in his *evaluation of the information* transmitted by the collection of chapters. We and we alone are responsible for its content.

Chapter 1

Information: Philosophical Analysis and Strategic Applications

1.1. Introduction

Nowadays, it is commonly considered that we live in an information society. Our civilization is abundantly fed by information and communication technology (ICT). In the military context, information has always been an invaluable and sought-after commodity to which special services are devoted. Leaders in all sorts of contexts – particularly military – have, for centuries, been aware of the importance of information. It is all the more paradoxical that in the area of philosophy, thinkers have largely ignored the concept of information. It appears only incidentally in philosophers' writings. It was not until thermodynamics, cybernetics and mathematical theorization of information took off that philosophers finally became interested in it, and even then, it was difficult to find a structured theorization centered on the notion of information.

In this chapter, we shall focus primarily on two aspects of this topic. To begin with, we shall look at the definition of an operational concept of information. In order to do so, following a brief state of the

Chapter written by Mouhamadou El Hady BA and Philippe CAPET.

art on current thinking about the notion of information, we turn our attention more specifically to the genealogy of the term, before going on to discuss two of the three thinkers whom we believe are the most important in the area of philosophy of information: Paul Grice and Fred Dretske. The work of these two philosophers will help to sculpt the precise definition of what information is, which will then be used in the second part of this chapter.

In this second part, we shall focus on the military domain, and see how the concept of information is used in that domain. In doing so, we shall present and critique the ideas of the third great contemporary thinker on information: Luciano Floridi.

Let us make it clear right now that while these philosophers help us to refine the concept of information which we shall use throughout this book, our ideas differ from theirs on a crucial point, because we reject the *alethic* conception of information – i.e. the idea that information must necessarily be *true*.

1.2. State of the art in philosophy

It is noteworthy that in the esteemed French reference dictionary of philosophical vocabulary – the Lalande – the term "information" does not appear. The work includes only the entry "to inform", which is given in the scholastic sense – that of "giving shape to, organizing matter". This view of the term comes directly from Plato's *Timaeus*, where the demiurge imposes order on a disorganized physical world by giving it a form reflecting the order reigning over the world of Ideas. Apart from this primary meaning of the verb "to inform", the Lalande recognizes a derived meaning, which is: "making somebody aware of something". Granted, the Lalande dates from 1927, but none of the later editions, including that from 2006, have the entry "information" – at least not in the body of the text. It is only half a century after the Lalande first appeared that the tenth edition included a separate supplement containing the entry "information". It is given a meaning derived from cybernetics: "an element of knowledge conveyed by a message which is its vehicle and of which it constitutes the meaning" [LAL 06]. In this definition, we can see the hallmarks of the work of Shannon. The persistent practice of affording only a very limited place to the concept of information in a philosophical dictionary which is highly influential – at least in the French-speaking world – highlights the recent and underdeveloped nature of the philosophy of information. It should be noted that this neglect of the concept of information is not specific to the French-speaking world. If we look at Simon Blackburn's *Oxford Dictionary of Philosophy* [BLA 08], we discover that even the second edition, revised in 2008, does not contain an entry for *Information*. It only has an entry for *Information theory*. This gives an indication of why philosophers gradually lost their indifference toward the concept of information during the latter half of the 20th Century. The domain known as "philosophy of information" first developed thanks to cybernetic research and the Mathematical Theory of Communication (MTC), then moved forward in the wake of philosophical explorations of the concepts of meaning and knowledge, and finally flourished due to the current development of the so-called "information society".

1.2.1. *History*

The Lalande shows that, historically, the word "information" arose later than the verb "to inform", from which it is derived.[1] In the work of both Plato and Aristotle, there is the idea that information is necessary for the passage of the *materia prima* from pure potentiality to actuality. This would remain the prevailing definition from Ancient times until the 17th and 18th Centuries, with the British empiricists (John Locke, David Hume). It is thanks to these empiricists that the verb "to inform" lost its original meaning and came to be understood in its current sense. The empiricists, abandoning the rationalistic credence whereby our minds come into this world already holding some innate ideas, attempted to explain how these ideas come into being. If the mind is not informed in advance, i.e. if it is not molded into a *form*, by the demiurge who leaves his mark upon it, imposing his seal which is constituted by innate ideas [DES 92], then we need a

---

1 For a detailed discussion of the history of the word "information" and its uses in Greek and Latin literature, we refer to [CAP 03], a version of which is available online at: http://www.capurro.de/infoconcept.html#Studies.

theory about the origin of our ideas. The choice of the empiricists, led by Locke [LOC 90] was to consider the mind as a blank slate upon which the world itself inscribes ideas when we interact with it. The second sense of the verb "to inform" and the notion of information as it is understood nowadays came from these considerations. The human mind is not naturally informed by any sort of demiurge; it receives its form from the outside world, which leaves its mark upon it. When we interact with the external world, it transmits to our mind some knowledge about reality. That is to say that the world *informs* our mind by imbuing it with certain ideas, certain knowledge. This gives us the derived meaning of the verb "to inform", which no longer means simply "to model" or "to mold", but also "to convey knowledge". Information, therefore, is no longer merely the act consisting of shaping a material object, but also the thing that is conveyed during the production of ideas. This second sense of the word "information" is the prevailing one now, and is the one of interest to us here.[2]

In spite of the introduction of this second sense of the word "information" by the empiricists, it should be noted that no "philosophy of information" worthy of that title would develop at that time. Information was to remain a blind spot for philosophy and epistemology until the latter half of the 20th Century. In the 19th Century, there would be a tacit revival of thinking about information, with the work done on thermodynamics, and in particular the link, demonstrated by Boltzmann in 1894, between entropy determined by the second law of thermodynamics and the amount of information accessible. In the 1950s, Claude Shannon used Boltzmann's work as the basis for the first mathematically rigorous definition of the concept of information. Paradoxically, it was only in the wake of Shannon's work that philosophers began to turn their attention to the notion of information. Of these philosophical works, particular mention ought to be given to the distinction drawn by Paul Grice between natural meaning and non-natural meaning, the use of the notion of information by Dretske in support of an externalist

---

2 It should be understood that for the time being, we are not formally defining the notion of information, but simply giving a preliminary analysis which we will improve once we have examined the relevant philosophical literature.

epistemology, and the recent work of Luciano Floridi, who has truly revivified the field of philosophy of information (PI).

1.2.2. *Information at the crossroads between epistemology and philosophy of language*

There are two main philosophical domains wherein the notion of information plays a crucial role: philosophy of language and naturalized epistemology. In philosophy of language, an important question is how to define the meaning of the expressions of the language. How can we say that someone understands a word or an expression? Shall we rely on behavioral indicators? Is to understand a sentence to be able to translate it into another language? For technical reasons neither of these solutions were satisfactory. This problem was solved by Donald Davidson[3], who posited that to understand an expression is to be able to state its truth conditions: this is the truth-conditional conception of semantics. In Davidson's view, the purpose of language is to provide us with information about the state of the world. Knowing the truth conditions of an expression is to know what state of the world would render that expression true. We can therefore consider that all expressions inform us about the state of the world. Hence, comprehension is nothing other than reception of the information encoded in language. One might therefore have expected logicians and philosophers of language who accepted a truth-conditional view of semantics to develop a school of thought centered on the notion of information. It did not happen. It was not until Dretske[4] reflected upon Paul Grice's work (see [GRI 89]) that information came in, one might say through a hidden door, to philosophy of language and epistemology.

1.2.2.1. *Meaning and information in Grice's work*

It is precisely because Grice did not blindly accept the conventional view held by analytical philosophers – according to which "the essential business of language is to assert or deny facts" [RUS 22] – that he reintroduced the notion of information to

---

3 See [DAV 67].
4 See [DRE 81; DRE 95; DRE 00; DRE 08].

philosophy of language, albeit in a roundabout way. In a 1957 article, he revisited the notion of meaning. As an ordinary language philosopher, he refuted the thesis according to which the only legitimate use of language was to describe states of the world that can be evaluated. He distinguishes two notions of meaning, of which he says the following two utterances are paradigmatic:

1) Those spots mean measles;

2) Those three rings mean that the bus is full.

Grice shows that the notions of meaning at play in the first and the second example are very different. If we consider the first example, the link between the spots and the measles infection is automatic and indisputable. For instance, it would be nonsensical to say "those spots mean measles but there is no measles infection". If the eruptions of the skin are indeed indicative of measles, their link with the disease is such that it is impossible to have them without being afflicted with measles. Furthermore, as Grice notes, it is impossible to deduce from "those spots mean measles" the consequence "measles is meant by those spots". Note that such a deduction would be entirely possible in the example of the bus, where we can understand sentence (2) as being equivalent to "the driver means, by those three rings, that the bus is full and about to depart".

Grice refers to the first sense of the verb *to mean* as *natural meaning*. In natural meaning, there is an unbreakable link between the two things being connected. One of these terms is an indicator of the other. The presence of a certain type of spots necessarily indicates that the person bearing them is infected with measles. In the case of natural meaning, it is (so to speak) intrinsically that the subject indicates the occurrence of what is meant. Hence, it would be contradictory to affirm at the same time that A means B and that A is occurring without B being the case. This is what led Dretske, commenting on this notion, to say that "natural meaning is information" [DRE 08]. Because natural meaning expresses an inalienable linking of two different things, it *is information*. This enables us to establish an initial link between the notions of meaning and information. One might, at first glance, imagine that meaning and information are one and the same thing, as suggested by considering only natural meaning. If we take account of the indicative link which exists within natural meaning, we can test whether the connection characteristic of the notion of natural meaning is always true. If, for instance, I say that the number of rings in a tree trunk indicates the age of the tree, I am saying that those rings give us information about the age of that tree, and that the age calculated using this method is always correct. The number of rings therefore literally *means* the age of the tree. Now let us look at the second sense of meaning envisaged by Grice to clarify the notion of information.

We saw earlier that in the case of a ringing tone on a bus, it is possible to deduce from the sentence "Those three rings mean that the bus is about to depart" the sentence "Somebody is indicating, by those three rings, that the bus is about to depart". Therein lies the main difference between natural meaning, which associates a symptom with its cause, thus giving us *objective information*, and the second sort of meaning Grice examines. In this second sort of meaning, the correlated variation between the two entities being linked is mediated by the human mind. There is necessarily a person who is using one entity to indicate the other. If, for instance, the public transport company instructs its drivers to ring three times to signal that the bus is full, that triple ring will come to *mean* that the bus is full. Each time a person who is aware of the local mores hears those three rings, he will inevitably understand that the bus is full. However, as Grice stresses, in this case there is not necessarily any causal link between the fact that the bus is full and the three rings. For example, there is no contradiction in exclaiming that "Those three rings mean that the bus is full, but the bus is only half full!" In the case of natural meaning, there is an impossibility of having A without having B given that A *means* B. For example, it is impossible to have a tree whose trunk has sixteen rings but whose age is not 16 years. On the other hand, the bus driver can ring three times whether or not the bus is full. This demonstrates that this second sense of *meaning* has an element of the arbitrary. It is for this reason that Grice dubs this *non-natural meaning*. With *non-natural meaning*, a connection is made *by the speaker* between two entities that otherwise would not necessarily have varied correlatively. It is the very fact that the person using

A to mean B, non-naturally, associates the two so that A ends up meaning B.

What are the exact characteristics of non-natural meaning? One possible definition would be that non-natural meaning is any association made between items that are not necessarily covariant, and intended to convey information. For instance, said Grice in this case, we would speak of non-natural meaning when a perpetrator leaves clues incriminating somebody else at the scene of his own crime. After all, the aim of such a tactic is to convey information (the culpability of an individual) by combining two items (in this case the crime committed and the clues left behind). Returning to the fictitious characters embroiled in the scenario around which this book is woven, suppose that General San-Gerio leaves the fingerprints of his enemy, General Quieto, on the weapon he has used to commit a murder. Would we, in this case, say "The presence of his fingerprints means that General Quieto is guilty"? Not really, Grice would maintain. We could certainly say "General San-Gerio is attempting to signify by these fingerprints that General Quieto is guilty", or more accurately, "General San-Gerio is attempting, by leaving these fingerprints, to convey false information incriminating General Quieto". Yet it would be a fallacy to affirm that: "The presence of his fingerprints means that Quieto is guilty". Nevertheless, San-Gerio undeniably has the intention of conveying information indicating that Quieto is guilty. What this demonstrates, according to Grice, is that the intention of the person who makes the two signals covary is not sufficient to bring out non-natural meaning. What, then, do we need in order to be able to speak of non-natural meaning? It is certainly essential, in the case of non-natural meaning, that someone attempt to communicate information. Yet this is not sufficient. We still need to take account of the fact that recognition of that intention is essential to the accomplishment of the transmission of information. If we look again at the case of the ringing bell on the bus, the three rings come to *mean* that the bus is full because, not only is the driver instructed to trigger those rings to indicate to the customers that the bus is full, but also because everybody knows that the sound is triggered to that effect. Hence, there is a coordination of the mental states (here, beliefs and intentions) of the different members of the relevant community, which results in a covariation between the sounds of the bell and the filling of the bus. Given that the non-natural lexical meaning emerges because of a coordination of the mental states of the people involved, it is not a case of transmission of an objective and necessarily true piece of information. In a given system, we can have an item A which comes to *mean* B even if the link between A and B is totally arbitrary and is valid only by virtue of the coordination of the mental states of the individuals who share in that code.

What do these musings of Grice's tell us about the notion of information? Firstly, we can accept that information is what is transmitted in our interactions. If, like Grice, we refuse to consider sense and meaning *in abstracto*, but attempt to understand them within a general theory of rational communication, we come to realize that information is what is transmitted in our meaningful interactions. In light of this, we can say that – unlike the view held by Bar-Hillel: that "semantic information intrinsically has nothing to do with communication" [BAR 55] – information, semantics and communication are interlinked. Without information, there is no meaning because information is the content that we try to capture and encode in language. The second thing which Grice shows us is that, in the same way that we can speak of *natural meaning* and *non-natural meaning*, we ought to draw a distinction between two sorts of information: *natural information* and *non-natural information*. This runs counter to the current consensus of practitioners of philosophy who are interested in information. This consensus is, in effect, that there is an inalienable link between information and truth.[5] We should not speak of information unless that which is being transmitted is true. Although there is consensus surrounding this view, we believe that taking non-natural meaning into account shows that it should not be accepted. Indeed, in cases of non-natural meaning, a piece of information is certainly transmitted by way of the recognition of our intention to form an association between two entities. If we accept, as our preliminary definition of the notion of information, that given by [LAL 06][6], we can see that non-natural meaning does indeed

---

5 For instance, see [BAR 64; DRE 81; FLO 10; FLO 11].
6 Reminder: "an element of knowledge conveyed by a message which is its bearer and of which it constitutes the meaning."

communicate to us an element of knowledge, if only relating to the thinking of our interlocutor. The difference with natural meaning is that while in the first case, it is objective and irrefutable information that is transmitted, with non-natural meaning, the information transmitted is mediated by the human mind. Hence, this sort of information is fertile soil for disinformation, deception and the different types of information warfare which we shall go on to discuss in the remainder of this chapter. If there were only the objective information encoded in natural meaning, such manipulations would not be possible. It is because we can also convey non-natural information using the recognition of our intentions that we are able to manipulate that recognition so as to convey false information.

Note that Grice himself did not appear to accept this notion of false information, as he wrote "False information is not an inferior kind of information; it just is not information" [GRI 89, p. 371]. In our view, however, there are three good reasons not to attach a great deal of importance to this reticence. The first is that accepting a notion of untrue information would help to better account for the genuine usages that are made in information warfare, where deception and the transmission of false information is important. The second is that the notion of non-natural meaning appears to directly legitimize the notion of false or non-natural information. The third and final reason is that this oft-quoted sentence from Grice is a lapidary affirmation concluding a discussion (itself only summative) of the maxim of quality in the retrospective epilog to [GRI 89]. Therefore, we do not think it is justifiable to take this sentence as expressing a fully worked-out thesis by Grice, as does [FLO 11], for instance. Before coming back to these questions, let us look at the other great thinker on information in the 20th Century: Fred Dretske.

1.2.2.2. *Information and knowledge in Dretske's work*

> "In the beginning there was information. The word came later."
>
> [DRE 81]

At its beginnings, Dretske's project was purely epistemological. His interest lay in giving a naturalistic analysis of the notion of knowledge in the purest analytical tradition. Because Gettier [GET 63] had shown that it was no longer possible to content ourselves with the conventional definition of knowledge as justified true belief, there was a need to produce a new definition of the notion of knowledge, and it is in this context that Dretske's work emerged. Using a naturalistic framework, Dretske believed it was essential to provide an objective and biologically-plausible description of the process by which humans went from perception to knowledge. Thus, he found himself developing a philosophical reflection centered on the nature of information. Actually, information was only of interest for Dretske because, according to him, "information is necessary for knowledge" [DRE 08]. The idea is that in order to know anything at all, we need to be *informed* of it. Knowing is nothing else than receiving, processing and understanding relevant information about the object of the knowledge in question. Hence, a naturalistic theory of knowledge cannot do without a theory of information. What *is* information, then? In order to answer this question, Dretske begins by drawing inspiration from Shannon and Weaver's mathematical theory of communication (MTC), but departs from it on a crucial point: the aforementioned two authors focus less on the content than on the informational channel.

Remember that MTC sought to measure the amount of information transmitted from one point to another. [SHA 48] only defined information incidentally. In order for there to be communication, Shannon tells us, there must be a source S, a channel c for transmission of the information and a receiver R of that information. If the source the source S has a set of possible states $s_1,...,s_n$, each with a given probability of occurrence $(p(s_1),..., p(s_n))$, then the quantity of information generated by the occurrence of the state s_i is given by the following formula:

$$I(s_i)= \log(1/p(s_i))$$

Whilst MTC is capable of quantifying the information generated by an individual occurrence, Dretske quite rightly points out that this theory is primarily concerned with statistics. It is significant that it is another formula – the one about the average amount of information generated at the source – that is best known in MTC. In this case, we speak of entropy. This formula is as follows:

$$I(S) = \sum p(s_i)I(s_i) = \sum p(s_i)\log(1/p(s_i))$$

This formula expresses that the average amount of information generated at the source is defined by the mean of the I(s) weighted by the probability of occurrence of each state.

Similarly, we can calculate the amount of information received at the other end. The receiver R also has a very definite number of possible states $r_{1...n}$, each with a given probability of occurrence (probabilities therefore ranging from $p(r_1)$ to $p(r_n)$); the amount of information generated by the occurrence of the state r_i is given by the following formula:

$$I(r_i) = \log(1/p(r_i))$$

Again at the level of the receiver, MTC averages the amount of information received using the following formula, which is exactly symmetrical to the one we saw earlier, except that it applies to the receiver rather than the sender:

$$I(R) = \sum p(r_i)I(r_i) = \sum p(r_i)\log(1/p(r_i))$$

Given these definitions, we can see that Shannon's concern was to quantify the information arriving at R based on the amount to be found at S by studying the degree of noise introduced by the channel c. His was a purely formal project, disregarding the content transmitted and focusing on the conditions of the transmission and the amount of information transmitted. Hence, MTC has no semantic concerns; its only goal is to calculate the quantity of information transmitted from S to R, and to determine the statistical properties of c. It is here that Dretske parts company with MTC.

Dretske's priority was to advance a *semantic* theory of information and to justify our ordinary concept of information. He felt that MTC was inadequate for this task because it tells us nothing about the particular piece of information that is transmitted, contenting itself to quantify that transmission indiscriminately. In [DRE 81], Dretske gives the following account of where he diverges from the MTC: "In standard applications of communication theory, the interest centers on the *source* of information and on the *channel* for transmitting this information, and for purposes of describing these aspects of communication, there is no reason to be interested in the particular messages transmitted. But we are here concerned with the particular messages, the particular content, the *information* that gets transmitted from a source over a channel" [DRE 81, p. 52–53]. If he felt compelled to take an interest not only in the amount of information transmitted but also in the very nature of that information, it is because in his view, perception is the basis upon which a naturalized epistemology should be constructed. Information is of interest to Dretske because it gives rise to knowledge by being perceived and processed by the knowing subject. In his theory, perception is none other than a "particular kind of information-carrying experience", and belief and knowledge are "merely specialized informational states in certain living organisms" (see [DRE 00: IX]).

Owing to this epistemological approach, Dretske needs a notion of information with very specific characteristics. In particular, he needs information to always be true. The reason for this requirement is that Dretske begins by defining knowledge as "information-caused belief" (see [DRE 81; DRE 00]). This definition of knowledge is modeled upon the features of perception: I know that s is P in the context of perception if, not only is it the case that s is P and that I believe s to be P, but also my belief is caused by the fact that s is P. For example, in the case of vision, it is not sufficient that I believe the sky is blue in order to know that the sky is blue; this belief has to be caused by the objective fact that the sky is blue. An immediate objection to such a definition is that it risks disqualifying cases where knowledge is acquired through testimony. Is it possible for a blind person to know that the sky is blue? However, this objection is not prohibitive. We can, in fact, answer simply by saying that the blind man knows that the sky is blue because someone who does know that has told him so, and that it is essential that that person know it because of direct access to perceptual information.[7]

---

7 Or indeed by the testimony of someone who has such perceptive access!

If we combine this definition of knowledge as "information-caused belief" with the fact that knowledge is supposed to always be true, we can see that information itself needs to be infallible. It is this infallible nature of information that Dretske encapsulates in his definition of the informational content of a signal:

> "A signal r carries the information that s is F=The conditional probability of s's being F, given r (and k), is 1 (but, given k alone, is less than 1)" [DRE 81, p. 65].

In this definition, k is the totality of the knowledge that the subject already holds. We can see with this definition that information is an objective property of the signals. More generally, Dretske holds that information is necessarily objective, natural and truthful. He clarifies his thinking on this point when he writes that "information is a commodity that, given the right recipient, is capable of yielding knowledge" [DRE 81, p. 47]. This means that although our capacity to glean information depends on the background knowledge we already have, the information in itself is independent of us and is capable of giving rise to knowledge, whether or not we are there to receive it. More clearly even than Grice, Dretske holds that information must necessarily be true. His arguments are, on the one hand, that our ordinary concept of information implies truth, and on the other, that if information were not necessarily true, it could not be used as the basis for a naturalistic epistemology, given that knowledge is necessarily true. We still believe that this view is flawed. First, it is not possible to rely on the fact that our ordinary concept of information implies truth to conclude that information is necessarily true. The aim of philosophy is precisely to analyze our ordinary conceptions and, if needed, reform them. As regards the statement that because information must serve as the basis for knowledge it must necessarily be true, it is a *petitio* principii. If we place ourselves in a strictly naturalistic context, there is nothing to guarantee the factivity of knowledge. The factive nature of knowledge could be an entirely unnatural conceptual elaboration.

Let us recap. In our foregoing discussion, we have seen that philosophy, for a long time, neglected the concept of information, and that it was only in the 20th Century, under the influence of science, that philosophers began to take an interest in it. We have also seen that the 20th Century's two main thinkers on information – Grice and Dretske – share the idea that information is an objective and necessarily true entity, serving as a support to meaning when that meaning is natural. This is the alethic view of information. Counter to this conception, we have advanced the idea that untrue information does not appear to us to be contradictory, or indeed to have been solidly debunked by the aforementioned authors. Thus, we propose to define information as that which is transmitted during our meaningful interactions. Therefore, as happens with meaning, we can distinguish between *natural information* which is naturally true and *non-natural information* which, depending on the coordination of the mental states of the agents, may be false. In what follows, we are going to focus specifically on the way in which these notions of information can be exploited in the military domain.

1.3. Information warfare

Meaningful interaction, as mentioned above, may take a wide variety of forms. In ideal cases of communication, it may certainly be benevolent or neutral. In other cases, it may take place within a hostile or even warlike situation. Considering – as we do in this chapter – that information may not necessarily be true enables us to continue to speak of "information" even when it is false, particularly in such conflict-ridden contexts. Whether someone deliberately omits certain pieces of information or transmits misleading ones, these pieces of information are like weapons in communication. The extreme case involving players in latent or open warfare lends information the status of a military tool.

In classic military treatises such as Sun Tzu's *Art of War*[8], information plays a crucial role in victory as a tool of "soft power" – either in addition to or instead of the weapons of the so-called *material* fields. By using it, the combatant is able to adopt a position in *immaterial* fields. As well as, or instead of, fighting in the physical areas of land, sea, air and space, he positions himself in the far more

8 See [SUN 94].

subtle theater of communication and cognition. Using the tool that is information, the combatant can continue to act in material fields – in an operation of war *by way of* information – or indeed act in the enemy's immaterial field – in an operation of war *on* information. Any operation by way of information requires a prior operation on information: an informational maneuver designed to lead the enemy into making in appropriate decisions in the material field is preceded by a maneuver in the immaterial field to shape the mental states of belief and intention of the adversary. The "art of war" has a component where information and its multiple facets play a crucial role in tactical and strategic successes or failures.

In spite of the antediluvian nature of information warfare, it has come to be of crucial importance from a military point of view, because of two concomitant and interrelated circumstances: the development of ICT, which means that anyone is capable of exchanging ample quantities of information, and the advent of so-called *asymmetrical* conflicts, wherein a State is forced to counter or combat a nebulous non-State entity, such as a terrorist organization, which is not highly structured and has far fewer material resources than its adversary, but has weapons of more or less equal power in the immaterial field of information. In order to take account of these changes, contemporary armies delimit the concepts associated therewith, constructing doctrines for what they call *information operations*, defined thus: "a set of actions carried out by the armed forces, directed and coordinated at the highest level, with the aim of using or defending information, the information systems and decisional processes, in support of a strategy of influence, and contributing, by these operations, to the achieving of the final target state, whilst respecting the defended values."[9]

Far from being limited to the military domain, information warfare has potential and homologous extensions in the domains of economics, politics, media and others. In his book *Information warfare* [VEN 09], in the introduction the author refuses to define information warfare, because the domains it affects and the disciplines concerned are so many…. However, we can give a number of

_____

9 See [CIC 12].

observations which help to understand the fundamental mechanics of information warfare, from a conceptual point of view, without departing from the philosophical viewpoints presented above.

1.3.1. *The role of falsehood and of intentions*

In the framework devised by Luciano Floridi to define information, a tree diagram is frequently used.[10] Figure 1.1 shows a reproduction of that part of the tree diagram which is of interest to us in this chapter.

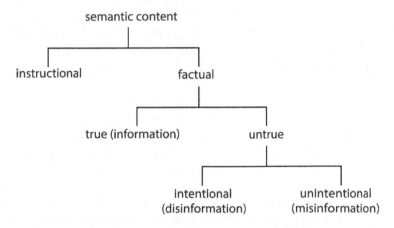

Figure 1.1. *Tree diagram of information, taken from [FLO 10]*

The *semantic content* at the root of the tree does not relate only to that which is informational. Content of an instructional nature corresponds more or less to what is found in a user manual for a machine, whilst factual content begins to look like information. According to Floridi, a piece of data cannot be defined as information unless it is *true*. Indeed, Floridi invokes Grice and Dretske to exclude the taking of false data into consideration as information. However, in the context of information evaluation upon which this collection is based, it is clear that this condition of truth cannot be retained. In the coming chapters, for the notion of information, we use the whole of the factual branch of Floridi's tree: the content is undoubtedly factual,

10 See [FLO 10; FLO 11].

but not necessarily true. Otherwise, to return to the military classification of information evaluation – where information is divided into two dimensions: source and content, evaluated on two distinct scales[11] – *all* information would have the maximum possible truth score, and it would be unimportant whether the source is more or less reliable, because that which is transmitted (the information) must *always* be taken as true... In the philosophical tradition, Floridi position is in line with the classical definition of knowledge[12]: a *true* and justified belief[13], although in more commonplace language the notion of knowledge does not presuppose truth (absolute certainty may in fact be wrong). A piece of information in the strictest sense must be true, whereas a piece of information in the broader (and certainly more usual) sense may be true, false, or of intermediate veracity, and it is this broader sense which we shall use here.

Now that we have established this, we also need to look at the other branches of the tree, starting from the node of factuality. If the content of what is communicated is not true, there is an alternative consideration: did the speaker or transmitter of the information have the *intention* to transmit false information or not?[14]

In the branch whose extremity represents what Floridi calls *disinformation*, the two notions present (falsehood and intentionality) form a fairly natural connection between the notion of disinformation and that of lying. Regardless of the definition we take for it, it is commonly accepted that a lie is intentional and is intended to affirm something which is false – or at least which the liar believes to be false. By introducing lying into the examination of information in the broadest sense, we are led to envisage a rather similar scenario but which has not yet been represented: that whereby the information transmitted is true, but the intention is that it not be. To begin with, an

---

11 Readers can refer to Chapters 3 and 4 for a discussion of these military classifications.

12 See section 1.2.2.2.

13 Note, however, that even this definition, taken from Plato's *Theaetetus* has largely been discredited by [GET 63].

14 The intention under discussion here relates to the information transmitted with falsehood; it does not relate to the transmission of the information. It is implicit that the transmission itself is intentionally made; the rest is debatable.

inexpert liar may behave in this way, transmitting true information without intending to. Floridi's tree diagram can therefore be extended, acquiring an extra leaf, which gives a more harmonious view of the notions hither to introduced:

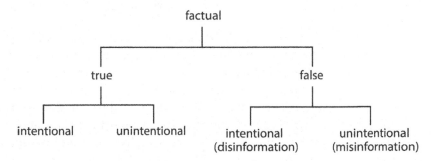

Figure 1.2. *Information tree: truth and intention*

With this symmetry established, other notions can expand the semantic information tree; we shall now introduce a number of such notions.

1.3.2. *Deception, simulation and dissimulation*

The term *deception* is widely used by the armed forces and is applicable to numerous paradigmatic scenarios in information warfare. According to the official NATO definition, deception is a set of "measures designed to mislead the enemy by manipulation, distortion, or falsification of evidence to induce him to react in a manner prejudicial to his interests."[15] These measures are sometimes taken in ways which are not related to information, but always have a definitive impact on the created information that the enemy receives. For example, the bombardment of an enemy city which is not of strategic importance, and which the attacker knows to be strategically unimportant, may be an operation of deception, the goal of which is to convey the idea, by the information transmitted to the enemy that the

---

15 See [NAT 12]; the definition has not been changed since it was first published in 1973.

bombardment has taken place, that the attacking forces have incorrectly assessed the priorities of the country they are attacking. The intended "error" caused in the minds of the enemy may come directly from the information, and sometimes, as in this example, indirectly *via* the material event which gave rise to the information.

Traditionally, there are two possible types of measures making up an operation of deception: measures of *simulation* and measures of *dissimulation*. General Francart recalls the distinction and contextualizes it in France's strategic approach: "In France, the term '*déception*' is specially reserved for simulation [a component in deception (active measures) whose effect is to fool the enemy about the allied intentions and possibilities by conveying false information to them] and dissimulation [a component of deception (passive measures) whose effect is to hide allied forces and their movements from the enemy's investigations]".[16] For example, an assault tank painted green and covered in foliage will be dissimulated (or hidden) from the sight of an enemy aviator; a lifesize cardboard model, carefully made and painted gray will suggest a tank and a target for the same aviator. In both cases, we are dealing with a piece of information that is ultimately transmitted to the enemy with the aim of duping them. Simulation and dissimulation are not mutually exclusive. The same tool, the very same practice may serve to transmit a message simultaneously by simulation and by dissimulation; if we slightly reinterpret the text of the *Aenid*, the Trojan Horse is a means of simulation of an offering left by the Greeks who had supposedly sailed away, and which the Trojans can therefore use to ensure the prosperity of their city, convinced by the arguments of the Greek spy Sinon, and also a means of dissimulation of Greek soldiers in its belly. In this case, there is a twofold message: information about the presence of an offering is transmitted, at the same time as the implication of the absence of the enemies responsible for the offering (*a fortiori* about their absence inside the offering) is also transmitted

---

16 See [FRA 00, p. 191-192]. At the start of the 17th Century, the distinction between the two concepts was discussed in an essay by Francis Bacon, *Of Simulation and Dissimulation*, reproduced in the collection [BAC 05].

by the silence about the maneuver. Misleading information induced in the mind of the enemy can also stem from a gesture implying that *another* piece of information was unknown to those performing the maneuver: Winston Churchill was aware of the Germans' plans to bomb Coventry, but he allowed it to happen so that the enemy would not suspect that the Brits had deciphered the secret German code used to communicate in preparation for the bombardment. Simulation of false knowledge (the city is not going to be bombed, so there is no need to evacuate it) helps the dissimulation of true knowledge (the secret code has been broken). The subtle distinction between these two joint types of information is, unsurprisingly, reminiscent of the distinction between a lie *by action* and a lie *by omission*.

It must be pointed out that here we are extending the definition of information proposed by Floridi still further. We accept not only that a piece of information can be false, but also that the *withholding* of information implies that a transmitter may possess information but not divulge it. The existence of information therefore no longer depends on the existence of any receiver or addressee. Overall, dissimulation is intended to withhold information: here, nothing is communicated, and yet we accept here that there is an implicit piece of information underlying that lack of communication. Therefore, Floridi's tree becomes even more denser, because before the branch-off between true and false, there is a division between transmission and withholding. The new tree therefore takes on the facet shown in Figure 1.3, if we leave aside the terminologics previously adopted by Floridi for disinformation and misinformation.

The methods typically used for simulation and dissimulation are many, and all of them find parallels in the animal and plant kingdoms (e.g. chameleons, stick insects or carnivorous plants). The historian Barton Whaley [WHA 82] subdivides the methods for simulation and dissimulation, associating them with categories of actions which have their correspondent in those kingdoms (see Figure 1.4).

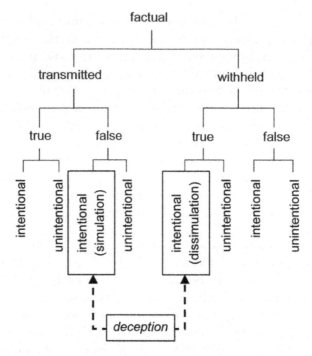

Figure 1.3. *Simulation and dissimulation
in the information tree*

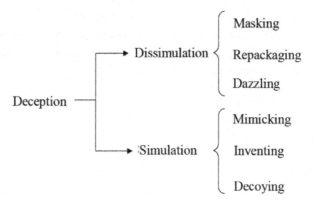

Figure 1.4. *Deception, simulation and dissimulation
according to [WHA 91]*

However, these verbs minimize the possibilities of resorting to dissimulation, and with good reason, because the same strategy has no genuine equivalent in animals or plants: nowadays in particular because of the existing techniques, it is possible to very effectively hide a piece of information, by communicating it to the enemy but *swamped* in an ocean of other information. At the opposite extreme to withholding information, the tactic here is to provide too much rather than too little. In both cases, the adversary is disarmed: the relevant information is not available to him, whether it has been hidden or transmitted. On that point, Figure 1.3 is no longer sufficient either, because Floridi's tree diagram makes no allusion whatsoever to the amount of other information surrounding the piece of information that is represented.

In [CAR 11], the philosopher Thomas Carson puts forward a succession of different definitions, first for lying and then for deception. For the latter, all the definitions proposed contain the following clause, unlike lying: a deception must necessarily be successful – there is no such thing as a failed maneuver of deception. If the Trojans had not believed that the horse was an offering, or if the Greeks had been discovered in its belly, the simulation or dissimulation would have failed, and the entire deception would have ended in failure in either case. It is true that lexically, just as happens with misleading or dupery, deception necessitates success: we can take back a lie, but we cannot take back a mislead, which must necessarily already have succeeded. In order to respect this linguistic obligation whilst remaining faithful to military terminology, let us say that it is an *attempt* at deception which can fail, and that deception in the true sense of the word corresponds to a successful attempt. Carson represents the different possibilities for relations between lying and deception as shown in Figure 1.5.

As we can see, in Carson's view, there are attempts at deception and indeed deceptions which are not mendacious. We shall come back to this point below, as we discuss disinformation.

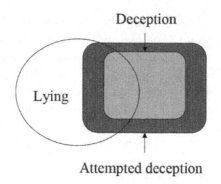

Figure 1.5. *Attempted deception and lying [CAR 11]*

1.3.3. *Addressees of information or the art of communicating*

Another way of deceiving someone using simulation and dissimulation simultaneously is to address many different people at once when transmitting a single piece of information. Let us return to the fictitious example used in this book of the troubles in Ektimostan, extended by the additional element that a spy in the pay of the dissident Usbek is sending reports from his post in the Ektimostanian Ministry of the Interior. Suppose that the spy is a double agent: he is in fact in the service of the Ektimostan regime and is duping Usbek. When he tells his hierarchical superiors that the 31 May attack is attributable to actions internal to the regime in place and is unrelated to the independence faction, the aim is to convince them that this is the case. Yet in the same message, he wants to convey to his true superiors (the Ektimostanians) that he is doing his job as a double agent. In any situation involving three or more visible people, the scenario can be reconstructed: X appears to address Y, but knowing that Z is listening. With modern-day technologies, it is still easier: if X writes an e-mail to Y and copies Z in (CC: Carbon Copy), Z knows that X has written to Y, but Y also knows that Z knows that X has written to him, and so on. This message is *common knowledge* (the term used in epistemic logic and game theory) between the three protagonists. In the fictitious scenario, the double agent sends his e-mail to Usbek, but puts the Ektimostan authorities in the BCC (*Blind Carbon Copy*) field. Ektimostan knows that Usbek has received the false message, whereas Usbek has no inkling that Ektimostan is aware that he has received the message at the same time.

Thus, information warfare uses interlinked pieces of knowledge on which the attacker can ably act, sometimes with identical messages: the informational content here comprises the content of the message *stricto sensu* (the body text of the e-mail), but also the visible or hidden addresses of the multiple addressees. To Usbek's eyes, the spy is *dissimulating* his true nature as a pro-Ektimostan double agent and *simulating* his role as a pro-Usbek spy.

1.3.4. *Information warfare as a play on beliefs*

In summary and more generally, simulating is tantamount to making somebody else believe something that we believe to be false, whereas dissimulating is tantamount to hiding our own beliefs, and more importantly our intention to hide those beliefs, from someone else. The beliefs and knowledge of the transmitter and the receiver of the information play an essential role in any information operation in a hostile context. With Floridi, these propositional attitudes of belief and of knowledge are essentially absent, which is legitimate in the context of his strict understanding of information, but is no longer legitimate with the broader acceptance adopted here.

Furthermore, in a simulation and in a dissimulation, the information transmitted may relate to something other than the simple object of its transmitter's belief. With lying (by way of action), the liar in his assertion may not necessarily make use of the fact that its content is true. He may use a different proposition, generally relating to the proposition in question but which is not necessarily identical to it. Hence, it may perfectly well be a question of communicating something about what he believes, in order to lead the target, in accordance with his probable ways of thinking, to infer from it that which the liar actually wants him to believe.

In philosophical literature, there are many definitions of lying, some of which are cataloged in [CAR 11]. To take only one forward here, we can cite the definition given in [CAP 12], where φ and ψ are two propositions:

1) the liar believes that φ is false;

2) he believes that if he tells his target that φ, then she will believe something about φ, notated as ψ;

3) he has the intention for her to believe that ψ;

4) he tells her that φ;

5) he has the intention for her not to believe that he believes that φ is false.

Similarly to in measures of deception, we see in this definition both simulating and dissimulating aspects. Clause 4 corresponds to a measure of a *simulation* of the liar's true beliefs. Furthermore, the intentions may be more numerous than simple simulation of his own beliefs: clause 5 reflects an intention of *dissimulation* – here to conceal his beliefs. Whilst clause 1 reflects the reality of the situation, the ultimate objective of the maneuver of deception, combining simulation and dissimulation, is expressed by clause 3. The beliefs of the actors in the play of information warfare clearly appear crucial for the success of that play. In that as well, Floridi's tree is altered: it is not so much a branch-off between true and false that needs to be considered, but rather between what is believed to be true and what is believed to be false by the transmitter of the information.

1.3.5. *Disinformation and associated notions*

The comparison of deception with lying is not meaningless. [GER 11, p. 96] holds that "deception is the truly military facet of disinformation". However, what is closer to lying than disinformation, if we accept the generic sense in the very abundant usage made of the term today?

Is disinformation mendacious in itself, though? Some definitions of disinformation given by a variety of authors are indicative of the difficulty in precisely defining the notion: "A punctual or continuous action, which consists, using any and all means necessary, of leading an adversary into error or favoring subversion in his mind with the aim of weakening him"[17]; "disinformation consists of deliberately propagating false information in order to influence an opinion and weaken an adversary"[18]; "disinformation consists of the elaboration and deliberate communication of a false piece information, carefully disguised to present all appearances of authenticity. In the context of wartime military operations, disinformation is identified with deception. [...] More specifically, disinformation appears to be a collective enterprise of design, manufacturer and diffusion of a falsified message, whose sole aim is to fool the targeted receiver in order to benefit from the positively erroneous usage he is liable to make of that information".[19]

It is difficult to argue with such definitions, which sometimes contradict one another, because the concept is so changeable and the word so recent, although the phenomenon which it denotes is as old as warfare itself. In order to better characterize the term, and force it to correspond with certain circumstances which we would tend to label as instances of disinformation based on our fictitious scenario; it is helpful to use some of the clauses of the definition of lying put forward above.

The well-known apologue of "The Boy Who Cried 'Wolf!'" shows us that if we wrongly claim something too frequently, no-one believes us when the claim is true. In an adaptation of this fable, suppose that an Ektimostanian blogger has always been considered by Usbek to be a puppet of the regime in spite of his claims to be an opponent: every entry on his blog makes reference to events to the glory of the Ektimostanian State – events which Usbek knows to be false, through other channels. For months, and each new entry on the blog confirms this, the blogger is believed to be a liar, and through lassitude, in the Usbek camp, people come to form the opinion that everything that he writes is false. On 3 June, on his site, the blogger champions the idea that the attack on 31 May is attributable to the *Free Resistance of*

---

17 *Dictionnaire de l'Académie française*, 9[th]edition.
18 For instance, see [HUY 00], or a number of texts by the same author.
19 See [GER 11, p. 58]. Note that for Géré, deception is closer to simulation than to dissimulation.

Dagbas (FRD). The scenario then changes: suppose that it is true that the FRD carried out the attack, and the blogger wants Usbek to believe the contrary. In this scenario, the information transmitted on 3 Jun is *true* (the individual *is not lying*), but it is tempting to label this operation as *disinformation*. In fact, it is not on 3 June that the blogger is sowing disinformation, but rather *throughout* the entire length of the existence of his blog – a means of the overall informational maneuver which comes to a head on the final day, when for the first time he tells a grain of truth. Thus, although lying is involved in this disinformation stratagem, it is not lies which, in the final analysis, are likely to fulfill the hopes of the disinformer, but rather the *truth* of his final statement! An extreme case would be a disinformer who has a reputation as a liar with his audience and knows it, but who has not in fact lied in the past. He need only cry "Wolf!" as soon as the wolf appears, the audience will be convinced of the contrary, and no false information has been disseminated. The constraint of being "counter to the truth" could therefore be superfluous in the definition of disinformation.

At a more fundamental level, the various definitions put forward above seem to lack an essential factor which is present any time disinformation occurs: *belief.* It must be recognized that Huyghe holds up the role of "influence", Géré that of the fact of "fooling the target receiver". This suggests that the disinformer wishes to act *on* the beliefs of his audience. Yet is this the only occurrence of beliefs in the process of disinformation? In the previous example, the blogger does not content himself with shaping Usbek's beliefs: constantly, the entries in his blog are based on Usbek beliefs, or more specifically, they are based on the belief that the blogger himself has of Usbek's beliefs. At least as much as an operation *performed on* beliefs, this is an operation *on the basis* of beliefs, beliefs about beliefs, etc., – in summary, on the basis of the *crossed beliefs* of the protagonists. Similarly, in the extreme example of the individual who has been nothing but truthful but has the reputation of being a liar, the fact that he uses his knowledge of his reputation with others – a reputation which itself expresses a belief on the part of his audience – enables him to carry out his operation without resorting to lies: the disinformer, as much as he wants to *alter* the beliefs and knowledge of his audience, uses *reason* in order to do so *on the basis* of those beliefs and knowledge (basing his reasoning on his own beliefs).

One thing appears to impose itself when we look at undeniable cases of disinformation: influencing the audience is always tantamount to (attempting to) inculcate a belief in them which is (or which the disinformer believes to be) false. It is here, rather than anywhere else, that truth or falsehood comes into play. It is not the information conveyed that needs to be false, but rather the future content of belief in the addressee's mind which is or needs to become false if we are dealing with characterized disinformation.

Thus, let us put forward a more precise (though of course imperfect) definition, more or less closely mimicking the structure of the definition of lying:

1) the disinformer believes that something about φ, notated as ψ, is false;

2) he believes that if he tells his target that φ, then she will believe that ψ;

3) he has the intention for her to believe that ψ;

4) he tells her that φ;

5) he has the intention for her not to believe that he believes that ψ is false.

Suppose that ψ is the opposite of φ. Note then that from the very first clause in the above definitions, lying is noticeably different from disinformation. Indeed, if the disinformer believes that φ is true (i.e. that its opposite is false), then by saying that φ, he is not telling a lie. By that clause, it is very possible that disinformation could be accurate, as in the case of the Ektimostanian blogger whose final act of disinformation is not untruthful.

Our definition enriches the presentation of disinformation by Floridi given in section 1.3.1: the role of the beliefs of the agents becomes highly important here. In addition, the intricate connections between beliefs and intentions are made explicit. Nevertheless, the relationship between disinformation and deception set out above remains compatible with considerations made in the definition of disinformation and the position of deception in Figure 1.3; it is merely suggested in addition that deception is a form of disinformation such as it is practiced in a military context. There is indeed dissimulation of belief and simulation of belief, more subtly than in the case of lying.

There is no consensus about the definition of disinformation; also, the definition put forward above can be broadly criticized, depending on the usage that each individual makes of the term. The same is true of other, similar notions, such as those of propaganda or intoxication. As we saw above, Géré states that deception is a form of disinformation considered to be military. To simplify the relationships between these notions, it is tempting to adopt a similar point of view to establish the implicit relationship between propaganda and intoxication: propaganda is aimed at a large crowd of people – as illustrated in the very well-known works of Tchakhotine [TCH 39] or Klemperer [KLE 03] – without the addressee having any connection to armies, and it is sometimes considered to be more closely related to publicity than to a warlike tactic, as in Bernays' well-known work [BER 07]. Conversely, intoxication, while the mechanisms involved appear to be very similar, seems to be reserved to the domains of warfare and espionage, so Table 1.1 gives a distribution of the notions on the basis of the addressees.

All addressees	Disinformation	Propaganda
Military addressees	Deception	Intoxication

Table 1.1. *Notions of information warfare, general or military contexts*

Yet this distribution is, doubtless, still open to debate, because it is possible to speak of self-intoxication without being able to see what self-propagandization might be (with the exception, perhaps, of a form of the Coué method). Self-intoxication occurs in cases where the source of information himself becomes intoxicated, e.g. in an intelligence service where one of the members considers an intoxicating piece of information emitted by one of his colleagues with different intended addressees to be worthy of interest. In this scenario, there is certainly no individual self-intoxication, but a collective self-intoxication which affects a department containing several people.

Regarding the relationship between disinformation and propaganda on the one hand, and deception and intoxication on the other, in view of examples which might be brought to mind from the existing body of literature, historical examples or examples from the cinema, it is helpful to consider that the second term is a very accentuated version of the first: Goebbels' propaganda was a barrage of disinformation, in the same way as intoxication is deception practiced in a high dose. However, these terminologies can be adjusted, doubtless at the cost of the clarification of the concepts which constitute these notions with fuzzy boundary.

1.4. Conclusion. Comprehending information in order to evaluate it

In this chapter, we have sketched the general form of the trajectory of the notion of information in philosophy. As it was not truly considered until the 20th Century, the three main philosophers mentioned here – Grice, Dretske and Floridi – all more or less held that a piece of information, in order to be worthy of the title, must necessarily be true. Because of the arguments championed here, and in order for the question of information evaluation to truly be posed, this near-axiom is rejected for our purposes, which opens the door to the considerations of conflictual contexts where information plays a crucial role.

With this in mind, we note that the tree diagram initially put forward by Floridi, in an extended view of information, proves highly inadequate: it could, once it has been developed, taking account of the intentions and beliefs of the protagonists, the means employed and their degree of usage in the particular domain in question, more closely resemble a true, bushy copse. Given the multitude of possibilities on offer for an information strategy, an adversary to whom information is addressed is faced with the difficulty of understanding which branch of the tree he is dealing with. This is precisely the problem with which an analyst, charged with evaluating the reliability of the source of a piece of information and the truth of its content, needs to overcome in order to achieve a proper *evaluation of the information*.

1.5. Bibliography

[ADA 03] ADAMS F., "The informational turn in philosophy", *Minds and Machines*, vol. 13 no. 4, pp. 471–501, 2003.

[BAC 05] BACON F., *Essays, or Counsels, Civil and Moral*, 1st edition 1625, Barnes and Noble, New York, 2005.

[BAR 64] BAR-HILLEL Y., *Language and Information*, Addison-Wesley, Reading, MA, 1964.

[BER 07] BERNAYS E., *Propaganda*, 1st edition 1928, Zones, Paris, 2007.

[CAP 12] CAPET P., *Qu'est-ce que mentir ?*, Vrin, Paris, 2012.

[CAP 03] CAPURO R., HJORTLAND B., "The concept of information", in *The Annual Review of Information Science and Technology*, Cronin B. (ed.), vol. 37, pp. 343–411, 2003. Available online at: http://www.capurro.de/infoconcept.html#Studies.

[CAR 10] CARSON T., *Lying and Deception*, Oxford University Press, New York, 2010.

[CIC 12] CENTRE INTERARMÉES DE CONCEPTS, DOCTRINES ET EXPÉRIMENTATIONS, *Glossaire interarmées de terminologie opérationnelle*, 2012.

[DES 92] DESCARTES R., *Méditations Métaphysiques*, 1st edition 1647, Garnier-Flammarion, Paris, 1992.

[DRE 81] DRETSKE F., *Knowledge and the Flow of Information*, MIT Press, Cambridge, 1981.

[DRE 95] DRETSKE F., *Naturalizing the Mind*, MIT/Bradford, Cambridge, 1995.

[DRE 00] DRETSKE F., *Knowledge, Perception, Belief Selected Essays*, Cambridge University Press, Cambridge, 2000.

[DRE 08] DRETSKE F., "Epistemology and information" in ADRIAANS P, and VAN BENTHEM J, (eds.), *Philosophy of Information*, Elsevier, Paris, pp. 29–472, 2008.

[FLO 10] FLORIDI L., *Information, A Very Short Introduction*, Oxford University Press, New York, 2010.

[FLO 11] FLORIDI L., *Semantic Conceptions of Informations*, Stanford Encyclopedia of Philosophy, available online at: http://plato.stanford.edu/entries/information-semantic/, 2011.

[FRA 00] FRANCART L., *La guerre du sens*, Economica, Paris, 2000.

[GER 11] GÉRÉ F., *Dictionnaire de la désinformation*, Armand Colin, Paris, 2011.

[GET 63] GETTIER E. "Is justified true belief knowledge?", *Analysis* no. 23, pp. 121–123, 1963.

[GRI 89] GRICE H. P., *Studies in the Way of Words*, Harvard University Press, Cambridge, 1989.

[HUY 02] HUYGHE F.B., *Terrorismes et guerres de l'information*, available online at : http://www.huyghe.fr/dyndoc_actu/424eb3aed503a.pdf, 2002.

[KLE 03] KLEMPERER V., *LTI, la langue du IIIe Reich*, 1st edition 1947, Agora Pocket, Paris, 2003.

[LAL 06] LALANDE A., *Vocabulaire critique et critique de la philosophie*, 1st edition 1927, PUF, Paris, 2006.

[LOC 90] LOCKE J., *An Essay Concerning Human Understanding*, 1st edition 1690.

[NAT 12] NORTH ATLANTIC TREATY ORGANIZATION, NATO glossary of terms and definitions, AAP-6, 2012.

[RUS 22] RUSSELL B., "Introduction" in WITTGENSTEIN L., *Tractatus logico-philosophicus*, 1st edition Kegan Paul, 1922.

[SHA 48] SHANNON C., "The mathematical theory of communication", *Bell System Technical Journal*, vol. 27, pp. 379–423, 1948.

[SUN 94] SUN TZU, *The Art of War*, Westview Press Inc., Oxford, 1994.

[TCH 39] TCHAKHOTINE S., *Le viol des foules par la propagande politique*, Gallimard, 1939.

[VEN 07] VENTRE D., *Information Warfare*, ISTE, London and Wiley, New York 2009.

[WHA 91] WHALEY B., BOWYER BELL J., *Cheating and Deception*, Transaction Publishers, Piscataway, 1991.

Chapter 2

Epistemic Trust

2.1. Introduction

In this chapter, I would like to take a broader perspective of information evaluation and see how it relates to the general epistemological question of the role of trust in knowledge. My perspective is that of *social epistemology*, i.e. the branch of modern epistemology which looks at the role of social processes in the formation and justification of knowledge. There are at least three aspects of the *social dimension of knowledge* which are of interest to epistemologists[1]:

1) *individual* – how individuals' beliefs are formed, and how they evaluate social sources of information;

2) *collective* – how social decision-making processes – such as assemblies or juries – operate, and how social aggregation of beliefs can yield accurate epistemic results;

3) *systemic* – what are the systemic and institutional constraints which steer the dissemination of information in a specific domain?

Chapter written by Gloria ORIGGI.
1 For this three-way division, see [GOL 11].

Social evaluation of information depends on all these dimensions. At an individual level, it is important to understand which indicators of information reliability an individual can use responsibly in the absence of direct *expertise* on the subject, in order to evaluate the *epistemic quality* of a piece of information. At a collective level, a group making decisions on the basis of information must share rules and procedures for consensus-reaching. At a systemic level, a system needs to be constructed in such a way as to take account of the weight of the different sources of information and the biases of the network – such as information cascades and contagion effects – which can be damaging for the aggregation of reliable information.

In what follows, we shall present a sketch of the social epistemology research program, before focusing on the epistemological dimension of trust, which is the main topic of this chapter.

2.2. What is social epistemology?

In the 1980s, social epistemology was defined as a philosophical or normative branch of sociology of sciences, born particularly out of the movement of STS (Science and Technology Studies), which placed social processes at the center of knowledge construction. The definition from the *Norton Dictionary of Modern Thought* gives a clearer idea of the intellectual motivations of this discipline in comparison to sociology of sciences:

"*Social epistemology*: An intellectual movement of broad cross-disciplinary provenance that attempts to reconstruct the problems of *epistemology* once knowledge is regarded as intrinsically social. It is often seen as philosophical science policy or the normative wing of *science studies*. Originating in studies of academic knowledge production, social epistemology has begun to encompass knowledge in *multicultural* and public settings, as well as the conversion of knowledge to *information technology* and *intellectual property*. [...] Despite their many internal differences, social epistemologists agree on two points: (1) classical *epistemology*, *philosophy of science* and *sociology of knowledge* have presupposed an idealized conception of scientific inquiry that is unsupported by the social history of scientific practices; (2) nevertheless, one still needs to articulate normatively appropriate ends and means for science, given science's status as the exemplar of *rationality* for society at large. The question for social epistemologists, then, is whether science's actual conduct is worthy of its exalted social status and what political implications follow from one's answer. Those who say "yes" assume that science is on the right track and offer guidance on whom people should believe from among competing experts, whereas those who say "no" address the more fundamental issue of determining the sort of knowledge that people need and the conditions under which it ought to be produced and distributed."[2]

As we can see from this quote, the *normative* component of this intellectual enterprise sets it apart from other, similar research projects such as sociology of sciences. Indeed, if science is merely a sphere of human activity like any other, subject to the same pressures and the same constraints, we could content ourselves with studying it as a field of inquiry like any other. However, science has a special status in our society – that of producing *epistemic norms* which are universally valid, against which we evaluate what is true and what is false, as well as the *rational approaches* that need to be followed if we wish to be able to state that we know something for certain. It is science which tells us that *astrology* does not correspond to these norms and practices, whereas *astronomy* does... Again, it is science which tells us that *homeopathy* is a remedy based merely on the *placebo effect*, whilst chemotherapy is based on causal principles... While for a sociologist of science there is no difference between studying the community of astrologers and the community of astronomers, as they both produce their facts and their objectives, for a social epistemologist the difference is crucial: astrology is a *corpus* of beliefs, which is certainly rich in history and tradition, but it now imposes no normative criterion as to what is true or false. Astronomy is something entirely different: its discoveries are supposed to respect epistemic norms and describe a state of the world which we accept as

---

2 Quoted in the foreword to the second edition of [FUL 88, p. IX].

the best *approximation of the truth*, given the state of our knowledge – and above all, whose truth we accept in our epistemic community, because we share the same criteria of rationality. This self-reflexive aspect of science as a field of inquiry is what interests a social epistemologist. We still need to understand the nature of the *epistemic norms* which govern our relationship with the truth. If, like most epistemologists, we recognize that epistemic vocabulary is imbued with a normative function, we then need to understand which categories these norms belong to: are they social or moral norms? Are there "epistemic duties" in the same way as there are moral duties? Who is the judge of this – the individual or society? Can I alone establish the norm which guides my scientific research, or do I need to share a set of norms and values which are socially determined? In the normative domain – e.g. in ethics – we can distinguish between *axiological normative concepts*, such as *good, bad*, etc., which express approval or disapproval, and *deontic concepts*, such as *permitted, obligatory*, etc., which evaluate a certain behavior from a procedural point of view.[3] In the case of epistemology, we can also express two types of normative judgments: "That is an intelligent theory" is a type-1 normative judgment, which relates to the expression of approval. "You shouldn't believe what you see" is a type-2 normative judgment. Thus, in the case of social epistemology, the problem of the nature of norms is as central as in ethics. Are we dealing with social norms of trust, reciprocity, honesty, or strictly epistemic norms which are the best approximation of the truth? When we look at the social aspects of knowledge, this question becomes a crucial one. The philosopher Alvin Goldman proposes *veritism* as an epistemic norm for social knowledge production: a system whose aim is to increase true beliefs to the detriment of false ones in a society is better than a different system which does not have the same effect.[4] The social interactions that are supposed to produce knowledge in the various systems – such as science, the media, the judicial system, etc. – must be designed to maximize that proportion. Yet if knowledge is socially constructed, how can the norm of maximization of true beliefs put forward by Goldman be defined independently of the social value of

---

3 See [ENG 07, p. 128].
4 See [GOL 99].

truth itself? What is the relationship between social norms and epistemic norms? The analysis of trust given in this chapter is an example of the difficulty in separating the two normative dimensions when we recognize the role of social links in the construction of knowledge.

2.3. History of the discipline

As an autonomous discipline, social epistemology became institutionalized in the late 1980s around the journal *Social Epistemology*, published from 1987 onwards by Taylor & Francis, and the work of philosophers very close to *Science Studies*, such as Steve Fuller.[5] It brings together a heterogeneous group of philosophers, most with a background in philosophy and history of science. They adopted a "militant" stance towards the criteria and norms of scientific rationality. The criticism of these norms and criteria is reminiscent of that of feminist philosophy, and a branch of *feminist epistemology* has developed within social epistemology. Authors such as Helen Longino[6] condemn the notion of a "community" of knowledge or discourse. In Longino's view, there is no perfect community, as any community is merely a series of sub-groups with different values and standards, which are necessarily renegotiated whenever a dialog takes place. The authority of discourse is asymmetrically distributed amongst those sub-groups. More recently, the philosopher Miranda Fricker has used the term *epistemic injustice* to describe the *deficit* of credibility from which a sub-group – e.g. women – may suffer within a community.[7]

Thus, from the very start, social epistemology is presented as an extremely interdisciplinary research program, much like social sciences, often based on *case studies* rather than on abstract theorizing, and open to the multicultural dimension and gender studies which were beginning to make their influence felt in all domains of philosophy: ethics, morality, aesthetics, etc.

---

5 See [FUL 88, SCH 94].
6 See [LON 90].
7 See [FRI 07].

In parallel to this *radical* tendency, which could be defined as *post-Kuhnian* – which called into question the very image of the truth as a balance between theory and nature – a different, more moderate tendency developed around the work of philosophers such as Alvin Goldman, Philip Kitcher and Hilary Kornblith.[8] Accusing the radical approaches to social epistemology of a constructivist drift, these authors emphasized the continuity between Quine's research program of *naturalized epistemology* and the research program of social epistemology. From this perspective, knowledge remains a natural phenomenon, even when we recognize the role of social factors in its production. It is a phenomenon which involves a relation between individuals and the outside world, which is then supposed to exist in a more or less organized form independently of our intellectual constructions.

2.4. Social epistemology and externalism

The task of epistemology is to understand the nature of the relationship between individuals and the world. In conventional epistemology, this relationship has two dimensions: a causal dimension (what is it about the outside world which causes my belief that a cat is standing in front of me?) and a dimension of justification (on what basis am I justified in believing that a cat is standing in front of me?). The two dimensions are well described in Plato's definition of knowledge as "justified true belief". It is not enough to have the correct causal relationship with the world in order to acquire knowledge about it. As a rational subject, epistemology also needs to be able to articulate reasons for that knowledge. A three-page article published by the American philosopher Edmund Gettier in 1963[9] put an end to this philosophical tradition. Through a series of ingenious examples, Gettier showed that we can have beliefs which are true and justified, yet which could scarcely be considered knowledge. If I look at the clock outside the Tower of London which says that it is four o'clock in the afternoon, I deduce from that observation that it is four in the afternoon and indeed it is four in the

8 See [GOL 99; KIT 93; KOR 94].
9 See [GET 05] and the previous chapter.

afternoon, but if the clock showed that time by accident because it is broken and always shows that time, then my belief that it is 4 p.m. is justified and true; yet I do not truly "know" that it is 4 p.m. Thus, we need something extra, in order to know something. We need to have the "appropriate causal relation" (a clearly normative notion) with the states of the world which cause a certain belief in our minds. This brief contribution turned a new page in naturalized epistemology: *epistemological externalism*, i.e. approaches to epistemology which base the analysis of the justification of knowledge on the analysis of the perceptual, cognitive and social processes which give rise to the representations that we have of the world. The approach centered on causality aims at understanding which are the "reliable" processes – i.e. those which favor truth – in the formation of beliefs. These processes are natural processes, organized at a variety of levels, which can be the subject of a true *naturalized epistemology*. Following Quine's ideas about naturalized epistemology, Hilary Kornblith stresses the importance of the organization of the world into "natural genres" in facilitating our inductive inferences. Granted, radical epistemologists would criticize him for an overly realistic attitude to those genres – which could themselves be a social construct. Goldman highlights the parallel between naturalized epistemology and cognitive sciences in the understanding of the causal relations which connect our beliefs with the world.[10]

2.5. Realism and constructivism in social epistemology

The emphasis on "reliability" and the desire to determine the processes which favor truth and fetter falsehood are symptomatic of this "conservative" tendency in social epistemology, as opposed to the radical tendency illustrated above. As Goldman says, the end goal of all epistemology – be it naturalized, social or conventional – is to "promote true beliefs and avoid false ones".[11] While the approach is in line with the aims of conventional epistemology, it is also to be found in trends in modern epistemology which break with the classical view

---

10 See [GOL 86].
11 See [GOL 04].

of knowledge, such as *feminist epistemology*. The philosopher Elisabeth Anderson defines social epistemology as follows:

"*Social epistemology* is a branch of naturalized epistemology that investigates the influence of specifically social factors on the production of knowledge: who gets to participate in theoretical inquiry, who listens to whom, the relative prestige of different styles and fields of research [and so on]. Feminist epistemology can be regarded as the branch of social epistemology that investigates the influence of *socially constructed conceptions and norms of gender and gender-specific interests and experiences* on the production of knowledge (...). A knowledge practice is rational to the extent that it promotes [...] critical self-reflections and responds to them by checking or canceling out the unreliable belief-formation mechanisms and enabling the reliable ones."

Hence, approaches which are critical of conventional epistemology, such as feminist epistemology, can still be concerned by truth and realism and consider them as the primary goal of epistemological research.

With regard to the radical agenda, the social factors that affect the cognitive processes refer to interests or biases relating to social class, gender, politics and the culture of every epistemic community. They are *external* factors which are foreign to epistemology in the true sense and to rationality. The conservative or realist agenda counts these social factors as being at the heart of the rational and epistemic processes which characterize the business of knowledge. For instance, the analysis of the advancement of science offered by [KIT 93] contains social elements: (1) consensual practices and (2) division of cognitive labor (who trusts whom). A *consensual practice* is a research practice which all members of a community accept "indirectly" by deliberately referring to other, authoritative scientists and experts. According to Kitcher, the *division of cognitive labor* is a crucial ingredient in the advancement of science: the progress of science is optimized by the distribution of the effort within the community. It is sometimes more propitious to deal with a new topic by directing the efforts of different people in different directions. It is also of greater strategic benefit for researchers to trust one another, and lend credulity to the results produced by a sub-group rather than having to carry out all the research necessary for their work for themselves. In the strategy proposed by Kitcher, there is no opposition between the epistemological and the social: the social dimension of knowledge is integrated into the epistemic[12] and cognitive processes of the individuals. So fully integrated is it, in fact, that certain philosophers hold that beliefs and knowledge should be attributed to social collectives rather than to individuals.

It is from this perspective that I shall now discuss the question of epistemic trust. Investigating the determining role played by trust relationships in the evaluation and acquisition of information does not mean to say that epistemology is founded upon sociological concepts (trust being a notion that has been studied and conceptualized particularly in social sciences) and it is thus "naturalized" in the social sciences, as some believe. Trust is an eminently epistemic tool: a procedure for rational and legitimate information extraction which any study of epistemic norms needs to take into account. Taking as a starting point this integration of the cognitive and social dimensions of trust, I shall present the debate about the role of trust in the information communicated and situate it within the philosophical debate regarding the epistemological status of testimony and communication.

2.6. Believing other people

I arrive at the train station in a foreign city, get off the train and ask a stranger for directions to the city's cathedral, which I want to visit. Of course, I have not simply asked "anyone at all": a quick assessment of the social environment around me has made me choose a person with seems to be a native – not a tourist like myself: a woman, whom I know to be more friendly and polite than men, and of a certain age, which reassures me about her experience of the city and the best ways to get around it. However, this assessment was only very superficial, almost instantaneous and I was hardly aware of doing it. This is my way of exploring the social world and deriving from it indicators of

12 See [HAR 91, pp. 693–708].

competence and benevolence which guide my choice of whom to trust. The lady answers my question, I thank her and trust her – that is, I follow her directions. Have I any reason at all to trust in what she tells me?

Believing other people in order to acquire information is one of the most common epistemic practices in our cognitive lives. Without that constant immersion in social life, without that sharing of cognitive labor with people like ourselves, our mental life would not be very different from that of animals. However, this observation is heavily charged with consequences for the received philosophical view of an epistemic subject who is autonomous, responsible and capable of basing her beliefs on well-founded reasons. Very often, the reasons that we have for believing other people are not clear to us; biases and prejudices are numerous, and the tendencies to defer blindly to authority are well documented. Our quick judgments about the reliability of others cause us to commit many epistemic injustices, to use the expression of Miranda Fricker, by attributing too much credibility to some people and too little to others. In brief, the vision of the epistemic subject is transformed by the introduction of trust into our processes of knowledge acquisition: rethinking our reasons for believing becomes a fundamental task in an epistemology that opens up to the social dimension of knowledge.

In a certain epistemic tradition, knowledge obtained from other people is considered as a degraded form of access to information – a resource that we are forced to use for lack of anything better. Here, I champion a more optimistic approach to the social dimension of knowledge: trusting others is a primary source of knowledge acquisition, which is essential for our cognitive development and the stabilization of the social structures for knowledge production and transmission. In societies with a high density of information, trust is a fundamental ingredient in knowledge, which cannot be substituted by individual procedures of knowledge acquisition. One could also state, as many philosophers have, that even in traditional societies, trust is a pillar of the acquisition and sharing of information, which enables us to accumulate a pool of shared knowledge about the world which constitutes the foundation of a specific, stable and transmissible culture. This optimistic vision of trust as an "epistemic tool" for knowledge acquisition requires us to rethink the criteria of independence and responsibility that a social group adopts in order for that sharing of knowledge to be possible and reliable. Other questions also arise – particularly about the connections between the trust in our interpersonal, social and political relations, and that particular form of trust which is at play when we believe other people in order to acquire information about the world. Are moral/affective trust and epistemic trust linked, and if so, how? Is it possible to reconstruct a different genealogy for these two forms of trust? Do the criteria of individual responsibility which we have to adopt when we believe other people's discourse have the same justification as the criteria which govern our relations of trust in our social lives?

2.7. Reductionism and antireductionism

This distinction traces back to the historical division between *reductionist* and *antireductionist* conceptions of the justification of testimony. Hume is the *locus classicus* for the reductionist view: trust in testimony is based on the same type of inductive inference that justifies any other belief – the *a posteriori* indicators that the testimony conforms to the facts. We trust those that experience has proven to be reliable; thus we have independent reasons to believe them. The opposing, non-reductionist view is that held by Thomas Reid, who considered deference to other people to be a primary source of information, i.e. which cannot be reduced to other sources and has no need for justification. Reid writes:

"The wise and beneficent Author of nature, who intended that we should be social creatures, and that we should receive the greatest at most important part of our knowledge by the information of others, hath, for these purposes, implanted in our natures two principles that tally with each other. The first of these principles is, a propensity to speak truth, and to use the signs of language, so as to convey our real sentiments [...]. Another original principle implanted in us by the

Supreme Being, is a disposition to confide in the veracity of others, and to believe what they tell us."[13]

According to Reid, our beliefs about what others tell us are guaranteed by the combination of a principle of veracity and a principle of credulity. The principle of credulity guarantees that recognition of a fundamental authority be afforded to certain people, from whom we accept what they say simply because they say it. Fundamental authority poses a far more difficult problem than derivative authority, which is afforded to people in whom we trust because we have independent reasons to believe that they are reliable. While the understanding of our reasons for deference to those whom we believe to be reliable is a clearly intelligible epistemological goal, it is far less obvious why the simple fact that other people believe something can be enough to justify our believing it ourselves. This problem is, to a certain extent, similar to that posed by moral and practical authority: recognizing the validity of a fundamental authority attributed to others seems, at first glance, to imply a sort of "capitulation of judgment", a relinquishing of reason which has often been cited in explanations for paradoxes of political obligation and morality.

We also need to distinguish fundamental authority from what could be called "Socratic influence". I may decide to abandon my own reasons and even my ways of reasoning, and accept those of somebody else because he has convinced me that his are better. The case of fundamental authority, though, is different: I believe what somebody says simply on the basis of the fact that he believes it. Are we ever justified in believing somebody else on that basis alone? The Reidian vision of having trust in others is attractive. Indeed, in our everyday practices, information exchange and trust in others often seem to precede reasoning about the reliability of our source of information. Yet if we accept the Reidian image of epistemic deference as a fundamental trait of our linguistic and cognitive practices, how can we go any further than simply invoking our "natural disposition" to believe, and attempt to justify the legitimacy of that invocation? An argument in support of the legitimacy of

13 See [REI 28].

fundamental deference places trust in others and the fundamental trust that we have in our own perception and memory on the same level.[14] Trust in the reliability of our own mental states is the starting point for any knowledge acquisition: without fundamental deference to ourselves, we could never form any knowledge at all. Yet if we trust our own beliefs by virtue of the simple fact that they belong to us, why should we deny the same type of trust to the beliefs that we acquire from others by way of communication? Do we really have the choice not to accept them when we accept those which we acquire through our own senses? Why should we be so "selfish" in epistemology? In addition, as highlighted by Allan Gibbard, the influence of others is omnipresent in our mental development – particularly in childhood. If we accept that the norms of reasoning that we use today have been influenced by others in the past, we have to recognize a degree of legitimacy of these norms, and we cannot rule out the possibility of other, similar influences in the future. Thus, in Gibbard's view: "[we] must accord some fundamental authority to others."[15] With this argument, the legitimacy of fundamental deference to others derives from the legitimacy of deference to ourselves: we cannot refuse authority to our own beliefs without condemning ourselves to a position of radical skepticism. Similarly, we cannot completely avoid the influence of others on our beliefs – at least in our past – so we must accord them some form of fundamental authority over ourselves. In the eyes of the epistemologist Richard Foley, it is by a process of "simulation" of the minds of others that we come to accord them fundamental authority, i.e. by considering them cognitive beings similar to ourselves.[16] However, it could be argued that the nature of the two situations of knowledge acquisition is so different that the argument gives us only a rationale to trust others, without shedding much light on the characteristics of the context of belief acquisition where that rationale would be effective. A better defense of the antireductionist view of deference would be to illuminate the nature of the cognitive mechanisms and interpretative practices underlying our trust in other people instead of invoking a general rationale. Language is certainly the first of these practices to

---

14 See the position of [FOL 94].
15 See [GIB 90, p. 181].
16 See [FOL 01].

explore in this quest for fundamental deference. As Hilary Putnam pointed out in his famous article in 1975, *The Meaning of "Meaning"* [PUT 04], the use of language is intrinsically deferential: I do not need to be an expert in chemistry to use the word "aluminum": as a competent speaker of my language, I can use the word even if I am incapable of distinguishing aluminum from steel, because the "division of the linguistic labor" relates each usage of the term to the relevant knowledge shared by metallurgy experts in my linguistic community. Language-learning clearly demonstrates this deferential component: children learn words sometimes without being able to associate the slightest inkling of meaning with those words. It is entirely normal for a child to ask questions such as: "Mummy, what does *"badger"* mean?" The child learns the word by deferring to public use of language, and accepts his mother's authority to establish the meaning of that word. Tyler Burge draws epistemic conclusions from the social and deferential nature of language. He defines an *acceptance principle*, whereby the acquisition of beliefs through other people is rationally justified: anyone is legitimized in accepting as true something which is presented as true and which they understand, in the absence of stronger reasons not to accept it as true.[17] That others are telling us the truth is a norm which we can presuppose unless we have reason to think that it has been violated. Even if we cannot deny the presence of a deferential component in language, is this sufficient to edify the trust that we attribute to others? Burge's argument about the *a priori* justification of beliefs which come to us by interlocution is based on the reliability and robustness of language as a means of transmission of information. In that sense, it is not overly different from the justification that Reid himself gave for his principle of credulity, based on the similarity between perception and language, which he considers to be crucial. From this point of view, language is merely one way of preserving information, much like perception or memory.

However, linguistic communication is far from a purely "preservative" process.[18] Every context of interlocution is a cause for distortion and uncertainty. We do not simply defer to the linguistic

---

17 See [BUR 93].
18 See [BEZ 98].

behavior of others. Rather, we attempt to give meaning to that behavior by supposing that the speaker has the intention of communicating something to us. It is on the basis of this critique of a justification of trust in testimony based on the preservative nature of language that this author has attempted in several publications to sketch out a *pragmatic theory of trust.*[19]

2.8. Trust and communication

Communication is a voluntary act. Every speech act affirms the authority of the speaker about what she is saying. Speaking to other people is one way of exerting pressure on them, asking them to accept what we are saying simply for the sake of communication. If someone intentionally decides to address us, this legitimately gives us the right to take a conversational stance which recognizes the interlocutor's authority about the subject of her discourse. By addressing me, my interlocutor communicates something to me about the world, and at the same time tells me something about herself: that it is worth listening to her and believing her. According to the philosopher Paul Grice[20], conversational exchange requires at least a form of trust in the other person, i.e. an assumption of the willingness of the interlocutor to cooperate for the success of the communication. This presumption of cooperation coordinates communication and maximizes mutual understanding. This does not mean that we have to passively accept everything said by the interlocutor. The presumption of trust enables the interlocutors to share a common context of hypotheses necessary for interpretation. It is precisely this cognitive vulnerability which we have to accept in order to acquire information through communication. Once the communication has succeeded and we have a shared context of hypotheses, we evaluate the credibility of those hypotheses on the basis of what we already know about the interlocutor and about the world. Eventually, we may be able to accept them as beliefs. The trust required to interpret others – i.e. the trust in their cooperation – is therefore both fragile and fundamental: while it

---

19 See [ORI 04; ORI 05; ORI 07; ORI 08; ORI 09].

20 With his analysis of *conversational maxims*, Grice is considered to be the founding father of modern philosophical pragmatics. See [GRI 91] and the previous chapter.

is a presupposition for any communication act, we may nonetheless decide to retract it later on if the hypotheses shared in the communication are revealed to contradict other information.

While this necessary deference may correspond to what we accept as true in the initial phases of our cognitive and linguistic development, once we have a certain command of the language spoken in our linguistic community, we are able to manifest a more skeptical attitude toward information given to us by others. This does not simply mean that we will verify the truth or estimate the probability of everything that is said to us. Indeed, in most cases, we will have no way of doing so. Rather, we seek to refine our understanding of the other people's intentions, and to develop more sophisticated heuristics to evaluate their credibility and sincerity. Over the past twenty years, developmental psychology has attempted to gain a fuller understanding of the capacity that human beings have to *mentalize*, i.e. to attribute a meaning to the behavior of others, attributing beliefs and intentions to them. Our *folk psychology* guides our *sense of other people*: it is as crucial a tool in acquiring information about the world as perception is.[21] Our interpretative capacities develop gradually, but they are present even at the earliest stages of our cognitive development. Recent studies show that in acquiring a language, a rudimentary folk psychology is indispensable, suggesting that this is an even more fundamental skill than language itself.[22] Understanding a language, understanding intentions and acquiring information from other people are all communicative activities which require a great capacity for social understanding. From this point of view, Reid's natural disposition to trust others is described in cognitive terms as an aspect of a cognitive competency which is fundamental for social understanding.[23]

Knowledge comes to us through communication, and communication is a far more creative process than is usually recognized: we do not merely accept information – we reconstruct it and process it on the basis of what we understand about our

---

21 See [ORI 07].
22 See [BLO 00; CAR 98].
23 See [SPE 10].

interlocutors. Trusting other people is therefore part of the constructive process that helps to share a context of hypotheses – something that is crucial in order to understand what is said. Blind trust does not exist in communication, except perhaps in extreme cases of social influence or during the very earliest stages of our development. Our deferential attitude is a part of the interpretative capacities which mold our understanding of the social world, and it is compatible with the epistemic strategies which enable us to evaluate the competence and goodwill of others. Our primary objective in the acquisition of knowledge through other people is to understand what is being communicated to us, by interpreting their hypotheses and beliefs in the light of our own beliefs. We are never passively "infected" by other people's beliefs. We share responsibility for the words and deeds of others. We also maintain a reciprocal relationship with a view to improving the quality of our conversation.

2.9. Conclusion

The social dimension of our beliefs is based on our activity as interpreters – an activity which we always share with others. A communication act is an involvement in an interaction which establishes not only a series of social attempts [GOF 67], but also a shared cognitive environment. We adopt a *stance of trust* in the conversation, meaning that we believe in the willingness of our interlocutor to participate appropriately in the conversation and engage in the construction of a mutual environment. This does not mean that we persist in believing everything we have accepted for the good of the conversation. A stance of trust is a fundamental ingredient in the process of conversation, but it is a virtual form of trust, which may be short-lived. Our cognitive labor, carried by our trust in our interlocutor's intentions, may greatly surpass, or deviate from, mere understanding of what has been said. The stance of trust that we assume in a conversation is a form of cognitive vulnerability. It is the cognitive risk which we accept in engaging in that exchange. As has been said, this trust is both fundamental and fragile: it is constructed dynamically in the conversation and some of the commitments of trust which we make during communication are not contextual and may be renegotiated. By the simple fact of addressing us, other people ask us to adopt such a stance of trust. The justification of that stance is not to be found in the properties of language, but rather in the cognitive and social specificity of our recognition of an intentional act addressed to us. This stance of trust may make us more disposed to believe, but it is not sufficient to make us credulous: along with our interlocutor, we create a shared cognitive environment whose epistemic consequences we are responsible for. In order to be in a position to believe what others tell us, we must accept the vulnerability that any communication exchange brings with it, but this does not mean that we have to relinquish our cognitive independence.

2.10. Bibliography

[BEZ 98] BEZUINDEHOUT A., "Is verbal communication a purely preservative process?", *The Philosophical Review*, vol. 107, pp. 261–288, 1998.

[BLO 00] BLOOM P., *How Children Learn the Meaning of Words*, Cambridge University Press, Cambridge, 2000.

[BUR 93] BURGE T., "Content preservation", *The Philosophical Review*, vol. 102, pp. 457–487, 1993.

[CAR 98] CARPENTER M., NAGELL K., TOMASELLO M., "Social cognition, joint attention and communicative competence from 9 to 15 months of age", *Monographs of the Society of Research in Child Development*, vol. 63, no. 4, pp. 1–174, 1998.

[ENG 07] ENGEL P., *Va savoir !*, Hermann, Paris, 2007.

[FOL 94] FOLEY R., "Egoism in epistemology", in SCHMITT F.F. (ed.), *Socializing Epistemology*, Rowman & Littlefield, Boston, 1994.

[FOL 01] FOLEY R., *Intellectual Trust in Oneself and Others*, Cambridge University Press, Cambridge, 2001.

[FRI 07] FRICKER M., *Epistemic Injustice*, Oxford University Press, New York, 2007.

[FUL 88] FULLER S., *Social Epistemology*, Indiana University Press, Bloomington, 1988.

[GET 05] GETTIER E., "Is justified true belief knowledge?", *Analysis*, vol. 23, no. 6, pp. 121–123, 1963.

[GIB 90] GIBBARD A., *Wise Choices. Apt Feelings*, Harvard University Press, Cambridge, p. 181, 1990.

[GOF 67] GOFFMAN E., *La présentation de soi*, Editions de Minuit, Paris, 1967.

[GOL 86] GOLDMAN A., *Epistemology and Cognition*, Harvard University Press, Cambridge, 1986.

[GOL 99] GOLDMAN A., *Knowledge in a Social World*, Oxford University Press, New York, 1999.

[GOL 04] GOLDMAN A., "Qu'est-ce que l'épistémologie sociale ?", in PACHERIE E., PROUST J. (eds.), *La philosophie cognitive*, Editions Ophrys, Paris, p. 159, 2004.

[GOL 11] GOLDMAN A., "A guide to social epistemology", in GOLDMAN A., WHITCOMB D. (eds.), *Social Epistemology*, Oxford University Press, New York, 2011.

[GRI 91] GRICE P., *Studies in the Ways of Words*, Harvard University Press, Cambridge, 1991.

[HAR 91] HARDWIG J., "The role of trust in knowledge", *Journal of Philosophy*, vol. 88, no. 12, pp. 693–708, 1991.

[KIT 93] KITCHER P., *The Advancement of Science*, Oxford University Press, New York, 1993.

[KOR 94] KORNBLITH H., "A conservative approach to social epistemology", in SCHMITT F.F., *Socializing Epistemology: The Social Dimensions of Knowledge*, Rowman & Littlefield Publishers, Lanham, 1994.

[LON 90] LONGINO H., *Science as Social Knowledge: Values and Objectivity in Scientific Inquiry*, Princeton University Press, Princeton, 1990.

[ORI 04] ORIGGI G., "Is trust an epistemological notion?", *Episteme*, vol. 1, no. 1, pp. 61–72, June 2004.

[ORI 05] ORIGGI G., "Peut-on être antiréductionniste à propos du témoignage ?", *Philosophie*, vol. 88, pp. 47–57, 2005.

[ORI 07] ORIGGI G., "Le sens des autres. L'ontogenèse de la confiance épistémique", *Raisons pratiques*, vol. 89, Editions de l'EHESS, Paris, 2007.

[ORI 08] ORIGGI G., "A stance of trust" in MORA MILLÁN M.L. (ed.), *Estudios en homenaje a José Luis Guijarro Morales*, University of Cadiz, pp. 187–200, 2008.

[ORI 09] ORIGGI G., "Confiance, autorité et responsabilité épistémique. Pour une généalogie de la confiance raisonnée", in LOBET-MARIS C., LUCAS R., SIX B. (eds.), *Variations sur la confiance*, Chapter 1, PIE Peter Lang, Brussels, 2009.

[PUT 75] PUTNAM H., The meaning of "meaning", *Language, mind and knowledge,* Minnesota Studies in the Philosophy of Science, vol. 7, 1975.

[REI 64] REID T., *An inquiry into the human mind on the principles of common sense,* 1764.

[SCH 94] SCHMITT F.F. (ed.), *Socializing Epistemology*, Rowman & Littelfeld, London, 1994.

[SPE 10] SPERBER D., ORIGGI G., *et al.*, "Epistemic Vigilance", *Mind and Language*, vol. 25, no. 4, pp. 359–393, 2010.

Chapter 3

The Fundamentals of Intelligence

3.1. Introduction

Information evaluation has always been a concern for intelligence agencies – particularly those in the field of military defense. While the concept of intelligence is not a new one, it is one about which there is very little theory. The same is true of the activity of intelligence, which is often conflated with the activity of the special services.

The contemporary definition of the term "intelligence" has been influenced by the military phenomenon and contemporary conflicts. Hollywood, in its depictions of competitive intelligence, has only picked up on espionage, which is more easily conveyed through media than the background work and reflection that is the counterpart to espionage, hidden beneath the surface.

Historically, in the military domain, conducting and preparing for a war requires us to try and crack the secrets of an adversary who was sometimes several days' travel away, who speaks a different language and looks like a foreigner. In addition, we need to steal information because usually, there is precious little information in circulation, and the task of gathering it – essentially a human task – is a very difficult

Chapter written by Philippe LEMERCIER.

one. "Human" espionage is commonplace, and can use any necessary ploy, including manipulation. This has earned the discipline a somewhat negative connotation – particularly in France, which we shall use as a case study throughout this chapter.

Very recently, in 2008, the topic of intelligence was first discussed in the *Livre blanc sur la défense et la sécurité nationale* (White Paper on Defense and National Security) [LBD 08a; LBD 08b]. This white paper defined five strategic functions, confirmed by the 2013 version [LBD 13]: knowledge/anticipation, deterrence, prevention, protection and intervention. Intelligence is included as one of the components of knowledge/anticipation.

The aim of this chapter is to set out the fundamental principles of competitive intelligence. Owing to the scarcity of theoretical writings on the subject, there is a tendency in the Anglo-American community to question whether the discipline is more artistic or scientific in nature. However, for our purposes here, we can adopt a scientific, analytical approach.

Hence, in this chapter, we shall discuss the uses of terminology, before going on to the terminological and methodological building blocks for a theory on intelligence.

3.2. Information evaluation in the language of intelligence

3.2.1. *A context which is not clearly defined, open to multiple interpretations*

To begin with, we are going to look at the definition of the word "intelligence"; then at the purposes of the activity of intelligence; then at the entities in charge of such activities; and finally the division of the activity of intelligence into different contributing sub-activities.

3.2.1.1. *Intelligence – a polysemic term*

Although to a large extent, the white papers [LBD 08a; LBD 08b] brought it back to center-stage, they do not rigorously define what intelligence is. Yet regardless of its purpose, it is associated with three notions:

– an activity that can be broken down into sub-activities;

– entities in charge of that activity;

– types of information used for that activity.

Furthermore, it is associated with numerous concepts and terms, as outlined by the graph in Figure 3.1.

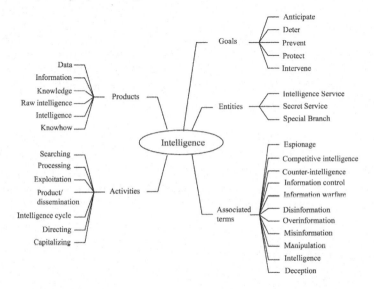

Figure 3.1. *Taxonomy of vocabulary associated with intelligence*

As we can see, the terminology is extremely varied and is characterized by empirical uses heavily influenced by the domain of the military and the "intelligence community" – particularly since the Second World War, when the first theoretical treatises on intelligence were published.

Consistency between texts is by no means assured, and interaction between the intelligence community and the people attempting to produce theory on its practices – either from within it or from a university environment – is the exception rather than the rule.

Therefore, for this chapter, it seems useful to adopt an approach typical of system specifications, involving a number of inevitable steps:

– defining the services to be provided, from the point of view of a backer and/or the beneficiary of the system;

– identifying use contexts;

– describing the modalities for each use context.

3.2.1.2. *Purposes which are clear but are still subject to interpretation*

The white papers [LBD 08a; LBD 08b] defined the aims of intelligence as "autonomy of appreciation, decision and action", and its beneficiaries: "for the highest authorities in the State, for our diplomatic corps, the armed forces and the homeland security and civil security apparatus".

There is widespread consensus about the overall aims of intelligence, but in a very general and imprecise sense: to illuminate the decisions of a decision-maker. There are many players who could serve this goal. We can easily identify a number of professional groups who might contribute:

– journalists;

– university researchers;

– independent experts;

– forensic police.

All of these can make a decision clearer for a decision-maker: the journalist explains to the reader, who then exercises free will; the researcher helps enlighten an engineer wishing to design an innovative device; the expert expresses an opinion to his backer; and the forensic scientist elucidates a situation for a police inspector and then a judge.

It is perhaps surprising, in this age where there are mechanisms for comparison or grading of most products and services, that most corporations appear to escape such assessment. However, the intelligence services operate according to an overarching plan, whereas most individuals tend to act mainly on initiative. Thus, the activity of intelligence is a generic process that is applied to a specific context, which we shall discuss below.

3.2.1.3. The entities in charge of intelligence

[LBD 08a; LBD 08b] gave a list of intelligence services, centered around "two departments of general competence: the *Direction générale de la sécurité extérieure* (DGSE – Directorate General of Foreign Intelligence Service), which is in charge of seeking out and exploiting intelligence data outside of the national territory, and the *Direction centrale du renseignement intérieur* (DCRI – Central Directorate of Homeland Security), whose activity of intelligence-gathering and judicial policing is directed at the national territory" and "four specialized services: two services which support the Ministry of Defense and the armed forces – the *Direction du renseignement militaire* (DRM – Military Intelligence Directorate) and the *Direction de la protection et de la sécurité de la défense* (DPSD – Directorate for Protection and Security of Defense Interests) – and two services specializing in import/export and financial issues – the *Direction nationale du renseignement et des enquêtes douanières* (DNRED – National Directorate for Intelligence and Customs Inquiries) and the service *Traitement du renseignement et action contre les circuits financiers clandestins* (TRACFIN – Intelligence Processing and Action Against Clandestine Money Rings)."

It should be noted, however, that other entities are at work in the sphere of intelligence activity, as suggested by the white paper *La France face au terrorisme* (France in the Face of Terrorism) [LBF 06] and echoed by the ORION group's report [ORI 12].

It may be surprising to learn that the armed forces' intelligence-gathering and analysis capabilities are not afforded the same status, and were not cited in the ORION report. In particular, we are referring here to specialized information-gathering units, the command centers for the airforce (*centre d'exploitation de l'armée de l'Air* – CRA), navy (*centre d'exploitation de la Marine* – CRMAR) and land forces (*centre d'exploitation de l'armée de Terre* – CERT...) and to the entities deployed in the theater of operations.

In view of the diversity of the organizations under discussion here and of their prerogatives, it is helpful to look at the activities which they perform. It seems no easy task to compare and evaluate them, as their fields of expertise are so dissimilar.

3.2.1.4. *Activities of the intelligence services*

The first definition of an intelligence cycle seems to have come from the American army, at the end of WWII. Intelligence is described by [WHE 11], reproducing the cycle attributed to [DAV 48], as an activity of collection of information made available for use after processing.

Note that the term "direction" is applied only to the collection effort, and that the processing of the information seems to be excluded from the field of direction. Note also that the driving force in this cycle is the military operations (missions) which make each of the cogwheels turn.

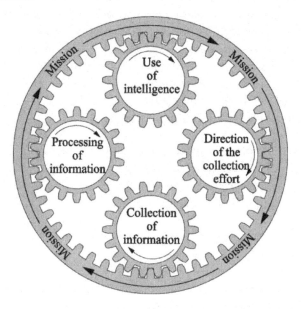

Figure 3.2. *The intelligence cycle from the time of WWII, attributed to Davidson and Glass by Wheathon [WHE 11]*

The definition given in the *doctrine interarmées du renseignement d'intérêt militaire* (DIA2 – Inter-Armed-Forces Doctrine on Intelligence of Military Interest) [CIC 10] is broader, and is in line with that given by NATO: "The intelligence cycle is defined as a 'sequence of operations by which information is obtained, classified, transformed into intelligence and made available to users.'

These operations include:

– the direction of information-collection efforts;

– the collection of information;

– the exploitation of the information collected;

– the dissemination of the intelligence.

The running of this cycle is not the effect of a spontaneous movement, but rather of a definite action by the controllers, referred to as the animation of the intelligence function."

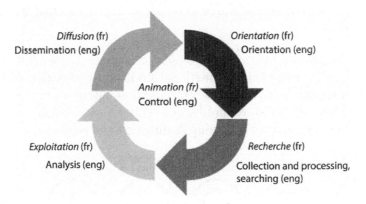

Figure 3.3. *National cycle of intelligence of military interest according to DIA 2 [CIC 10]*

Two activities (animation and orientation) control the other three activities, which aim to transform the raw material (information) into product (intelligence).

In addition, the same document introduces the notion of intelligence elaboration (*élaboration de renseignement*), which covers searching (collection and processing) and exploitation. One might reasonably wonder about the relevance of the word "elaboration" to cover these two notions, given that the *Académie française* defines the verb as "to prepare and produce, by an assiduous work of the mind", and the Collins Concise English Dictionary defines as "to produce by careful labor". Indeed, the analytical aspect is predominant, whereas the terms "exploitation" and "searching" evoke activities of an industrial or mining-related nature: "searching" (prospecting) for a resource, followed by extraction/exploitation.

The two terms "exploitation" and "elaboration" seem to be more mutually complimentary than mutually opposed. Indeed, when we find the enemy's plans, it is sufficient to do a swift check; after that, we can simply exploit the intelligence. However, when we have no information at all, or – on the contrary – have an ocean of information, it is necessary to perform a critical analysis in order to find the missing pieces of the puzzle, or to dispense with pieces that are wrong or irrelevant.

For its part, the American intelligence community (see [ODN 11]) has adopted a non-cyclical functional division of activities into four services relating to the flow of information (Collection, Processing & exploitation, Analysis & production and Dissemination) and two relating to management (Planning & direction and Evaluation).

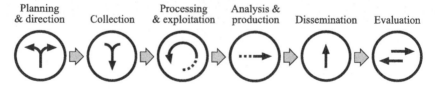

Figure 3.4. *Process of intelligence used by the Americans [ODN 11]*

This helps to distinguish phases wherein different skills are put to use. Collection is the business of specialists who are expert with the sensor in question (electromagnetic signals, photographs, non-electromagnetic signals, humans, open sources[1] such as the Internet, space imaging, etc.). Processing makes the collected data intelligible for analysts. Analysis involves weaving together pieces of information which may be contradictory and incomplete. Dissemination boils down to making the intelligence available to its beneficiaries. Exploitation is associated with processing, and analysis is separate from it. For a fuller examination of the different cycles in the intelligence process, readers can refer to [IRS 11] and [WHE 11].

3.2.1.5. Overview

The military entities involved in intervention (to again use the terminology employed for the five strategic functions in [LBD 08a; LBD 08b]) have adopted the terminology "exploitation", while the ODNI (Office of the Director of National Intelligence), which is at the highest level in the American State machinery, draws a distinction between "exploitation" and "analysis".

In view of [LBD 08a; LBD 08b] it appears that the decisions which are illuminated by intelligence may be strategic in nature (i.e. they affect the State at the very highest level, in the long or short term), or may be more operational (they do not involve high-level State personnel and are not long-term) or tactical. Therefore, there are many different entities in charge of illuminating these decisions and, a priori, the issues with which they deal and the means they use to deal with those issues may be very different.

Increasingly regularly, decisions need to be taken in emergency situations and, regardless of their scope, it is always best if these decisions can be anticipated. Therefore, we can consider two different types of intelligence organizations: those in charge of capitalizing on and producing intelligence, which will then be consumed (used) by those organizations in charge of supporting operations – military, police, security-related, medical, etc. operations. We are also led to

---

1 Open sources are sources which contain so-called "white information" (i.e. easily and legally accessible) and "gray information" (legally accessible but not widely known about or difficult to access) in the definition given by AFNOR, the French standardization agency (X50-053). This precludes "black information", which is "of restricted availability *and* whose access or use is deliberately protected".

consider intelligence as a process whereby the quality of the information is improved.

As information is the primary material used by these services, it is useful to specify the transformations that the information undergoes, so as to identify the points where measures would be most relevant.

3.2.2. *An informational model historically based on the evaluation of information and of sources*

The activity of intelligence acquires added value by way of the quality of the information: we need to analyze its characteristics from the viewpoint of what it adds, rather than the viewpoint of its various competing sub-activities. We shall now examine a number of classic models which are used to put information, and its variants with differing values, into perspective, before going into greater depth about the notion of information evaluation, looking at different situations.

3.2.2.1. *Knowledge pyramids*

From the intelligence cycle, it appears that the main added value of the discipline of intelligence is to collect information and produce enhanced information. This can be represented diagrammatically as a qualitative pyramid. There are numerous variants of such pyramids, presented   in   [ROW 06]: DIKW (Data, Information, Knowledge, Wisdom), DIKUW (Data, Information, Knowledge, Understanding, Wisdom) or SDIK (Signal, Data, Information, Knowledge). Note the distinction between understanding and knowledge, which gives rise to a degree of abstraction and conceptualization.

In general, the notion of raw data is confined to the area of technological sensors. Also the terms "signal" and "data" are, for simplicity's sake, often omitted.

France's military intelligence service retains three levels in the DIA2 (see [CIC 10, paragraphs 111, 112 and 113]).

"*Data* characterize elements corresponding to facts, states or events. They may come in a variety of forms: textual, graphic, signal from sensors, transcoded for all types of supports."

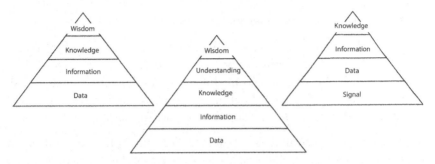

Figure 3.5. *The DIKW, DIKUW and SDIK pyramids*

Using one or more datasets, an analysis – sometimes automated or reduced to its simplest expression – is performed to give the data meaning. The end product is now called *information* and is intended to be communicated.

Finally, intelligence is "the result of the exploitation of the pieces of information. The elaboration of intelligence, which takes place in parallel to the mastering of the information, is represented symbolically." Figure 3.6 illustrates this hierarchy between data, information and intelligence.

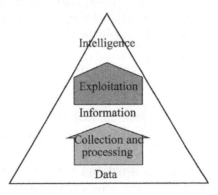

Figure 3.6. *Knowledge pyramid for intelligence of military interest (DIA2 in [CIC 10])*

It is universally acknowledged that the higher up the pyramid one goes, the more valuable the information (in the generic sense) becomes.

However, we can consider two viewpoints:

– that of the process, whereby signals can be transformed into data, data into information, information into knowledge, knowledge into understanding and understanding into wisdom. We then need to ask the question of where the added value comes from at each stage, and the amount of time that is needed for the transformation;

– that of the terminology, whereby we can define a relation of hyponymy between the terms: data are a particular form of signals; information is a particular form of data; knowledge of information; understanding of knowledge; and wisdom of understanding.

3.2.2.2. *Evaluation of the information collected by sensors and of human sources*

Evaluation of sources was first developed with regard to human sources, and then extended to apply to information gathered by technological sensors (to use conventional terminology) – particularly electromagnetic sensors.

Among the elements which are liable to skew the information provided by a human source, we can identify his capacity to objectively perceive facts and to reformulate them objectively, using a language and lexicon that are shared with a technological sensor, but also his desire to influence the receiver.

Note that a primary source may prove to be a prevaricator, in which case we are essentially dealing with an operation of influence or deception.[2]

The rating attributed to a primary source appears to be the result, based on experience regarding that source, of his attributable reliability. The rating for information therefore relates to the average which is used to evaluate the sources. Equally, the rating for the

---

2 See Chapter 1 and its section on information warfare.

information contributes to the rating of the sources which provided it. Figure 3.7 illustrates this cycle of rating.

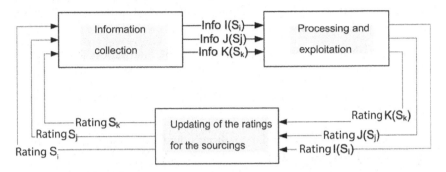

Figure 3.7. *Feedback in terms of the evaluation of information and of information sources*

A piece of information $I(S_i)$ from a source S_i will, *a priori*, inherit the reliability rating of the source (Rating S_i). After processing and exploitation, the product – intelligence – created by comparison with other referential pieces of information or with models, will be used to assign a rating to that information *a posteriori* (Rating $I(S_i)$). In order to ensure the consistency of the model, the rating of the source (Rating S_i) needs to be updated on the basis of the rating of the information most recently provided (Rating $I(S_i)$). It is quite easy to see the limitations of such an approach:

– is the source equally as reliable (or unreliable) in all the domains in which it produces information?

– when the source no longer has the same reliability, how are we to retrospectively re-evaluate all the information it has provided in the past?

– when the source is not a primary source, what value does the rating have?

We are going to attempt to identify cases which are typical in terms of the conditions in which the information was collected, the interactive nature and the richness of the type of media used:

– evaluation of a physical source (a scene);

– evaluation of a primary source considered interactively using rich modalities;

– evaluation of a primary source considered interactively using impoverished modalities;

– evaluation of a primary source without interaction (unbeknown to the source);

– evaluation of a secondary source considered interactively using rich modalities;

– evaluation of a secondary source considered interactively using impoverished modalities;

– evaluation of a secondary source without interaction (unbeknown).

3.2.2.2.1. Evaluation of a scene

Here we discuss the situations encountered during the collection of image data – particularly images acquired from a distance – and the collection of signals that are not associated with an interaction between people.

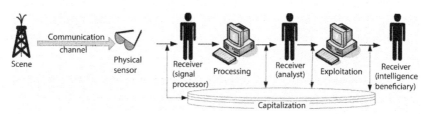

Figure 3.8. *Evaluation of a scene*

It is also necessary to think about the reliability of the sensor and the possibility of manipulation of the scene by a third party.

From this, we can deduce the factors influencing the rating of a scene (which acts as a source in the sense of information theory).

Rating of the scene (source) = function (reliability of sensor, existence of a deceptive third party).

3.2.2.2.2. Evaluation of a primary source considered interactively using rich modalities

This involves an interview in the same place. The source may be collaborative and be aware of the intentions of the human sensor (interviewer/agent), or semi-collaborative if he is unaware of them.

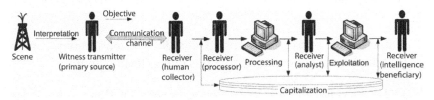

Figure 3.9. *Evaluation of a primary source by interaction*

The richness relating to the interaction can be used by an expert in human intelligence to evaluate context-based elements – particularly non-verbal factors. Obviously, the source may have an influence strategy (a personal objective), may have interpreted whatever he witnessed or indeed may recount what he has seen subjectively. These three parameters can be viewed as determining the reliability of the source.

Rating of the source = function (reliability of the primary source, skill of the human collector).

3.2.2.2.3. Evaluation of a primary source considered interactively using impoverished modalities

The scenario is similar, but because of the communication medium being used, the modalities are impoverished, so the human agent will have greater difficulty in steering the conversation.

The impoverishment may relate to non-verbal factors – e.g. the lack of interaction, no sound, no image (harder to gage reaction, to identify the interlocutor, etc.), sound quality (harder to assess the prosody), emotions, etc.

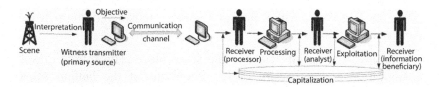

Figure 3.10. *Evaluation of a primary source over a noise-afflicted channel*

Rating of the source = function (reliability of the primary source, skill of the human collector, restrictions due to the medium).

3.2.2.2.4. Evaluation of a primary source without interaction (unknown to the source)

This is an extrapolation of the previous scenario, with the interaction reduced to zero. The likelihood of influence (i.e. personal objective) is less, except if the source suspects he is being monitored.

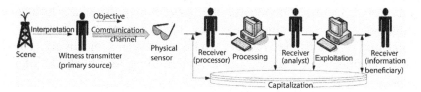

Figure 3.11. *Evaluation of a primary source without interaction*

The human collector is always reliant on his ability to identify certain contextual elements:

– with images and video recordings, these contextual markers could be facial expressions, body language, etc.;

– with conversations, the prosody used by the speaker is a useful marker;

– with digital documents (texts, images, sounds, video recordings), technological traces are left which can be assessed.

Rating of the source = function (reliability of the primary source, skill of the human collector, restrictions due to the medium, reliability of the physical sensor).

3.2.2.2.5. Evaluation of a secondary source with interaction using rich modalities

This involves interactive exchanges where the human intelligence specialist is able to spot contextual elements which could reveal things that are not explicitly said.

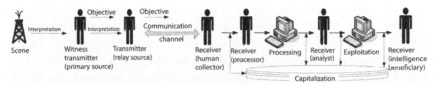

Figure 3.12. *Evaluation of a secondary source via a reliable interactive channel*

Unlike the case of the primary source with the same modalities, we need to take account of the reliability of the secondary source, and we cannot rule out the possibility that other secondary sources may have interposed between the primary source and the relay source. Each source may have a personal objective in terms of influence. The skill of the human collector is relativized.

Rating of the source = function (reliability of the primary source, reliability of the secondary source(s), skill of the human collector).

3.2.2.2.6. Evaluation of a secondary source with interaction over a noise-afflicted channel

The same remark as above applies. This scenario corresponds to interactions using means of communication – particularly the Internet (e-mail exchanges, online discussions, teleconferences, etc.).

Figure 3.13. *Evaluation of a secondary source via a noise-afflicted channel*

Rating of the source = function (reliability of the primary source, reliability of the secondary source(s), knowhow of the human collector, restrictions due to the medium).

3.2.2.2.7. Evaluation of a secondary source without interaction (unknown to the source)

The same remark as above applies. This scenario corresponds to intercepted communications. Unlike the case of the primary source with the same modalities, we need to take account of the reliability of the different secondary sources and any possible personal objectives they may have. The skill of the human collector is relativized. Processing and selection become more difficult because of the lack of interaction.

Figure 3.14. *Evaluation of a secondary source without interaction*

Rating of the source = function (reliability of the primary source, reliability of the secondary source(s), reliability of the physical sensor, restrictions due to the medium).

3.2.2.3. *Evaluation of information gathered from artificial technical sources*

The gleaning of information from artificial technical sources (e.g. a weapons system, a telecom source, a nuclear, radiological, biological, chemical, seismic, etc. system) provides elements of information governed by physical laws, which can be used to perform an analysis.

The sensors provide contextual information which can be analyzed and used to form hypotheses about the systems which produced those data. To do this, we need to use physical models that offer a full understanding of those systems. Evaluating a piece of information produced by such a device involves evaluating the confidence that we can invest in the model used as a benchmark for the technical analysis of the signal.

As one might imagine, a particular source will emit signals in different modes depending on the situation (peace time, crisis state, period of maintenance, etc.). Thus, exhaustive knowledge of these modes is a major factor which contributes to the attribution of a particular rating to a given piece of received information.

Therefore, by evaluating a sensor and its processing device, we contribute to the calculation of the rating for the information it provides.

Note that it is far more difficult to generate false physical signals to disseminate disinformation than it is to lie in a documentary source. Also, by their very nature, such signals afford us reliable avenues for investigation which it would be a shame not to exploit. For example, if we have an in-depth knowledge of the models of photographic sensors (cameras), we can verify whether or not a given image was taken by a particular sensor. Of course, it is much easier to prove that an image is inconsistent or incompatible with a particular type of sensor than to prove that it is authentic.

3.2.2.4. Deconfliction of sources and information

In order to prevent phenomena of amplification, whereby we are led to believe that different sources – which are actually correlated – are independently verifying the same piece of information, the intelligence service has historically and empirically set up an organization whose purpose is to confirm a measurement (with a technological sensor) or a piece of information (with a human source):

– successively with the same sensor;

– comparatively using several sensors of the same type (images, electromagnetic data, human sources, etc.);

– comparatively using different collection domains (humans, images, electromagnetic data) or different services.

Historically, technological sensors are referred to on the basis of the type of signal recorded: SIGINT for Signals Intelligence, IMINT for (spatial or aerial) Imaging Intelligence. Information from human sources is HUMINT (Human Intelligence). Freely accessible information founts are referred to as "open sources" (OSINT). The evaluation of sources and information, in theory, offers a weighting system to valorize certain sources rather than others and favor their use.

By way of example, we could put into perspective three pieces of information gleaned from open sources (a certain country is building a detection system in a particular place), HUMINT (intense activity in the vicinity), and IMINT (confirming that major work is being done there), even if no electromagnetic sensor had detected the signal (SIGINT) normally emitted by this type of system.

Technological sources require specific treatments to make the content usable. These treatments are grounded in signal-processing or transformation techniques (image adjustment, for instance) or indeed translation, speech-to-text conversion, etc. Historically, the agencies which have this type of sensors have developed entities devoted to the processing of each of them. This has also resulting in the grouping together of personnel who specialize in recognizing certain hardware (IMINT), certain types of signals (SIGINT), etc., leading to organizational structures such as that presented in Figure 3.15.

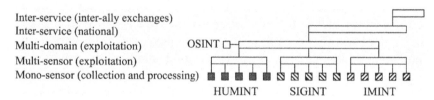

Inter-service (inter-ally exchanges)
Inter-service (national)
Multi-domain (exploitation)   OSINT
Multi-sensor (exploitation)
Mono-sensor (collection and processing)
          HUMINT   SIGINT   IMINT

Figure 3.15. *Historical diagram of deconfliction of multi-sensor, multi-domain intelligence data*

This comparison of information proves problematic when only open sources are available, so that it is difficult to be certain of the authenticity or truth of the sources. Indeed, such sources often promulgate declarative information, which is easily manipulated and frequently imprecise.

Also, this type of organizational structure has two consequences:

– the human resource cost of this deconfliction increases;

– it becomes tempting for teams to recruit people with skills which no longer relate to the type of information being processed, but rather to the subject being studied, causing a largely unnecessary duplication and redundancy of skill-sets.

An alternative is to group entities by homogeneous skills (e.g. specialization in technical data collection, processing, exploitation). This specialization has its limitations in human intelligence, because in order to be able to conduct exchanges with an expert, it is crucially important for the human intelligence specialist to also have a rudimentary knowledge of the particular subject in question. Therefore the organization needs to remain decentralized. While it is possible for a specialist in human intelligence to familiarize himself with a geographic zone, it is trickier for him to acquire expertise in explosives, for instance.

The same is true of open sources, which are directly intelligible for the consumers. Centralizing the collection of such data would cause a loss in reactivity and quality (in terms of accuracy and noise). The cost of collecting them is marginal (off-the-shelf tools are sufficient) but could be optimized by a harmonized acquisition policy.

Figure 3.16 illustrates the possibility for deconfliction in this context:

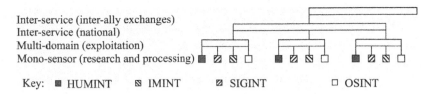

Figure 3.16. *Suggested diagram of deconfliction up to the point of exploitation*

This leads to the introduction of experts, investigators, analysts, etc. into the heart of the intelligence apparatus, as is done in agencies which do not have technological sensors. In such a case, the specialists have access to all of the information collected. The richness is greater, although the specialists need to learn about the foibles of the different sensors underlying the different technologies. The relevant pieces of information can always be selected on the basis of their rating.

3.3. Attempt to formalize generic models appropriate for the new issues facing the intelligence services

Based on the observed uses, we can now attempt to lay the foundations for an epistemology or theory of intelligence. In order to do so, we shall adopt a functional analysis method, considering the environment in which contemporary intelligence activities take place, with a view to identifying invariant factors and ultimately proposing perennial definitions.

3.3.1. *Functional analysis as a support for definition*

Functional-analysis-based methods such as SADT[3], the public version of which is known as the IDEF0 method (*Integration Definition for Function Modeling*) outlined in [NIS 93], involve the description of every activity in terms of the products that it generates, the products that are needed to carry it out, the constraints and mechanisms by which it is controlled, and finally the resources needed to perform it. By applying this to the activity of intelligence, we obtain a diagram similar to Figure 3.17.

Thus, we have identified that the activity *intelligence* produces *intelligence products* intended for the use of beneficiaries who have expressed a *request for intelligence*. The activity of intelligence is performed on the basis of the *information collected*. In order to perform this activity of intelligence, it is necessary to have *staff, methods* (procedures) and *means of collection, processing, exploitation of and capitalization on* the information gathered. This activity is performed under constraints which will be discussed later on.

---

3 *Structured Analysis Design Technique*, trademark of the companies SofTech and IGL Technologies.

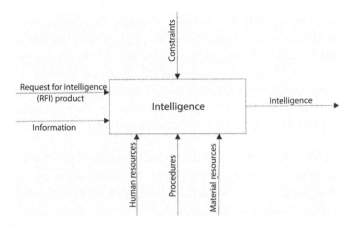

Figure 3.17. *Preliminary functional analysis of the activity of intelligence*

3.3.2. *Paradigm shifts*

In the almost-half-century since the first theory of intelligence emerged, many major changes have taken place. These changes have implications for the balance between searching and exploitation. We shall discuss these implications before going on to characterize the economy of knowledge of the issues that arise in the area of intelligence, and then distinguish the major areas which are affected by all the activities of the intelligence services. Finally, we shall attempt to infer a number of essential invariants from these results.

3.3.2.1. *Intelligence, information-seeking and information-exploitation*

During the 20th Century, there were two major breakthroughs: the emergence of remote information collection using technological means and the opening up of societies, caused by the globalization of the economy.

3.3.2.1.1. Emergence of remote information-collection techniques

Since WWII in terms of IMINT and SIGINT, the intelligence community has been developing assets based on increasingly complex technological systems, shrouded in secret (see the British/American agreement made public in 1988 by Duncan Campbell in [CAM 88]).

Hand in hand with this comes a major constraint: we have to recruit technicians who specialize in photography (development of films, "revelation" of photos and then interpretation of the results obtained), or in transmissions (identification of signals, decoding, locating, transcription, identification of senders, emotions (prosody), or translation). Thus, departments are created which specialize in the gathering of photographic or electromagnetic data.

Consecutively, entities develop which specialize in the collection, then processing and finally exploitation of the information gleaned by the sensors. Most of the time, human and open sources remain close to the analysts.

3.3.2.1.2. Opening up of societies due to globalization of economies

Under pressure from colonial empires looking for economic outlets, since the mid-19th Century, borders have gradually been opening up, providing easy access to even the most isolated of societies. The fall of the Berlin Wall and the opening of China for trade are the most recent concrete examples of this – particularly in terms of free circulation of people. In terms of the free circulation of ideas, the dawn of the Internet and satellite broadcasting does not render particular government sensors unusable. On the contrary, it helps to direct them better and therefore "economize" on their use. Using an image published on the Internet with geolocation data, it is easier to conduct additional investigations using government resources. At least in the short term, therefore, the collection of information seems to be easier, or within the reach of any and everyone. The flip-side of this is that we need to carefully asses the reliability of that information.

3.3.2.2. *Informational economy of the problems posed for the intelligence community*

If we take as our starting point the principle that intelligence illuminates decision-making, four types of problems are posed for the intelligence services depending on the informational richness of the request and the availability of relevant expertise (see Table 3.1).

	Experts are available (problem known)	No experts are familiar with the issue
The beneficiary knows what he wants (inquiry)	Apply a trusted model	Improve an existing model
The beneficiary does not know what he is looking for (prospective) Production is mostly unsolicited	Devise new models	Conceive of new problems and the models associated therewith

Table 3.1. *Typology of problems the intelligence service may need to deal with*

These four types of problems are:

Apply a trusted model: the expert configures his sensors and performs a simplified exploitation using the data obtained. The behavioral models are already in existence. The products serve explicit needs of the beneficiaries. The qualities expected of such work are rigorousness and reactivity. Capitalization on the information gathered and on the knowledge is essential. The definition of the model is scientific and remains valid unless it is invalidated or *falsified*, to use the expression employed by Karl Popper [POP 07]. It is particularly well suited for phenomena governed by the laws of physics or established on the basis of scientific principles.

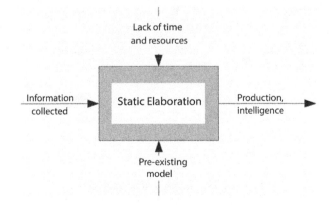

Figure 3.18. *Elaboration of intelligence using a static knowledge model*

The model needed to describe the problem at hand is known and does not change. The resources needing to be devoted to the analysis are not extensive, and the time-period is short;

Improve an existing model: in order to do so, we need to develop expertise, often by trial and error. It is very difficult to deliver reactivity.

Most of the time the products serve explicit needs of the beneficiaries, but the processes may be initiated by the specialists in information collection or exploitation who have identified the unusual events.

The qualities required are initiative and perseverance so as not to abandon avenues of inquiry which seem fruitless. It is necessary to allow a certain degree of initiative to the collection and exploitation experts, who will produce knowledge that can be used to form new models.

The evolving knowledge model is amended by the addition of specific rules to take account of the cases which falsified the original model.

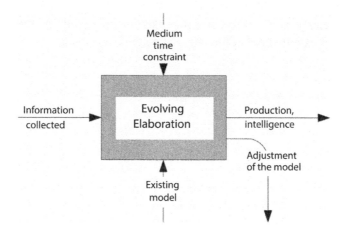

Figure 3.19. *Elaboration of intelligence using an evolving knowledge model*

The model needed to describe the problem at hand is known and changes only little. The resources to be devoted to the analysis and the time-period allowed are variable;

Devise new models: the enemy uses conventional or dual means, but diverts them from their typical usage. The agencies need to be creative and imagine novel scenarios. This is an extension of the previous case, requiring a certain degree of creativity;

Devise new problems and the models associated therewith: the agencies need to make hypotheses, or gamble as to what might happen, and define the relevant alert indicators, which they will ask the sensors to detect. Often the experts will have to imagine indirect ways of accessing these indicators.

By their very essence, the production activities take place on the initiative of the exploitation team, and serve as an early warning system. The aim, therefore, is to formulate models to detect new indicators or to combine existing indicators leading to problematic situations. The terminology "speculative elaboration" could usefully replace "detection of weak signals", which remains anchored to an issue of detection, and therefore of sensors, whereas in fact the issue is to characterize a system by analysis.

The agencies need to be allowed the initiative to work on unexpected scenarios. "Anything goes" to create the model on an empirical as well as theoretical basis. Such a model will never be static, and the constant proposition of new hypotheses will help to improve and enrich it. This approach is particularly well suited to phenomena involving people whose interactions may be extremely difficult to characterize.

The model needed to describe the problem at hand is not or is only partially known, or changes rapidly. The resources to be devoted to the analysis and the time-period allowed may be up to several months.

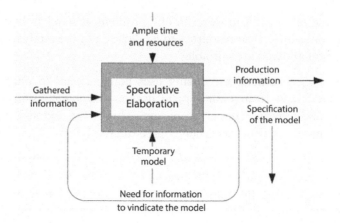

Figure 3.20. *Elaboration of intelligence*
using a speculative knowledge model

3.3.2.3. *Fields of investigation dealt with by intelligence agencies*

The analysis of threats in military intelligence brings to light three main areas of interest: the vectors and players involved in the threats, and the environment in which they move, interact and change. We propose to characterize a threat by a capacity which acts as a vector of a players intentions, with the threat likely to apply differently depending on the environment in which it takes place.

3.3.2.3.1. Capacities, threat vectors

Corresponding to the threat vectors there are physical models (hardware, constraints of support, commitment, usage, maintenance, performances, etc.) or logical models (access time, response time, etc.) which can be used to produce debatable hypotheses. Thus, there is an epistemological substrate which can be used to gain a high level of confidence of a certain level of physical performance (speed, power, penetration capacity, etc.).

This leads us to develop assorted models of threats with sometimes surprising variants (e.g. diversion of a system from its usual purpose). The non-typical NRBC (nuclear-radiological-biological-chemical) or de-materialized threats (e.g. cyber threats, trafficking, including white-collar crime) fall into this category, because the corresponding models are models of expansion, propagation and effects.

The problem at hand, therefore, is one of having the appropriate models, developing variants of them (often by pushing the limits) and looking for measurable elements that can be used as evidence.

However, there are limitations to which this approach is subject. These include technological breakthroughs and the measurability of certain physical parameters for evidence.

3.3.2.3.2. The intentions of potentially threatening actors

In this domain, the models appear to be less deterministic, and are grounded in the unfairly-labeled "soft" sciences (sociology, ethnology, psychology, etc.), although scientific proof has been emerging for years (from cognitive sciences) to support the often excellent theories of their experts.

The problem lies in knowing the psychology of the players, their culture, their training, their fantasies or their obsessions. Behavioral models are not hugely deterministic, and media focus or geopolitical pressure can influence the behavior of the participants at play, etc. but also that of their enemies.

As human behavior is, in fact, rarely deterministic, it is misguided to attempt to precisely model the behavior of the players, with the exception of certain very widely applicable phenomena. The avenues glimpsed by Serge Galam [GAL 03], through the lens of sociophysics, appear interesting and innovative in this respect.

More generally, it is possible to establish alternative scenarios [HEU 06] and envisage the consequences of those scenarios – particularly the quantifiable effects in the real world (transfers of funds to finance acquisitions, communications to influence enemy and third-party actors, etc.).

With empiricism and creativity, it is possible to generate very rich (usually prospective) scenarios, for which we then need to define the consequences and the measurable elements, and then begin the leg-work of gradually discounting those which are least plausible. However, this approach leads to an explosion of possibilities, which very rarely satisfies decision-makers.

3.3.2.3.3. The environment in which the threats take place

By nature, the environment is accessible and observable by many players – both civilian and military. It includes those who are under threat, those who are threatening (or potentially threatening) and the conflict space (either geophysical or virtual) which is governed by stable rules, which can be modeled and are often clearly understood.

3.3.2.4. *Consequences of these paradigm shifts*

3.3.2.4.1. Information collection has become easier, but the importance of capacities for information storage and valorization has greatly increased.

The explosion in the amount of accessible information, particularly by public processes (open sources), but also the widespread digitization of communications, have utterly reversed the situation: instead of the scarcity of primary material that was experienced up until the late 1980s, we now have an (over-) abundant quantity of primary material.

The consequence of this is that we need to manage the *capitalization* on that primary material, both for its proven and its potential value (e.g. retain information about second-order areas or topics for preventative purposes).

It therefore becomes essential to have *processing* tools capable of *rendering* the information gathered *intelligible* (translation, transcription of soundtracks in different languages into text), in order to *select* what will be kept, but also to facilitate later use of those data by analysts (it is helpful for an expert working on China to be able to read what its neighbors are writing, in Russian, Japanese, Korean, etc.).

The quantity of information accumulated poses – and will continue to increasingly pose – the problem of the quantity of information thrown up by search engines which, in any case, will always present documents at the top of the list, using criteria which are rather difficult to apprehend. *Treatments for valorization* of the capitalized information (grouping together of similar pieces of information, detection of links, co-occurrences, temporal forecasting, geographic projections, etc.), but also quick *retrieval* of the relevant information, buried deep within an enormous volume of heterogeneous multimedia information, constitute new challenges.

These four functions of *capitalization, rendering intelligible, valorization* and *retrieval* of informational capital have become essential components for the experts who exploit information to produce intelligence.

3.3.2.4.2. Consumers with rare or dual fields of expertise

The elaboration of intelligence, for its part, requires increasingly interdisciplinary expertise, in view of the issues dealt with, and is dependent on the quality of the treatments carried out beforehand. In addition, the consumers need to be increasingly specific in the expression of the need for information, and if possible, be aware of the capabilities of the sensors and sources so as to avoid requests which are impossible to implement – because they are either too unwieldy or incompatible with the reactivity required.

3.3.2.4.3. Detectable invariants

Analysis of the founding texts of the six French intelligence services shows that certain highly-integrated agencies have acquired a decisive advantage by placing the exploiters, analysts or investigators at the heart of the apparatus and surrounding them with experts in searching (information is thus readily available and easily accessible) and their beneficiaries in charge of neutralizing the threat.

Reactivity seems to be essential and variable even within the same agency. It is easier to react to events in real time when we have anticipated their occurrence. Agencies which mobilize their resources only in response to events, without capitalizing on the knowledge gathered and without the benefit of experience, are unlikely to remain at a high level for long. The more extensive an agency's knowledge and the further back it goes, the easier it will be for that agency to adapt to an event which was unexpected from the point of view of its beneficiaries.

In addition, intelligence contributes to anticipation, and the intelligence services themselves need to anticipate events and threats to gain better knowledge of them, and be able to feed that knowledge to the beneficiaries. They therefore need to have a *capacity for initiative* that enables them to set aside a portion of their resources to compile unconventional dossiers.

Finally, the launch of an operation decided upon by the government or other authority to overcome a major threat requires *protection* of the whole of the operational chain involved in the preparation and execution of the operation – all the more so when the stakes are strategic and the decisions involve the higher strata of the state framework. The need for protection of activities other than intelligence seems less urgent, although it remains covered by "military secrecy". Indeed, the consequences of failure are often felt at an infraministerial level.

We can see the emergence of a crucial element which helps explain why some of the agencies mentioned in the [LBD 08a; LBD 08b] have adopted a very integrated structure (from collection to intervention): the need for *reactivity* and for *protection* between the collection of the information, its exploitation and the action which is to be carried out.

It is also noteworthy that certain agencies, whose mandate is applicable for the national territory, need to provide proof of guilt for the crimes and misdemeanors noted. This constrains these agencies to respect the procedures of the penal code.

3.3.2.4.4. Need for evaluation of intelligence production

Evaluating the production of intelligence may seem somewhat paradoxical. The intelligence services use authoritative experts and sources of information. We can therefore imagine that if they have good experts and rigorous methodology, it would be difficult or even impossible to make a contradictory judgment *a priori*. Yet there is still the possibility of adopting a constructivist approach whereby we can estimate the quality of the overall process of the elaboration of intelligence. Although information evaluation is based on experience and is therefore ill-suited to surprise situations, the evaluation needs to provide *a priori* guidance for a decision-maker.

The three modes of intelligence elaboration (static, evolving and speculative) could therefore be qualified using the following criteria:

– for the static mode of elaboration, the quality is established when the model is designed, based on the exhaustivity of the human and technological sources taken into account, and therefore the availability of the associated sensors and the quality of those sources. The possible scenarios are evaluated at the design phase and are stabilized for a given duration. A preliminary judgment is made to define the cost/efficiency ratio of the device put in place;

– for the evolving mode of elaboration, it is necessary to introduce mechanisms to identify seemingly trivial changes (new sources, new sensors, new practices) and take them into account. The overall quality can be evaluated on the basis of the reliability of these mechanisms. The possible scenarios and the percentage of evolution are evaluated at the design phase and are stopped for a given duration. A graded distribution will be needed, based on the aforementioned percentage of evolution (~5%, ~20%, etc.);

– for the speculative mode of elaboration, information evaluation is no longer of any use, and only the forecasting method of constantly re-evaluated scenarios, popularized within the intelligence services by R. Heuer [HEU 99], seems relevant. The richness of the scenarios envisaged and the falsifiability (*à la* Popper) of the hypotheses chosen are then considered.

3.3.3. *Attempt at a rigorous definition of intelligence*

Two points of view can be adopted here: an external (black box) view of a service rendered, and an internal (white box) view that gives a functional description of the activities involved.

3.3.3.1. *External model of intelligence*

This model discusses the intelligence service from an outside point of view. We can add to the initial diagram presented in Figure 3.21.

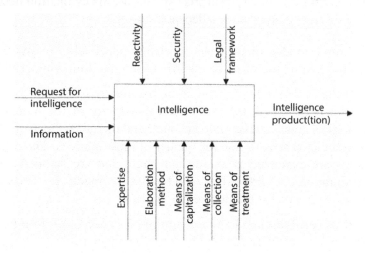

Figure 3.21. *External model of the activity of intelligence*

– Input:

   - collected information;

   - request for intelligence products or intelligence data;

– output:

   - intelligence or intelligence products;

– constraints:

   - a need for reactivity (time for production);

   - a legal framework;

   - security requirements;

– support (resources):

   - human expertise;

- methods and knowhow;

- means of capitalization, collection and processing of the information.

Let us now describe the entities which are in charge of intelligence, the activity, the characteristics, the informational added value and the terminology associated therewith.

3.3.3.1.1. Intelligence agencies

The following definition is suggested:

"State bodies in charge of providing elements of decision support or aid to the conducting of action at governmental level. They are subject to particular requirements in terms of reactivity, neutrality and secret-keeping, and have a specific legal and regulatory framework."

3.3.3.1.2. Intelligence defined as an activity

The following definition is suggested:

"An authoritative activity entrusted to organizations with particular prerogatives in terms of information collection, to provide state decision-makers – within predefined time periods and to a degree of confidence proportional to the stakes that the decisions represent – with information offering knowledge or understanding, justifiable by way of argumentation or investigation, of an issue or a situation, with a view to a decision or an action."

3.3.3.1.3. Intelligence characterized by the fields of knowledge, skills and aims which it involves

It appears that intelligence can be viewed in the light of three periods of time (prospective time, reflective time and real time to action) [CSD 12], three fields of knowledge (capacities[4], intentions,

---

4 In the sense of the definition given by the inter-armed forces glossary of operational terminology [PIA 12]: "The operational capacity of a unit is determined by the number, availability and skills of its personnel; by the number, availability and capability of its major pieces of equipment; and by its organization, training and cohesion."

environment) and two modalities of intervention (1: knowledge for anticipation, and 2: knowledge for action or alert).

The time periods correspond to the reactivity which can be expected of the intelligence services, or more generally of the knowledge/anticipation service: the *prospective time* (years), the *reflective time* (years or weeks) and the *real time* or *action time* (weeks or hours).

The fields of knowledge are the *capacities* (what is a player capable of?), the *intentions* (what might he want to do?), and the *environment* – geophysical, geopolitical (services with an extra-national mandate), social, sociological, economic, religious (services with national mandate) – in which the players can exercise their intentions by use of their capacities.

Finally, it is necessary to specify the purposes of the intelligence, depending on whether we wish to understand in order to anticipate, to act or to alert.

Thus, *knowledge and understanding for the purpose of anticipation* are of a particular type which facilitates anticipation and therefore helps lay the groundwork for *deterrence*, *prevention* and *protection*. They are found in the *reflective time*, and to a lesser extent the prospective time, and are used for the purpose of *early warning*. They have earned their stripes in the field of capacitating, where the definition, design and realization of capacities can take several years, which means that counter-measures can be taken. As regards the *environment*, knowledge of it can be anticipated, and the relevant expertise is often available in the civilian community. Intentions are, by their very nature, fluctuating and changeable, and are therefore less easy to anticipate.

Knowledge for the purpose of action or alert, for its part, is found in the real time or action time. It is initially fed by knowledge and understanding for the purpose of anticipation, and is updated over time as experience is gained. It can be used for *reactive alerts*.

Figure 3.22 shows all of these time periods, fields of knowledge and modalities, where the darker areas are of higher priority in terms of the stakes and the room for maneuver for those carrying out these activities.

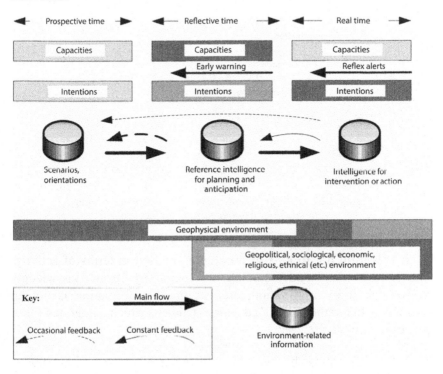

Figure 3.22. *Services provided by intelligence*

This terminology is applicable to all intelligence services, and gives us a functional description, based on the time periods and purposes, of the main categories of topics dealt with.

3.3.3.1.4. Intelligence defined as high-added-value information

The hierarchical terminological relation of the term "intelligence" appears to be compatible both with the term "knowledge" and the term "understanding", with the latter bringing a more conceptual dimension into play.

The knowledge pyramids introduced earlier on express that relation, which can in fact be better expressed by an imbricated relation (see Figure 3.23).

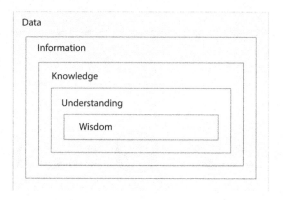

Figure 3.23. *Lexicographical model of the information-related terminology associated with intelligence*

It is helpful not to look at this representation in terms of activity, considering that understanding is extracted from knowledge, knowledge from information, etc., as the transformation is not an extraction but rather an added value activity, which integrates other pieces of knowledge.

Information must be considered to be a hypernym of the nouns "knowledge", "understanding" and "intelligence", because these latter are more restrictive.

Knowledge is a hyponym of the term "information" which adds the notion of appropriation by a person – in this case an expert in the employ of the agencies. This tacitly introduces comparison of the information with the knowledge previously acquired by the expert.

Note that in the area of the environment, and to a lesser extent than the intentions, the skills are shared with a university environment, which is a potential recruiting ground for the intelligence services. With regard to capacities, equivalent skills are to be found in industry.

Understanding (comprehension) is defined in the official dictionary of the *Académie française* as a conceptualization of knowledge. This lends it a more factual aspect. It is therefore positioned as a piece of meta-knowledge – a model or a theory. Obviously, intelligence uses models (ballistic, economic, sociological, criminological, etc.), but has to change them or create new ones when breakthroughs occur.

The French term *renseignement* is polysemic. Historically it has been used to denote knowledge collected in a context which deviates from common law; etymologically, it is synonymous with the understanding of a problem, a threat, of the interactions between players and of the environment in which they occur.

The younger English term *intelligence*, for its part, seems because of its Latin roots – the verb "intelligere", meaning to understand, conceptualize – to be closely related to the term "understanding/comprehension". It entails necessary reflection, questioning of modes of thinking, of the referential knowledge, to establish models which offer an understanding of the subjects being studied.

We propose, therefore, to retain these two uses in their own right, and to distinguish them by way of two definitions: intelligence-knowledge and intelligence-understanding (in French "renseignement-connaissance" and "renseignement-intelligence" respectively).

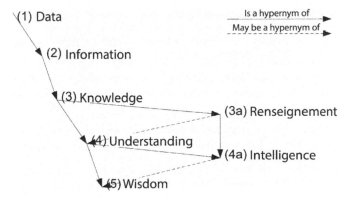

Figure 3.24. *Reworked ontological diagram*

This enables us to preserve the historical consideration, which is that intelligence penetrates the secrecy of the enemy's vaults, and the etymology whereby intelligence is responsible for penetrating the secrecy of knowledge.

The former relates to the action time and knowledge, whereas the latter relates to the reflective time of anticipation.

Two definitions stem from this observation:

"Intelligence-knowledge is a form of knowledge that relates to threats and actors, or to the understanding of situations. It results from the exploitation of information whose reliability has been evaluated previously, and involves the use of tried-and-tested, conscientiously-established knowledge models. Intelligence-knowledge can be used by a head of state to conduct an action."

"Intelligence-understanding is a form of understanding of a situation or a complex issue relating to threats and players shifting within their complex environment. It is elaborated from information, referential knowledge and models established on scientific or empirical bases. Their quality needs to be proportional to the stakes in play and help to gain an *a priori* determination of the level of confidence that the beneficiary can attach to them. Intelligence-understanding helps a state leader prepare for a decision, and more infrequently leads to an action."

3.3.3.1.5. Connected terms and notions

The terms "inquiry" and "investigation", taken from the police, are very similar to that of intelligence as we have just defined it. Indeed, the intelligence agencies do act as agencies of inquiry and investigation, but only on subjects of strategic importance. However, the intelligence services do not tend to systematically intervene, and often rely on other services to accommodate them (in France, for instance, the DRM relies on the head of the armed forces; the DCRI on the general police directorate, etc.).

3.3.3.2. *Internal model of intelligence*

Leaving aside the intelligence cycle in favor of a more functional approach, but one which is richer than the approach of the ODNI discussed above, a general functional model can be put forward. We shall now detail the function of exploitation/elaboration and deduce a typology for intelligence services.

3.3.3.2.1. Overall functional view

Drawing inspiration from the structure of a commercial company, the major operational departments (in the sense that they contribute directly to the value of the finished product) could be:

– direction, which is divided into three sub-functions:

- operational prospective (strategy/marketing department of a company),

- planning of resources allocated to the other three functions,

- counter-intelligence and defense of secrets and knowledge;

– collection (purchasing department of a company), divided into:

- search engineering (where and how can we find the information?),

- capitalization on the searched information (handling of the sensor parameters, descriptions of sources),

- engineering of technical search tools,

- animation of the searching function;

– information management, divided into:

- treatments to render the information intelligible,

- manual or computer-assisted enrichment of the information,

- conservation of the information,

- extraction of the information of interest, and retrieval of the relevant information);

– exploitation and elaboration of intelligence (production department of a company):

- exploitation of the information,

- elaboration and engineering of comprehension models,

- animation of the exploitation/elaboration function,

- production of the referential intelligence data;

– dissemination (sales and customer relations department of a company):

- tailoring of the products for the beneficiaries;

- relations with the beneficiaries.

To go into detail about all of these functions would exceed the scope of this book. Instead, what we shall do is concentrate on the exploitation/elaboration, particularly to attempt to define the elements on which it is based which are likely to relate to information evaluation.

3.3.3.2.2. Exploitation and elaboration of intelligence as a process of enrichment of knowledge

It seems possible to give a generic description of the process of creation and enrichment of knowledge, considering:

– the pre-existence of a basic knowledge model which is at least methodological and independent of the issue under examination, used to:

- constitute models in the scientific sense of the term (physical, behavioral models, etc.). Knowledge can be viewed as an accumulation of facts, modeled by a black-box approach, whereas understanding would be viewed as a white-box modeling process;

- compare incoming information with the referential information and models;

– the existence of a flow of incoming information which is compared to the referential knowledge.

This can be illustrated as shown in Figure 3.25.

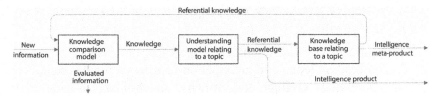

Figure 3.25. *Conceptual model of exploitation of information/ elaboration of intelligence*

The exploitation or elaboration of intelligence therefore consists of contrasting new information with the reference knowledge and, depending on the case, will result in:

– non-credibility of the incoming information;

– enrichment of knowledge on the topic;

– amendment of the comprehension model on the topic.

Intelligence therefore appears to be a particular form of knowledge or understanding of a threat, which can be used to prepare for a decision or carry out an action.

Thus, it is possible to consider that exploitation in the initial sense defined in the context of the intelligence cycle ought to be specialized into two variants, characterized by their level of maturity:

– exploitation, consisting of the contrasting of information against referential knowledge and comprehension models;

– elaboration of intelligence, which can – in addition to exploitation – come to amend or even create new knowledge- or comprehension models.

This is consistent with the rhythm suggested earlier on, with the reflective time offering the opportunity to elaborate knowledge- and comprehension models, while during real time or action time, it is only possible to implement the existing models.

3.3.3.2.3. Typology of intelligence services

A *typology of intelligence services* can be compiled on the basis of the above elements:

– specialized entities, intelligence agencies, the essence of whose profession is knowledge and anticipation of threats, for the benefit of the governmental, civilian and military stateholders in charge of dissuading, preventing, protecting and intervening. This is in line with the description given in the [LBD 08a; LBD 08b]. These entities elaborate intelligence;

– specialists charged with remaining informed of threats, particularly to the specialized services, to assess those threats in terms of the consequences for the fulfillment of their mission of deterrence, prevention, protection or intervention. These specialists exploit information and produce conventional intelligence products, without calling into question the underlying comprehension models. This is in line with the historical description of military intelligence.

Hence, the beneficiaries of the intelligence services are the governmental decision-makers, but also the organizational stateholders in charge of implementing the plans of action on a daily basis.

Their respective rhythms cannot always be synchronized: the former need to privilege and preserve background work but accept marginal incursions of real life or operational emergency; the latter need to privilege reactivity, not expect the intelligence service to make decisions for them and only call on that service in case of very high stakes. This brings the notions of documentary intelligence and situational intelligence back to the fore. The two are mutually complimentary. The elaboration of documentary intelligence facilitates anticipation, but cannot keep up with the pace of real life. Conversely, the exploitation of situational information certifies a factual truth, which is given the status of situational intelligence. It is useful for feedback, for the elaboration of documentary intelligence, particularly by enriching the knowledge bases and understanding models.

This distinction by no means takes away from intelligence or the entities which produce it. On the contrary, it is one explanation of some of the differences between them, and can be used to highlight the best practices.

These two types of intelligence data are not elaborated in the same way. Documentary intelligence uses dynamic or speculative methods of elaboration, with emphasis placed on the richness of the analysis; situational intelligence uses more fixed methods (static or dynamic), and places emphasis on collection and reactivity.

This leads us to identify two axes of governance for the intelligence services:

– an axis of coherence, sharing of good practices and sharing of the information collected, to create intelligence that is as rich as possible, making an effort proportional to the stakes in the decision or the action;

– an axis of customer/supplier relations, associating particular beneficiaries with each service in charge of elaborating intelligence.

Introducing the notion of a customer/supplier does not mean succumbing to excess measurement of performance, which is intensified and inappropriate for an intelligence agency. However, it is desirable to adopter a pragmatic, beneficiary-oriented organization.

We can therefore understand the advantage to keeping the French intelligence services within the ministries which they serve. Yet consistency in terms of their means and of their methods can only develop transversally.

3.4. Conclusion

In France, the intelligence community was founded only very recently, and is constructed empirically. Theorizing about the issues involved in intelligence leads us to identify invariants and practices which improve its efficacy or efficiency. These musings are only in their infancy, and the richness of the dialogue between the services and the university and industrial hubs of expertise is the gauge of their efficacy.

It is clear, having come to the end of this chapter, that in order to theorize on intelligence, it is essential to examine it through the lens of the knowledge sciences. Intelligence is founded on two historical pillars:

– the collection of information revealing facts about capacities, intentions and the environment in which they are felt; this is intelligence-knowledge;

– the understanding of these facts in order to illuminate the path of decision-making or action; this is intelligence-understanding.

No longer is it the capacity to collect streams of information which can make or break a modern agency, but the capacity to exploit them, valorize them and understand them.

The evaluation of incoming information of intelligence-knowledge type has limitations, which intelligence-understanding can overcome by evaluation of the intelligence products. This leads us to evaluate the underlying comprehension models, whether implicit or explicit.

A move towards the knowledge sciences in both their informational and cognitive aspects is merely one step in the right direction, etc. and the report and guide published by the American academies on the subject (see [NAP 11a; NAP 11b]) are, of course, worth reading.

3.5. Bibliography

[CAM 88] CAMPBELL D., "Somebody's listening", *New Statesman*, article 12 August 1988.

[CIC 10] CICDE, Doctrine interarmées (DIA 2), Renseignement d'intérêt militaire et contre ingérence (RIM & CI), 2010.

[CSD 12] CONSEIL SCIENTIFIQUE DE LA DÉFENSE, Technologie et renseignement, edited by Alain Juillet, 2012.

[DAV 48] DAVIDSON P., RIGBY R., *Intelligence is for commanders*, Military for Service Publishing, Harrisburg, 1948.

[GAL 03] GALAM S., "Global physics: from percolation to terrorism, guerrilla warfare and clandestine activities", *Physica A 330*, pp. 139–149, 2003.

[HEU 99] HEUER R., *Psychology of intelligence Analysis*, Center for the study of intelligence, Central Intelligence Agency, Washington, 1999.

[HEU 06] HEUER R., "Analysis of Competing Hypotheses (ACH)", www2.parc.com/istl/projects/ach/ach.html, 2006.

[IRS 11] IRSEM, Etudier le renseignement, état de l'art et perspectives de recherche sous la direction d'Olivier Chopin, 2011.

[LBD 08a] LIVRE BLANC, *La défense et de la sécurité nationale*, Documentation française, Paris, 2008.

[LBD 08b] LIVRE BLANC, *La défense et de la sécurité nationale*, Odile Jacob, Paris, 2008.

[LBD 13] LIVRE BLANC, *Défense et sécurité nationale*, Documentation française, Paris, 2013.

[LBF 06] LIVRE BLANC, *La France face au terrorisme*, Documentation française, Paris, 2008.

[NAP 11a] NATIONAL ACADEMIC PRESS, *Intelligence analysis for tomorrow*, www.nap.edu/catalog.php?record_id=13062, 2011.

[NAP 11b] NATIONAL ACADEMIC PRESS, *Intelligence Analysis: Behavioral and Social Scientific Foundations*, www.nap.edu/catalog.php? record_id=13040, 2011.

[NIS 93] NATIONAL INSTITUTE OF STANDARDS AND TECHNOLOGY, Integration Definition for Information Modeling, www.itl.nist.gov/fipspubs/idef02.doc, 21 December 1993.

[ODN 11] OFFICE OF THE DIRECTOR OF NATIONAL INTELLIGENCE, *National Intelligence: A consumer's guide*, www.dni.gov/files/documents/IC_Consumers_Guide_2011.pdf, 2011.

[ORI 12] ORION, *Le renseignement en France. Quelles perspectives ?*, www.jean-jaures.org/Publications/Les-essais/Le-renseignement-en-France.-Quelles-perspectives, 2012.

[PIA 12] PUBLICATION INTERARMÉES, Glossaire interarmées de terminologie opérationnelle, www.cicde.defense.gouv.fr/IMG/pdf/20120205_NP_CITA_PIA-7-2-6-3-GIAT-O.pdf, 2012.

[POP 07] POPPER K., *Logique de la découverte scientifique*, 1st edition 1935, Payot, Paris, 2007.

[ROW 06] ROWLEY J., "The wisdom hierarchy: representation of the DIKW hierarchy", *Journal of Information Science*, 33, pp. 163–180, 2006.

[WHE 11] WHEATON K., *Let's kill the intelligence cycle*, mciis.org/files/Wheaton_LetsKillTheIntelligenceCycle.pdf, 2011.

Chapter 4

Information Evaluation in the Military Domain: Doctrines, Practices and Shortcomings

4.1. Introduction

Information evaluation, the fundamental theme of this book, is by no means a new idea, and is profitably used in a number of domains (physical, economical, biological, demographical and many more). Yet the establishment of a method, and the attempt to establish a certain rigor of this practice as part of an overall process, are, without a doubt, attributable to the domain of Defense. The origin of information, as well as its content, plays a crucial role both in a strategic and tactical context. Far from being reserved for espionage or data encoding, information evaluation is quite rightly considered to be an essential step in the preparation of a maneuver, the understanding of a situation in a theater of operations, or the making of a decision at a politico-strategic level.

In this chapter, we begin by presenting the doctrines in force regarding information evaluation (which does not necessarily mean that they reflect the real-world uses and practices of military

---

Chapter written by Philippe CAPET and Adrien REVAULT D'ALLONNES.

intelligence personnel). Then, from a purely conceptual point of view, we hold up some of the shortcomings of these definitions and their associated underlying uses. These various theoretical difficulties could potentially cause very damaging practical consequences, in that they make any attempt at information evaluation impossible and, therefore, may have repercussions throughout the process of which information evaluation is a part. These open-ended issues, which are by no means exhaustive, will serve us in putting forward possibilities for solutions, which will certainly need to be further developed, but which outline the work which remains to be done. The fictitious scenario presented in the introduction to the book is used for three illustrations: the presentation of the existing concepts, some of the pitfalls relating to these, and the avenues opened up by the initial suggestions. The chapter refers directly to the previous one, focusing on points about information evaluation that were not expanded upon in Chapter 3, and also serves to establish useful perspectives for several of the chapters which follow.

4.2. Presentation of the existing situation

Information evaluation is essential to intelligence, helping guide highly important decisions by handling sensitive information. Hence, it is an integral part of the process of validation of information and, therefore, is subject to directives and guidelines.

Before describing the habits in force, it should be pointed out that, historically, such evaluation plays a part in the management of situations of open conflict – i.e. when surveying battlefields. However, the functions and requirements of intelligence have evolved; nowadays they are geared more towards peacekeeping, monitoring the stability of regimes or asymmetrical conflicts such as the struggle against terrorism. Therefore, the requirements and the materials have changed. Firstly, because their perimeter is less restrictive than the identification of troops mobilized in a conflict zone, the analysis of clandestine groupuscules or political forces requires in-depth investigation. The appropriate reactions can only be determined once these investigations have been carried out, when knowledge has been constructed and established. Nowadays, the volume of sources has burgeoned, and the urgency to respond is less critical than in a traditional context. Decisions are made on the basis of more information, possibly gleaned from less stringently identified sources. Furthermore, the near impossibility of manually handling such volumes of data gives rise to a need for computer assistance in the processing of the information, as we can no longer rely solely on the expertise of a human operator.

Here, we present the existing doctrines and the underlying concepts, which are supposed to dictate the practices in force. The limitations of these practices will then be used to envisage the changes that are needed – particularly the clarifications and formalizations which are indispensable for semi-automated handling of information evaluation.

4.2.1. *Information evaluation in the intelligence cycle*

The activity of intelligence services – military, economic, public or private – is the series of operations whereby, following an initial request, information is gathered, assembled and then enriched and, finally, made available to the client [MIN 01]. When the response is given, it is possible that new questions will emerge and the process will have to start all over again. For this reason, we speak of the intelligence cycle.[1]

This cycle varies slightly according to cultures and customs, and therefore exhibits a variable number of stages. The version presented below, in Figure 4.1, includes the basic four stages found in all formulations of the model, which we briefly outline below, basing our explanations on the available doctrines.

The initial phase – orientation – is where the end user expresses his needs. In the historical context of military intelligence mentioned above (the surveillance of battlefields), the commander establishes zones of interest and plans the collection efforts – i.e. the list of

---

1 See Chapter 3 for further discussion of the cycle.

services to be requested. The plan of action thus constructed provides the direction for the search for information.

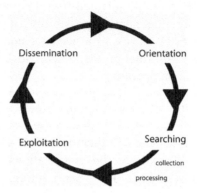

Figure 4.1. *The military intelligence cycle (simplified view)*

Secondly, the phase of searching, carried out by human agents of the collection planning services, begins with the search for relevant sources. This collection of information procures the raw data upon which the following phases of construction of knowledge are based.

Exploitation – and the processing which immediately precedes it – are carried out to enrich the raw data thus extracted. It is mainly this phase which is of interest to us here. The five tasks which make it up, illustrated by Figure 4.2, are described here as they are in [TTA 01]. In France, the terminology has evolved slightly since 2001 – particularly with regard to information evaluation. We shall come back to this later. The first task is *grouping*, the task of classifying pieces of information of the same nature, i.e. relating to the same object. Then comes *information evaluation*, the evaluation of the quality of the information and of the sources consulted. This is followed by *analysis*, which aims to extract from the information those elements which are most significant for the response to the initial orientation. The next step is *fusion*, where the informational elements contained in different information items are integrated into one framework, in order to obtain enriched content. Finally, in the *interpretation* stage, we evaluate the reach – the set of implied consequences – of the information.

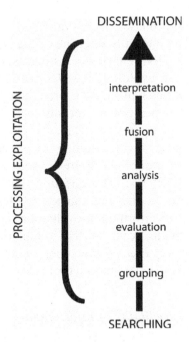

Figure 4.2. *Detailed representation of the exploitation phase in the intelligence cycle*

During the final phase – dissemination – the intelligence constructed in response to the initial question is given to the commander and to any agencies that it may concern. These addressees may then be led to redirect the search, triggering an iteration of the intelligence cycle.

Thus placed, information evaluation can therefore be considered as a *task* during the *phase* of exploitation, fed by the *grouping* of information and feeding material to the *analysis*, i.e. a relevance filter for the next stage of the exploitation.

However, this placement of information evaluation within the process of intelligence production is sometimes called into question by other doctrines on the subject. Note, for instance, that the French inter-armed-forces doctrine [INS 03, p. 56] states that "information evaluation begins even during the first stage of the processing/exploitation phase. It is validated or modified during exploitation [...]". The inter-ally doctrine of the North Atlantic Treaty Organization (NATO – [NAT 03]), for its part, states that information evaluation is a stage in exploitation *stricto sensu* in the intelligence cycle, meaning that it takes place *after* processing. The French armed forces glossary of operational terminology gives information evaluation a similar place in the cycle: "a step in the exploitation phase of the intelligence cycle leading to an appreciation of raw intelligence in view of the reliability of the source and the credibility of the information" [DEF 04]. The question thus arises of the exact place of this activity in the intelligence cycle. As this question determines the object of information evaluation, i.e. what it relates to, it raises the problematic point of the granularity of the piece of information – either a piece of raw data or an enriched piece of intelligence – which is touched upon later in this chapter.

4.2.2. *Reliability and credibility of information*

In the task of information evaluation which takes place after grouping, which in turn follows on from the search phase, the agent in charge of exploitation uses a two-dimensional scale to evaluate the *source* of the information, on the first dimension, and its *content*, on the other. According to the NATO doctrine [NAT 03] for a given piece of information, the ratings of the *reliability* of the source and the *credibility* of the information are measured on the two six-graded scales shown in Tables 4.1 and 4.2 respectively. Note that this official classification is the same in France as that given by NATO, which explains the meaning of each grade in the right-hand column of the two tables. Up until quite recently, France's armed forces used terms which are slightly different to those used now: the *qualité* (quality) of the source of the information and the *valeur* (value) of the content. Certain definitions of the ratings have also changed with a view to harmonization with NATO's glossary.

This double scale thus attaches to a piece of information a couple of values, referred to as a *rating*, which are supposed to report the results of the evaluation of that information in order to be able to analyze it in the strictest sense. For instance, the information transmitted after direct observation of a tank by a combatant[2] can be rated B2, to express the fact that the soldier providing the information is certain of the fact, but may, in the eyes of the receiver of that information, be mistaken. The rating B2 means, however, that it is probable that a tank was in that particular place in the observed situation.

At first glance, in view of these definitions and their associated examples, information evaluation is firmly embedded in the intelligence cycle, and can officially and unambiguously be put into practice. However, is it all that certain? The next section of this chapter looks at the limitations of these directives.

A	Completely reliable	Refers to a tried and trusted source which can be depended upon with confidence.
B	Usually reliable	Refers to a source which has been successful in the past but for which there is still some element of doubt in a particular case.
C	Fairly reliable	Refers to a source which has occasionally been used in the past and upon which some degree of confidence can be based.
D	Not usually reliable	Refers to a source which has been used in the past but has proved more often than not unreliable.
E	Unreliable	Refers to a source which has been used in the past and has proven unworthy of any confidence.
F	Reliability cannot be judged	Refers to a source which has not been used in the past.

Table 4.1. *Reliability of the information source: grade, label and description [NAT 03]*

---

2 Example taken from [TTA 01].

1	Confirmed by other sources	If it can be stated with certainty that the reported information originates from another source than the already existing information on the same subject, then it is classified as "confirmed by other sources" and rated "1".
2	Probably true	If the independence of the source of any item of information cannot be guaranteed, but if, from the quantity and quality of previous reports its likelihood is nevertheless regarded as sufficiently established, then the information should be classified as "probably true" and given a rating of "2".
3	Possibly true	If, despite there being insufficient confirmation to establish any higher degree of likelihood, a freshly reported item of information does not conflict with the previously reported behaviour pattern of the target, the item may be classified as "possibly true" and given a rating of "3".
4	Doubtful	An item of information which tends to conflict with the previously reported or established behaviour pattern of an intelligence target should be classified as "doubtful" and given a rating of "4".
5	Improbable	An item of information which positively contradicts previously reported information or conflicts with the established behaviour pattern of an intelligence target in a marked degree should be classified as "improbable" and given a rating of "5".
6	Truth cannot be judged	Any freshly reported item of information which provides no basis for comparison with any known behaviour pattern of a target must be classified as "truth cannot be judged" and given a rating of "6". Such a rating should be given only when the accurate use of higher rating is impossible.

Table 4.2. *Credibility of the information content: grade, label and description [NAT 03]*

4.3. Illustrative scenario with multi-sourced information

The methods set out in the doctrines seem accurate: with the definitions and criteria formulated here, an officer charged with evaluating a piece of information in terms of its reliability and credibility has a circumspect and clear framework upon which to base his evaluation. Using the example of the fictitious scenario described in the introduction to this book, enriched with elements that are particular to this chapter, we are going to see the ambiguities and difficulties – both conceptual and practical – that still arise during the process of information evaluation, rendering it impracticable or devoid of meaning and applicability, if we adhere to the original doctrinal model. Let us return now to the case of the bomb attack perpetrated in the capital of Ektimostan on 31 May, and attempt to examine it through the eyes of, and through the lens of the knowledge held by, the agents of Usbek, a dissident now living in exile in a foreign country, and an unofficial supporter of the rebellion. Many different pieces of information, of diverse natures, are considered by these agents:

a) on 1 June, Captain Ixil, head of the Free Resistance of Dagbas (FRD), denies that his rebel movement is responsible for the attack;

b) on 31 May, in the wake of the attack, the minister Balldar, chief of the Ektimostanian police, *conditionally* incriminates the FRD;

c) the Ektimostanian head of State, Colonel al-Adel, states with certainty, on 2 June, that the FRD is behind the attack;

d) previously, a spy in the pay of Usbek who is part of the Ektimostanian police communicated to his interlocutors linked to Usbek that anti-governmental political groupuscules had been identified, were under heavy surveillance and were preparing to carry out violent actions against the regime, but are unconnected with the rebellion;

e) finally, on 3 June, a post by a very active and very widely read Ektimostanian blogger supports the idea that the FRD is behind the attack.

The sources of information are varied in nature: some of the reports are obtained by human intelligence *via* the spy in place (case *d*), others by intelligence of open-source origin such as the blogger (case *e*). The others are public declarations, so are also open-source, but with the peculiarity that they are relayed by press agencies or usual or authoritative Websites.

In reality, the information under examination refers to the same event with the five chosen sources: according to three of these sources, it is *true* that the attack was carried out by the FRD (this proposition is denoted as "φ" hereafter); according to the other two, it is *false* that the FRD are the perpetrators of this attack – in other words, for these two sources, "not-φ" is true.

A number of elements from this scenario are used later on in this chapter to illustrate the limitations of the doctrines presented above.

4.4. From an inaccurate definition to an attractive but unusable concept

Now let us look at the way in which information evaluation is put into practice in order to gain a better understanding of its limitations. Significant criticisms can be leveled at the existing system for information evaluation. Indeed, before even thinking about whether or not the information evaluation accurately represents the realization of the fact that it qualifies, let us look at the way in which it can be apprehended – its intelligibility. Problems emerge with regard to each of the following four points: the reliability of the source, the credibility of the information, the combination of these two aspects to form a rating and, finally, the granularity of the objects being handled, ranging from raw information to enriched intelligence. Below, we shall examine each of these points in turn, and illustrate the limitations using the fictitious example presented in the introduction.

4.4.1. *Estimation of reliability*

4.4.1.1. *Reliability of the source: a question of point of view*

The use of the information evaluation scale is reliant upon the hypothesis that the first dimension, which only describes the source, is independent of the information. Viewed thus, the value of the reliability is supposed to be stable for all the information the source provides, independently of its content. However, according to the usage recommendations [DIS 01], it must reflect the trust that the analyst has in the source but can also indicate the conviction that the source has in the information that he offers, as well as his capacity to judge what he is providing. Indeed, all these elements seem judicious for the evaluation of the trust that can be placed in the information, but they run counter to the linguistic labels in Table 4.1, which, for their part, describe only different levels of reliability. This confusion obscures this first dimension, leaving users to fall back on standard ratings. Thus, as we saw earlier, a reliability rating of B will be attributed to a field agent who is certain of what he has seen, or to a technological sensor. The top rating, A, is not given so as to allow for possible failures on the part of the man or the machine.

It is therefore implied by the reliability scale that the source is rated regardless of his domain of expertise. The degree of trust that we are supposed to have in that source should normally be immutable. However, things almost never work that way: we give our trust[3] to a given person in a particular domain; less so in another, or perhaps more so, depending on the experience or knowledge that we have had of that source (I trust my plumber to repair a broken pipe, but not necessarily so much to remedy a power outage). The Ektimostanian blogger may be very knowledgeable about the economic environment, but no better informed than the man on the street with regard to the political issues in his country. The pro-Usbek spy may be specialized in financial or military issues in Ektimostan without knowing anything about the country's strictly interior policy.

Apart from the transmitter of the information, the receiver also has his own specific areas of expertise: how is an intelligence analyst specialized in the domain of economics to adequately judge the credibility of a piece of information in a domain which he knows nothing about, such as Ektimostanian politics and, directly related to reliability, grade a source whom he has never dealt with, or with whom he has dealt in circumstances which have misled him as regards the source's trustworthiness (e.g. not knowing that the same source had provided erroneous information on the subject on other occasions)?

The last impediment to the universality of the reliability of the source also relates to the receiver. Indeed, the evaluation of the source depends, as we have already stated, on shared history. This history is unique to the auditor. In addition, the auditor's subjectivity – or his allegiance – also influences the measurement. In fact, it is desirable

---

3 See Chapter 2 for an in-depth discussion of the notion of trust.

that Usbek's intelligence services should not evaluate the reliability of Colonel al-Adel in the same way as his subordinate, Minister Balldar, would.

4.4.1.2. *Implementation*

The reliability of the various sources obviously depends on multiple factors: traditional objectives of the source as estimated by the intelligence agencies in the pay of Usbek, the antecedents, proclaimed or hidden interests relating to the stated information, etc. In a simplified approach[4] taking account of some of these factors, based on the definitions of the scale used to evaluate the sources, there is no real doubt about the reliability of the sources mentioned, depending on the adjustments which need to be made in the specific context.

In case *a*, the rebel Ixil sometimes denies actions which his movement has undeniably carried out and, conversely, vainly attributes to his own followers acts of violence for which others are responsible, or which have never even taken place. He is estimated to be "not usually reliable" and his reliability is evaluated at D.

In cases *b* and *c*, the Ektimostan leaders can be reliable, but have also been known to be propagandists. For example, it has been proven in the past that their declarations were true, exaggerated, played down or quite simply barefaced lies. Usbek's agents could therefore attribute them a rating of C, based on the (highly debatable) principle that the ambivalence of the mode of declaration of the two personalities yields that average.

In case *d*, the active spy is considered to be a safe bet, because of his past history and his status with Usbek's intelligence agents. His reliability is therefore maximum, and is rated A.

Finally, in case *e*, the blogger has in the past proved his excellent knowledge of Ektimostanian environments and his blog seems to be objective, although it tends to lean in favor of the regime. Our agents therefore find him to be "usually reliable" – a reliability rating of B.

---

4 See Chapter 5 for further details about methods for evaluating the reliability of sources.

Table 4.3 recaps the evaluation of the reliability of the various sources by the pro-Usbek agents, and recalls the position advanced by each one.

Information source	Ixil	Balldar	al-Adel	Pro-Usbek spy	Ektimostanian blogger
Reliability rating	D	C	C	A	B
Proposition	not-φ	φ	φ	not-φ	φ

Table 4.3. *Reliability of sources, evaluated approximately on the basis of their past history and the knowledge that Usbek's agents have*

4.4.2. *Estimation of credibility*

Once the reliability of the sources has been evaluated, the credibility of the proposition remains in doubt. By examining various questions among possible others, we shall now see that this credibility proves even more difficult to evaluate than reliability.

Similarly to that of reliability, the interpretation of credibility poses a problem. This dimension is supposed to represent the degree to which the information is credible, as indicated by the labels of the final four predetermined levels on the scale (graded 2 to 5). However, because the maximum level is reserved for information "confirmed by other sources" – not to mention the problem of information granularity, to which we shall return later on – this is more an indicator of *confirmation* than of *credibility*. Section 4.4.2.1 looks particularly at this point.

4.4.2.1. *Acceptance and debatable role of corroboration*

Of the two contradictory events related by propositions φ and not-φ, which are we to believe? Do we believe the positive information transmitted by the three sources of middling reliability between B and C, or the negative information transmitted by the two sources whose reliability ratings are very different (one is A, and the other is D)? How do we evaluate the credibility of that information, in view of these very different and heterogeneous reliability ratings? As the information φ appears to be more widely corroborated than the contrary, it would be legitimate to give it the rating of 1.

Indeed, level 1 in terms of credibility indicates that a piece of information is corroborated by several sources: when we receive information from one source, we note that its content is identical to that of a piece of information received previously from a different source. Its (maximum) rank indicates that therefore the information is as credible as it can be, and we can assume that the more sources agree on a piece of information, the more credible it will be judged to be. However, what can we actually conclude from a corroboration, without any other specification? We can easily see at least three difficulties in the definition and use of corroboration.

Firstly, in our example, the spy seems to be a better choice to provide information to Usbek, for whom he works from within the Ektimostanian system, unlike the political personalities and blogger, who are all Ektimostanian. Yet the spy is the only one (besides a doubtful individual) who claims that φ is false. The statement that the attack was perpetrated by the FRD is corroborated by three individuals, whom one might imagine to be even more numerous, unlike its contrary which, if we ignore Ixil, who is too unreliable in the example, has no corroboration. Should we infer from this that φ is true?

It is not coincidental that the doctrine has come to include the reference to a *convention* of use of the rating 1 when the source is marked A. Indeed, "by convention, the evaluation of A1 is reserved for exceptional cases when doubt is impossible" [INS 03]. Yet apart from these "exceptional cases" where corroboration no longer appears, *any* corroboration does not, in itself, indicate anything about the credibility of the information. For instance, a rumor may be shared and propagated through a crowd without its content necessarily being further validated. The voice of the people (*vox populi*) is not necessarily the voice of an omniscient being (*vox Dei*); the common affirmation of a crowd is not necessarily credible, even if there is only one person who says the opposite.

Secondly, a piece of information and its opposite may both be corroborated. In our initial example, we have an almost equal proportion: three sources against two support the proposition φ, i.e. two contradicting corroborations – for φ on the one hand, and for not-φ on the other. The easiest way to resolve this ambiguity would be to impose a condition, so that in order to obtain a rating of 1, the information must be confirmed by a large majority of sources providing information about that subject, and undermined by few or no sources, with the use of a threshold to be determined for the proportion of corroborations. As with the previous point, the rate of high reliability for such a corroboration, as opposed to a low average reliability for the contradictory sources, needs to be taken into consideration. Yet even so, multiple possibilities would subsist, making it impossible to make a clear judgment: the question is more complex than it is with a vote, where the majority wins, because here, the "election" also needs to consider the reliability of the voters. Hence, a vote would need to be weighted by the reliability of the person casting it, using a formula which remains to be defined.

Finally, the last problem, the relationships between the information sources corroborating a piece of information ought not to be ignored: if two enemies are promulgating the same information, this means something different than if it were two allies, two people connected by the same interests. In our fictitious example, what advantage do we gain by noting that Balldar supports the same statement as his boss? Rather it is the opposite that would be surprising and worthy of interest. In reality it is more a question of *redundancy* than meaningful corroboration, and that redundancy should add nothing to the evaluation of the credibility of the information. Similarly, if we consider that the pro-Usbek agent shares neither Ixil's positions nor his objectives, the coincidence of their affirmation is informative *because of the fact* that they are supposed to be possible adversaries, and not in itself and independently of the pre-existing relations between sources. However, that coincidence (which resembles a corroboration) says nothing about the credibility of the information in itself; it informs the analyst, or at least piques his interest, about something entirely different. It is highly preferable for the sources corroborating a piece of information to be *independent* if its credibility is to increase; yet this is not what is said by military doctrine, where *any* corroboration seems to entail an increase in the credibility of the information.

4.4.2.2. *Problems in accessibility and unused top levels*

These difficulties in the apprehension of credibility, which may be at the root of the lack of objectivity in the usage and consistency between operators, are, without a doubt, partially resolved by the skill of the specialists. However, many of these operators struggle to avoid these problems. In cases where credibility can be evaluated, only the four levels qualifying doubt (grades 2 to 5) are used, and the integration of the confirmation (level 1) is left up to the services responsible for analysis, which perform matching prior to fusion of various pieces of information, once again posing the problem of the granularity.

In addition, from a purely semantic point of view, other problems arise with the evaluation of credibility. In our example (point *b* above), Balldar suggests *conditionally* that the FRD is to blame. In reality, how are we to rate the credibility of the transmitted information? Balldar himself gives a sort of score to the statement that the FRD is to blame (it *could be involved*, he says: a rating of around 3 on the scale). In view of this moderate presentation, we should not assign the same rating to the ensemble of the information (source and content) as if Balldar had declared the same thing with categorical certainty, or if he had been highly doubtful but stopped short of rejecting that hypothesis. The source remains the same in all three cases; the event (*stricto sensu*) has not changed; but the overall rating should change depending on the certainty or doubt expressed by the source.[5] In other words, semantic elements included in the information immediately alter the credibility that should be attached to it.

Furthermore, this problem cannot simply be rectified by incorporating a sort of "doubt coefficient" provided by the source itself, because linguistically speaking, many other nuances would then

---

5 See Chapter 7 for details about how allowances are made for this uncertainty expressed by the source, by a semi-automated method of evaluation.

need to be given similar consideration. There is clearly a difference in meaning between "the Minister stated that a given event could have taken place" and "the Minister could have stated that a given event has taken place": the doubt expressed by the conditional is applied in turn by the source – i.e. the Minister – and by the press agency reporting his comments. Yet in a strictly by-the-book approach to information evaluation, these two expressions should be taken to attach the same level of credibility to the same event, although the doubt is not expressed by the same source. Here, we touch on the tricky question of consecutive sources (and of the independence between source and content when evaluating each of them respectively): one reporting that another has suggested that a third party may have said that... etc. This question is specifically dealt with in Chapter 8.

4.4.3. Combining dimensions – what is the comparability of the ratings?

Information evaluation on a double scale, in addition to ensuring it properly represents the desired dimensions, is supposed to enhance the immediate readability of the rating. It seems, however, that operators are not all of that opinion: in addition to the difficulty in assigning a level of trust, the problem with readability of the resulting rating also stems from a lack of comparability. Indeed, it is difficult to tell which piece of information is more credible if one is rated B3 and the other C2 – two levels which should, in theory, be comparable. The specialists with whom we have been able to speak on this subject maintain that only the known values, i.e. the "default values" often cited here, are expressive and therefore interpretable. A piece of information gathered by a drone, which is therefore considered to be theoretically certain, is evaluated as B2, establishing a form of benchmark, which is unfortunately impossible to compare against other, less objectively envisaged situations.

Another weak point of such an expression of the evaluation, as a combination of ratings, stems from the interpretation of the credibility. Indeed, construed as an indicator of confirmation, the scale it uses runs from invalidation to confirmation. Thus, it is a signed (positive and negative) scale, constructed around a neutral value. Indeed, two pieces of information may more or less confirm or undermine one another, or they may be completely unrelated. Reliability, on the other hand, describes a progression from low or non-existent activation to an absolute maximum. The combination of values on these two differently constructed scales increases the margin for interpretation by the users and, along with it, the risk of inconsistency between their perceptions.

With Tables 4.1 and 4.2, the intermediary ratings (B-D and 2-5) use adverbs and adjectives which are supposed to characterize the different levels: *usually*, *fairly* and *not usually* for reliability and *probably*, *possibly*, *doubtful* and *improbable* for credibility. With regard to reliability, these terms correspond to an approximate average of the credit attributed to a source after the analyst's findings; with regard to credibility, to a level of belief of the analyst on the basis of his expertise and his experience. While the order of these words is more or less undisputable because there is little risk of its varying from one analyst to another, the boundary between one class and another may be extremely variable with different experts. Quite apart from the subjectivity of the analyst, the choice of a level, with corresponding opinions, depends on the sensitivity of each analyst to the qualifiers used.

In our example, one analyst may well estimate that the Ektimostanian blogger is "usually reliable", whereas another would say that he is "not usually reliable", depending on the particular analyst's past experiences of reading the posts on his blog, and his particular knowledge, but also on the subjective expectations that each analyst has: even supposing that the two analysts have read the same things on the blog and have the same knowledge of the domain, one may employ the adverb "usually" where the other would use "rarely" (or "not usually"), and the rating is therefore merely a question of point of view.

As there is no other criterion that is more objective than this use of subjective terminology, information evaluation is "fuzzy"; the same is true of credibility. However, the two scales for information evaluation have only six degrees each. These *discrete* grades are based on fuzzy adverbial estimations which in fact more closely reflect a certain *continuity*. The multi-valued logic with 6 values of truth implicitly present in these scales expresses an assumed position which fuzzy logic [BOU 93], or "Computing with words" [ZAD 02], seems better able to express if we wish to preserve these adjectives and adverbs and the gradation of the scoring system attached to them.

4.4.4. *Raw data, enriched intelligence – can information evaluation qualify everything?*

As previously stated, depending on the particular doctrine in question, information evaluation takes place at different stages in the intelligence cycle. The French manual for joint forces [INS 03], for instance, specifies that it is applied to information[6] rather than to intelligence, although the producer of intelligence does pair it with an evaluation. A distinction indeed needs to be drawn between information – facts *reported* to the agencies by a source – and intelligence – the agglomeration of knowledge from relatively diverse sources, *produced* by the agencies. In addition, during the enrichment of the data and the production of intelligence, it is clearly stated that these two types of data are mixed, so a piece of intelligence may be built on raw data and other pieces of intelligence. The choice not to measure trust in the same way for these objects of different granularities is, doubtless – at least in part – a consequence of the choice of scoring system. Indeed, the notion of source reliability poses a problem for a piece of intelligence, because it is the product of the fusion of different snippets of information from different sources. However, the evaluation of the sources is still relevant in order establish trust in a piece of intelligence.

In addition, as these evaluations are not, as we have seen, comparable, the construction of a rating for a piece of intelligence by aggregation of the ratings for the different pieces of information is not a clearly formalized operation. In practice, the analyst responsible for that aggregation demonstrates his skill by writing up accompanying remarks. These operations are further complicated when creating intelligence that combines pieces of information and other intelligence, which itself has been created by the fusion of data. The

---

6 Here, for simplicity's sake, we count the raw data to be information.

analyst then forms an opinion about the trustworthiness on the basis of different types of indicators, which are therefore incomparable. The skill of the analysts is, of course, unquestionable. However, this simply makes the formalization of information evaluation, either to facilitate its automation or to improve its readability, more confusing. Suppose that, rather than raw data, the report of the pro-Usbek agent forms part of an enriched piece of intelligence; where and how does his reliability fit in to the overall evaluation of that intelligence?

If we look at the problem of granularity, we see the inconsistency of the top level of credibility. Indeed, the maximum degree of credibility of a nugget of information depends on confirmations – or invalidations – by other sources. As information evaluation takes place before grouping and fusion, taking other pieces of information into account runs counter to the definitions of a given atomic element and its evaluation. Note also that this divergence introduces the combination of sources, which is difficult, as we have just pointed out. While this observation seems to provide an argument for abandoning corroboration when evaluating the quality of information, the search for confirmation to relieve a doubt is so widespread and so often appropriate that we are led to stick with this approach.

Section 4.5 briefly runs through some of the publications on the subject, before the rest of the book goes on to detail some of these proposals and offers new ones.

4.5. A few suggested refinements to information evaluation techniques

Military research in general, and research into issues relating to intelligence in particular, are experiencing rapid growth. While information evaluation is not the most widely studied domain in this context, in this section we introduce a number of articles which deal specifically with the issue as defined above. Our introduction to each of the articles on the subject contains some of our own remarks about the existing model of information evaluation. The proposed methods are usually anchored in the maintaining of consistency in a system or the combination of degrees of uncertainty, which are classic tasks of uncertain information fusion.

Thus, Cholvy and Nimier [CHO 03] focus on maintaining consistency in a knowledge base, and look at various operators that can be used for fusion, weighting the distances between possible worlds according to the reliability of the sources. Cholvy [CHO 04] reuses the initial information evaluation grid to qualify the elements inserted into a database storing the history of the pieces of information and their sources. The responses to requests to the database are chosen by a vote between conflicting elements. This history contributes to the construction of a piece of information enriched by the fusion of the stored elements.

In the same vein, most of the articles discussed here consider the problem of information evaluation to be a fusion problem. Nimier [NIM 04], for instance, proposes a description of it using combination operators in three formalisms: the first probabilistic, the second possibilistic and the last based on Dempster–Shafer theory.

In greater detail, Besombes and Cholvy [BES 09] propose a complete architecture for an information fusion system. In order to perform fusion, the pieces of information are mutually correlated, the correlation measurement covering the whole of the scale, from invalidation to confirmation. The authors then introduce a calculation to update the evaluation on the basis of this correlation. Although they do not detail the fusion process, they examine different methods for calculating the correlation.

These articles thus envisage information evaluation as an estimation, in a more or less closed world, of the contradiction between known facts. We have seen that credibility can be viewed as a confirmation indicator, essential in the evaluation of trust. However, we have also seen that to consider only that factor is not at all satisfactory, and is among the problems with the existing approach to information evaluation. In addition, these models, however rich they may be, assimilate the evaluation of a piece of information to its consistency with existing knowledge about the world, leading to disagreement as to the mode of production or summarizing it as the relative importance of the reliability of its source.

Another point of view is proposed by Baerecke [BAE 10], who, in addition to the dimensions usually taken into account, considers the confidence that the source attaches to his information, the recentness of the information and the amicable or hostile relations between sources. Uncertainty is given as distributions of possibility moderated by the reliability of the sources. Elements are then fused according to the friendship partition, i.e. two sources in conflict with one another but providing the same information corroborate one another more than two friendly sources doing the same.[7] This formulation reuses certain aspects of information quality [BER 99] to determine the factors needing to be taken into account in its evaluation. The authors add notions of subjectivity and propose an interesting model of the repercussions of their dissemination.

In [REV 11], we put forward a different view of information evaluation, whereby it is understood less as an evaluation of the reality of the fact described than as an estimation of the faith that can be invested in the information describing that fact. We will come back to these works in Chapter 9.

4.6. Conclusion and future prospects

The conclusion drawn from the above discussion should not be too pessimistic: the inclusion of information evaluation in the phase of exploitation of the information is crucial, and to deprive it of its role would be calamitous for any labor of intelligence: the information would then only need to be relativized, in the postmodernist sense where "everything is of equal value". However, we still need to know how to cater for the need for information evaluation in the restricted context of military intelligence, using proposals for reform of the two original dimensions, balancing the specific levels of each of them and

---

7 See Chapter 7 for an example of how to take account of these relations between sources in the information evaluation process.

a possibility of usage, even if it requires a prioritized enrichment of the doctrines of other dimensions of information evaluation.

Yet there are crucial questions which remain. Thus, even if these dimensions of evaluation are refined, the relationship between the source and the content needs to be far more clearly defined. In many scenarios, though, there is probably a certain degree of dependency between them, whether we are working in an overall framework or one relative to the information received. In addition, throughout the process, the human agents will inevitably remain subjective. This crucial issue, and that of the scales used for evaluation, merit in-depth theoretical studies using a variety of possible models (fuzzy logic, multi-valued logic, etc.), necessarily followed by tests using experts in the domain to refine the classification scales thus constructed. By doing this, the practice of information evaluation would be greatly facilitated, whilst the role of information evaluation would be enhanced throughout the phase of processing and exploitation of the information.

Indeed, if we look again at Figure 4.2 representing that phase, and consider the decrease in the limitations to the methods and practices laid out in this chapter, not only would information evaluation continue to play the key role in the information exploitation stage to valorize it for military intelligence, but it could acquire an even greater role, throughout the whole length of this phase: at each step, from grouping, through analysis, fusion and interpretation to the beginning of the dissemination phase, it would likely be performed again each time the process advances to the next phase, whilst helping the enactment of each one. Acquiring an additional status, at all times during the processing and exploitation of the information, information evaluation would thereby gain the respectability which it doubtlessly deserves.

4.7. Bibliography

[BAE 10] BAERECKE T., et al., "Un modèle de cotation pour la veille informationnelle en source ouverte", *Colloque international veille stratégique, scientifique et technologique, VSST'2010*, 2010.

[BER 99] BERTI L., *Quality and Recommendation of Multi-source Data for Assisting Technological Intelligence Applications*, Lecture Notes in Computer Science, Springer, Berlin, 1999.

[BES 09] BESOMBES J., CHOLVY L., "Information evaluation in fusion using information correlation", *International Conference on Information Fusion*, pp. 264–269, 2009.

[BOU 93] BOUCHON-MEUNIER B., *La logique floue*, Presses Universitaires de France, Paris, 1993.

[CAP 12] CAPET P., DELAVALLADE T., "La cotation de l'information : approches conceptuelles et méthodologiques pour un usage stratégique", in *La qualité et la gouvernance des données au service de la performance des entreprises*, Hermès, Paris, 2012.

[CHO 03] CHOLVY L., NIMIER. V., "Information evaluation: discussion about STANAG 2022 recommendations", *NATO-IST Symposium on Military Data and Information Fusion*, Prague, Czech Republic, 2003.

[CHO 04] CHOLVY L., "Information evaluation in fusion: a case study", *International Conference on Processing and Management of Uncertainty in Knowledge-based Systems, IPMU 2004*, Perugia, Italy, 2004.

[DEF 04] MINISTÈRE DE LA DÉFENSE, Glossaire interarmées de terminologie opérationnelle, Paris, 2004.

[DIS 01] DEFENCE INTELLIGENCE, SECURITY SCHOOL, DEFENCE INTELLIGENCE, SECURITY CENTRE, Intelligence Wing Student Précis, 2001.

[INS 03] INSTRUCTION INTERARMÉES SUR LE RENSEIGNEMENT D' INTÉRÊT MILITAIRE, TITRE I, Doctrine interarmées du renseignement, PIA 02-200, Paris, 2003.

[MIN 01] MINISTÈRE DE LA DÉFENSE. Commandement de la formation de l'armée de Terre (COFAT), Manuel du cadre de contact (TTA150), 2001.

[NAT 03] NORTH ATLANTIC TREATY ORGANIZATION, Standardization Agreement, Intelligence Report, STANAG, no. 2, p. 511, 2003.

[NIM 04] NIMIER V., "Information evaluation: a formalisation of operational recommendations", *Seventh International Conference on Information Fusion*, Stockholm, Sweden, pp. 1 166–1 171, 2004.

[REV 11]   REVAULT   D'ALLONNES   A.,   Evaluation   sémantique
d'informations symboliques : la cotation, Doctoral thesis, Université
Pierre et Marie Curie, Paris, 2011.

[TTA 01] TRAITÉ TOUTES ARMES, *Renseignement*, no. 150, titre VI, Paris,
2001.

[ZAD 02] ZADEH L.A., "From computing with numbers to computing with
words. From manipulation of measurements to manipulation of
perceptions", *International Journal of Applied Mathematics and
Computer Science*, vol. 12, no. 3, pp. 307–324, 2002.

Chapter 5

Multidimensional Approach to Reliability Evaluation of Information Sources

5.1. Introduction

Knowing the reliability of one's information sources is useful for a number of reasons: it helps to order them, sort them and also to exploit the information which they transmit. In particular, if a source provides testimony in the form $\omega \in A$, where ω denotes, e.g., the type of weapon used in the 31 May bombing in the capital of Ektimostan[1], and A is a subset of the set Ω of the different possible types of weapons, and if that source is reliable to a degree α, between 0 and 1, then the operation of *discounting* introduced by Shafer [SHA 76] attributes the coefficient α to the fact of being able to categorically state $\omega \in A$, and the coefficient $1-\alpha$ to $\omega \in \Omega$. This transformation of the information emitted by a source is based on the following model of the notion of reliability: if a source (a sensor, an agent) is considered to be reliable, we agree to enrich our knowledge base with the information which that source gives us, and if he is not reliable,

Chapter written by Frédéric PICHON, Christophe LABREUCHE, Bertrand DUQUEROIE and Thomas DELAVALLADE.
1 See the general introduction to the book for the description of the fictitious scenario set in Ektimostan.

we do not take the information transmitted into account [SME 93]. This commonly-accepted view of reliability is similar, though different, to other notions such as sincerity of sources or trust (see [DES 11] for a comparison of these notions). Note that information provided by an unreliable source may very well be true. For instance, a broken clock will show the right time twice a day, but since there is no way of knowing whether the information transmitted is correct or not, it cannot be used.

There are different methods for estimating the reliability of a source depending on the nature of the available data about that source. If we know the veracity of the information provided by the source – in other words, to use the vocabulary of machine learning theory, if we have a labeled dataset – the reliability of that source can be estimated by comparing the information provided by the source to the expected values [ELO 04; DES 08]. However, it is not always possible to obtain such a dataset; indeed it is sometimes impossible to estimate the veracity of certain assertions.

An alternative approach is to compare the information provided by the source against information provided by other sources, making the hypothesis that the majority opinion represents truth [KLE 10; SCH 11]. Yet veracity estimation by consensus constitutes a last resort, which it is not really desirable to employ. Indeed, if we construct a model considering that an assertion is true simply because most people who have expressed a view on the matter believe it to be true, this model can easily be fooled by rudimentary disinformation maneuvers. For instance, it is sufficient, on a given subject, to artificially generate a large number of comments leaning in the same direction as what is reported by a source who we wish to appear reliable.

A third way of working to estimate the reliability of a source is to consider different attributes of the source which give indications as to his reliability and whose values can be obtained without needing access to labeled data, as is the case in [MOR 12; CAS 11; DES 11; DIA 12]. For example, we see in [MOR 12] that an opinion about the reliability of a Twitter account can be formed on the basis of simple attributes such as the username and image (or "avatar") of the account. Higher-level information may also be relevant for the reliability estimation, and may include ratings awarded by other users [YU 02; RAM 04] or the reputation of the source [ULI 11], which can be obtained by content analysis [CHA 08] or by relational analysis.

In order to be usable, methods based on different attributes providing information about the reliability must satisfy numerous constraints. Firstly, it is important that the reliability ratings computed by these methods be easily interpretable so that a user can easily understand both what the ratings represent and the way in which they have been calculated. Indeed, their use context is that of a semi-automated processing chain, at the center of which is a human operator who needs to be able to have access to the automated operations and challenge them. This aspect is crucial in order for users to accept such a processing chain. The approach championed in [DES 11], for instance, includes a means of identifying those criteria which have most impact in the establishment of the rating. In [CAS 11], where the aim is to estimate the credibility of a piece of news rather than the reliability of a source, a technique is also used to determine the most discriminating criteria.

In addition, as these methods are generally founded on expertise, another desirable characteristic is the existence of a simple methodology to extract the expertise. The approach of [DES 11], for instance, enables the expert to express himself in the form of linguistic terms, whereas in [CAS 11], concrete examples which are representative of the domain in question are presented to the experts for them to evaluate their credibility on an overall and binary basis.

In this chapter, we present a new method to evaluate the reliability of a source by way of a combination of the evaluations of different dimensions (or attributes) that characterize that reliability. The method is based on a multi-criteria aggregation function [GRA 03] known as the Choquet integral. This function has a certain number of "good" properties which have led researchers in different domains to use it, successfully. In particular, there is often a natural order with the attributes. For example, the more a source actually cites his own sources of information, the more reliable he may be considered to be –

all other things being equal. From this order on each attribute, we induce an order on the sources, which is expressed by the property of "monotonicity". This is the essential property which all aggregation functions satisfy. The Choquet integral also comes with a complete methodology for implementation, including – amongst other things – numerous means of collecting expertise and of explanation of the obtained decisions [GRA 10]. The method which we put forward in this chapter to evaluate the reliability of a source differs from [DES 11] in that the latter approach is based on the fusion of multiple models of uncertainty, whereas ours uses an aggregation function. It is also fundamentally different from the approaches grounded in machine learning and based on supervised classification such as that presented in [CAS 11]: these techniques do not satisfy the property of monotonicity and accept contradictory learning examples, quite unlike ours.

This chapter is organized as follows. In section 5.2, the basic notions of multi-criteria aggregation are recalled, and the Choquet integral is presented. At the end of this section, we also propose a way of exploiting the Choquet integral in order to establish the degree of reliability of an information source. After a succinct state of the art in section 5.3 about the problem of reliability evaluation of Twitter accounts, in section 5.4 we illustrate the proposed approach on this particular type of sources. Section 5.5 concludes this chapter.

5.2. Multi-criteria aggregation by the Choquet integral: application to the evaluation of the reliability of sources

This section presents the aggregation of the preferences in general and the Choquet integral model in particular. The advantage of this model is that it exhibits a good compromise between expressivity and readability. The approach used to construct such a model will be outlined from a practical point of view. The application of that model to the problem of estimation of the reliability of an information source is discussed at the end of this section.

5.2.1. *Multi-criteria decision support*

Multi-criteria decision support seeks to represent the preferences of a decision-maker regarding several alternatives (here the information sources), on the basis of multiple attributes $X_1,..., X_n$. An alternative x is characterized by a value representing each attribute and is therefore identified with a point in the Cartesian product:

$$X = X_1 \times ... \times X_n$$

meaning that:

$$x = (x_1,...,x_n)$$

where $x_i \in X_i$, $i = 1,..., n$. We use the notation $N = \{1,..., n\}$ for the set of attribute indicators.

Modeling a decision-maker's preferences regarding the alternatives of X involves constructing a binary relation, known as a preference relation, $\succeq_X$, whereby $x \succeq_X y$ means that from a certain perspective, the decision-maker prefers x to y, or at least he judges them to be equivalent. Here is an example to illustrate this, where the preferences between alternatives (which in this case are blogs) are expressed from the perspective of the influence of those blogs.

EXAMPLE 5.1.– The influences of four blogs are evaluated on the basis of their values for the three attributes listed below.

Blogs	1: Subscribers	2: Messages	3: Update frequency
a: Blog1	7,000	700	High
b: Blog2	9,000	700	Medium
c: Blog3	7,000	200	High
d: Blog4	9,000	200	Medium

In accordance with the notations used, we have N = {1, 2, 3}. The attribute associated with the criterion subscribers is the number of subscribers in the interval $X_1 = [0; 20,000]$; that associated with the number of messages is $X_2 = [0; 1,000]$; and finally the attribute associated with update frequency is $X_3 = \{$Very Low, Low, Medium, High, Very High$\}$. The four blogs a, b, c and d are viewed as elements of $X = X_1 \times X_2 \times X_3 \times X_4$. One way of illustrating the preferences of an expert between two alternatives is to consider an expert stating that Blog4 is more influential than Blog3.

Decision support applies in a wide variety of domains, as indeed do evaluation and classification of projects in response to a call for tender exhibiting different characteristics, or the evaluation of students after exams on multiple subjects.

5.2.2. Multi-Attribute Utility Theory

With this formalism, the objective of the multi-attribute utility theory (or MAUT) is to numerically represent an expert's preferences in the form of a complete $\succsim_X$ preorder using a function $u: X \to \mathbb{R}$, called the *global utility function* satisfying the following property:

$$\forall x, y \in X, x \succsim_{XY} y \Leftrightarrow u(x) \geq u(y) \qquad [5.1]$$

The function u is therefore constructed in such a way that the greater the global utility associated with an alternative, the more that alternative is "preferred" by the expert.

Classic methods based on multi-attribute utility consider the function u to be decomposable in the following way [KEE 76]:

$$\forall (x_1,\ldots, x_n) \in X, u(x_1,\ldots,x_n) := A(U(x)) \qquad [5.2]$$

where $A: \mathbb{R}^n \to \mathbb{R}$ is a so-called aggregation function, which yields a unique value $A(z)$ in $\mathbb{R}$ as a transformation of an element $z = (z_1,\ldots, z_n)$ in $\mathbb{R}^n$ such that A is increasing in each of its arguments (see [GRA 09]), and $U(x) = (u_1(x_1),\ldots, u_n(x_n))$, where the functions $u_i: X_i \to \mathbb{R}$, $i = 1,\ldots, n$ are marginal utility functions. They serve to transform the attributes (quoted in different units) onto a common scale which is interpretable as an intensity of preference. The utility u_i then corresponds to a relation of preference $\succsim_{Xi}$ over the attribute X_i:

$$\forall x_i, y_i \in X_i, x_i \succsim_{Xi} y_i \Leftrightarrow u_i(x_i) \geq u_i(y_i) \qquad [5.3]$$

[KEE 76] gives axioms which characterize the representation of $\succsim$ by equation [5.2].

The construction of the aggregation function and of the utility functions is based on notions of *measurement* which are discussed in the next section.

5.2.3. *Concepts of measurement and construction of utility functions*

The aim of *measurement* is to construct a *numerical representation* (also known as a *scale*) of a relational structure $\mathcal{E} = (E, \succsim)$, where E is the set of objects to be evaluated and $\succsim$ is a binary relation expressing, e.g., a decision-maker's preferences regarding the set E. The scale is therefore a function $f\colon E \rightarrow \mathbb{R}$ compatible with $\succsim$. This general framework will be applied in turn to all of the attributes $(X_i, \succsim_{Xi})$ to deduce the scale u_i. Note that although this framework can also be applied to $(X, \succsim_X)$ to construct the aggregation function, we shall use a different technique to construct it. The rest of this section focuses on the relational structure $(X_i, \succsim_{Xi})$.

In what is known as *ordinal* measurement, we simply impose condition [5.3]. This implies that the function u_i cannot be unique, as any strictly increasing transformation $\phi \circ u_i$ of u_i also satisfies [5.3]. More generally, the set of functions $\phi\colon \mathbb{R} \rightarrow \mathbb{R}$ such that $\phi \circ u_i$ remains a numerical representation is called the *set of admissible transformations*.

The different *scales* are characterized by the set of admissible transformations. The best known are:

– the *ordinal scale*, where the admissible transformations are the strictly increasing functions. Examples of ordinal scales are the Mohs scale and the Mercalli scale;

– the *interval scale*, where all functions $\phi(t) = \alpha t + \beta$, $\alpha > 0$ are admissible (positive affine transformations). Examples of interval scales are temperature in degrees Celsius or degrees Fahrenheit.

An ordinal scale is a poor structure which cannot be used to manipulate numbers, and particularly to define a degree of reliability, because the arithmetic operations are not invariant to the admissible transformations. It is therefore necessary to construct an interval scale. On such a scale, the notion of difference in score has meaning. In order to construct the scale, we construct a *quaternary* relation $\succsim^*_{Xi}$ comparing one pair of elements in X_i to another pair in X_i. The meaning of $x_i y_i \succsim^*_{Xi} z_i t_i$ is as follows: the difference in intensity (e.g. of reliability) between x_i and y_i is at least as large as the difference in intensity between z_i and t_i. The scale f must therefore satisfy the following condition:

$$\forall x_i, y_i, z_i, t_i \in X_i, x_i y_i \succsim^*_{Xi} z_i t_i \Leftrightarrow \quad u_i(x_i) - u_i(y_i) \geq u_i(z_i) - u_i(t_i) \quad [5.4]$$

It has been shown that, under certain conditions on $\succsim_{Xi}$ and $\succsim^*_{Xi}$, such a function u_i exists, and that it defines an interval scale [KRA 71]. Thus, the ratio $\dfrac{u_i(x_i) - u_i(y_i)}{u_i(z_i) - u_i(t_i)}$ makes sense (invariant with any admissible transformation).

The MACBETH method [BAN 94] is an approach which can be used in practice to construct an interval scale. A decision-maker's interview on the basis of a quaternary relation is very complex. The idea then is, for each pair (x_i, y_i) in X_i such that $x_i \succsim_{Xi} y_i$, to ask the decision-maker to estimate the intensity of preference between x_i and y_i from the values *very low, low, moderate, high, very high* and *extreme*. The scale thus obtained is fixed, to a particular affine transformation. As the utility functions are aggregated through A, the scales constructed on the different attributes must be *commensurate*. This means that for any $x_i \in X_i$ and $x_j \in X_j$, the relation $u_i(x_i) \geq u_j(x_j)$ implies that the decision-maker considers x_i to be at least as good as x_j. In order to satisfy this property, it is thus sufficient to fix the two degrees of freedom of the interval scales by setting the value of the scale on the basis of two reference levels. We suppose that for every attribute X_i there is an element denoted by $\mathbb{0}_i$ such that the criterion is not at all satisfied for that value. Such an element is a saturation level in the sense that $x_i \succsim_{Xi} \mathbb{0}_i$ for all $x_i \in X_i$. Similarly, we also suppose that for each attribute X_i, there is an element notated as $\mathbb{1}_i$ such that the criterion is perfectly satisfied for that value, i.e. $\mathbb{1}_i \succsim_{Xi} x_i$ for all $x_i \in X_i$.

The elements $\mathbb{0}_1,..., \mathbb{0}_n$ have the same meaning and correspond to reference levels. The same is true of $\mathbb{1}_1,..., \mathbb{1}_n$. The scales are then normalized so as to satisfy the relation:

$$u_i(\mathbb{0}_i) = 0 \text{ and } u_i(\mathbb{1}_i) = 1 \qquad\qquad [5.5]$$

5.2.4. *Aggregation function A: limitations of the weighted sum*

Before demonstrating the way in which the aggregation function is constructed, let us look for a moment at the expression of A. The most commonly used aggregation function is the weighted sum:

$$A(U(x)) = A(u_1(x_1),...,u_n(x_n)) = \sum_{i=1}^{n} v_i u_i(x_i)$$

or more simply:

$$A(a_1,...,a_n) = \sum_{i=1}^{n} v_i a_i$$

where the weights v_i represent the *degrees of substitution between criteria* (gain on a criterion compensating a loss on another) and where $a_i = u_i(x_i)$, $i = 1,..., n$. Thus, this model conveys the idea of possible *compensations* between criteria. While it has the advantage of being simple to understand and manipulate, the weighted sum does exhibit certain limitations, as demonstrated in example 5.2.

EXAMPLE 5.2.– Suppose that our expert assessing the influence of blogs thinks that the update frequency is important, especially if the total number of messages is high, but far less so if not. More specifically, suppose that he estimates Blog1 to be more influential than Blog2, and Blog4 to be more influential than Blog3.

If we wish to represent the expert's preferences using a weighted sum, then if v_i represents the weights and u_i the functions normalizing the attributes on a scale of 0 to 1, we would have:

Blog1≻Blog2 $\Rightarrow$ $v_1u_1(7,000) + v_3u_3(\text{High}) > v_1u_1(9,000) + v_3u_3(\text{Medium})$
and Blog4≻Blog3 $\Rightarrow$ $v_1u_1(9,000) + v_3u_3(\text{Medium}) > v_1u_1(7,000) + v_3u_3(\text{High})$

These two constraints lead to a contradiction. It is therefore impossible to represent this expert's preferences by way of a weighted sum.

In [GRA 04; GRA 10], we can find other phenomena which cannot be modeled by additive models such as the weighted sum – e.g. the existence of a *veto criterion*. A veto criterion is a criterion which, when it is not satisfied, leads the expert to be unsatisfied regardless of the values of the other criteria. In order to get around these difficulties, non-additive models have been suggested. The next section relates to one such model: the Choquet integral.

5.2.5. *The Choquet integral*

The Choquet integral is very widely used in multi-criteria decision support. In its simplest form, it can be written thus:

$$C_\mu(a_1,...,a_n) = \sum_{i=1}^{n} v_i a_i - \frac{1}{2} \sum_{i,j \in N} I_{ij} |a_i - a_j| \qquad [5.6]$$

where the v_i values represent the importance of the criteria (much like the coefficients in a simple weighted sum) and the I_{ij} are the interaction coefficients. Note that there is a more general form of the Choquet integral [GRA 10]. The advantage to this formulation lies in the ease of interpreting it, and the fact that it is capable of representing most decision-making strategies which are encountered in practice. The expression [5.6] clearly appears as a generalization of the weighted sum, with the interaction terms being seen as a disturbance in the linear part. The coefficients I_{ij} correspond to notions of positives or negative synergies. If $I_{ij} > 0$, the more different a_i is from a_j, the more the phenomenon of interaction drags down the overall score $C_\mu(a_1,...,a_n)$. More specifically, if $a_i > a_j$, the good evaluation of the criterion i is penalized with a degree $I_{ij}/2$ by the poorer evaluation of the criterion j. If $I_{ij} < 0$, then the greater the difference between a_i and a_j, the more the phenomenon of interaction pulls up the overall score. More specifically, if $a_i < a_j$, then the low score for the criterion i is compensated by the better score for j. To illustrate, we can again us the example of evaluation of the influence of the blogs.

EXAMPLE 5.3.– The application of the Choquet integral necessitates the use of commensurable scales. Therefore, we again use utility functions u_1, u_2 and u_3 which bring the numbers of subscribers, messages and update frequency of the blogs to normalized scores, between 0 and 1.

Blogs	1: Subscribers	2: Messages	3: Update frequency
a: Blog1	0.35	0.7	0.75
b: Blog2	0.45	0.7	0.5
c: Blog3	0.35	0.2	0.75
d: Blog4	0.45	0.2	0.5

If we take the following values: $v_1 = 0.25$, $v_2 = 0.35$, $v_3 = 0.4$, $I_{12} = 0$, $I_{13} = 0.5$, $I_{23} = 0.3$, we obtain:

$$C_\mu(Blog1) = 0.35v_1 + 0.7v_2 + 0.75v_3 - 0.4\ I_{13}/2 - 0.05\ I_{23}/2 = 0.525$$

$$C_\mu(Blog2) = 0.45v_1 + 0.7v_2 + 0.75v_3 - 0.05\ I_{13}/2 - 0.2\ I_{23}/2 = 0.515$$

$$C_\mu(Blog3) = 0.35v_1 + 0.2v_2 + 0.5v_3 - 0.4\ I_{13}/2 - 0.55\ I_{23}/2 = 0.275$$

$$C_\mu(Blog4) = 0.45v_1 + 0.2v_2 + 0.5v_3 - 0.05\ I_{13}/2 - 0.3\ I_{23}/2 = 0.325$$

With this form of coding it is therefore possible to represent the preferences Blog1 > Blog2 and Blog4 > Blog3 of the expert by a Choquet integral.

5.2.6. Determination of the aggregation function A

When the aggregation function used is a weighted sum, we need only determine the coefficients of importance v_i. It is not desirable to directly ask the decision-maker to provide the values of these weights, because the values thus obtained would be biased by some of that decision-maker's cognitive tendencies. In order to limit such biases, it is preferable by far to infer the values of the weights for the responses given to a question based on comparisons between alternatives. Looking at equation [5.5], we can see that, for the weighted sum, $v_i = u(r^i)$, where $r^i = (\mathbb{1}_i, \mathbb{0}_{\{1,...n\}\setminus\{i\}})$ denotes the so-called reference alternative whose value is $\mathbb{1}$ for the attribute i and $\mathbb{0}$ for the other attributes. Hence, in order to determine the weights, we merely need to ask the decision-maker about the alternatives $r^0 = \mathbb{0}$, r^1, r^2,...,r^n [BAN 94].

The above approach may be generalized in the context of the Choquet integral (equation [5.6]) [MAY 10]. The alternatives needing consideration are then $R = \{r^0, r^1, r^2,..., r^n\} \cup \{r^{i,j}: i,j \in N\}$, where $r^{i,j} = (\mathbb{1}_{i,j}, \mathbb{0}_{N\setminus\{i,j\}})$ denotes the reference alternative whose value is $\mathbb{1}$ for attributes i and j, and $\mathbb{0}$ for the other attributes. In order to construct the parameters v and I of the Choquet integral, we then ask the decision-maker to compare the alternatives in R using the MACBETH method described in section 5.2.3. Thus, we ask him first to rank the alternatives in R, and then to quantify the intensity of his preference between the pairs of alternatives in R from the values *very low, low, moderate, high, very high* and *extreme* [MAY 10]. We shall illustrate this approach in section 5.4.

5.2.7. *Multi-level preference models*

In most applications, the number of criteria can quite easily be greater than fifteen. Such is the case, for instance, with the model for evaluating the reliability of a Twitter account, which will be presented in section 5.4 (see Figure 5.1). In this case, it is no longer possible to simultaneously aggregate all the criteria as described in the model given by [5.2]. Indeed, the questioning of the decision-maker would be too complex (see section 5.2.6) because he would have to compare alternatives which have different values for all of the attributes. In order to limit the decision-maker's cognitive workload, the aggregation function A is organized hierarchically in the form of multiple aggregations. Each aggregation uses a Choquet integral and gathers together a homogeneous set of viewpoints. The questioning method is then applied to each aggregation.

5.2.8. *Estimation of a degree of reliability via the multi-criteria approach*

It is not possible to construct a rating for the reliability of an information source without looking at its semantics, or without knowing what the user will do with that reliability. In order to be able to give a tangible interpretation of that rating, we need to place ourselves in a specific context of usage of reliability. Here we envisage the interpretation of a reliability rating as a *degree of reliability*, with the major advantage lying in the fact that it helps to modulate (particularly to attenuate) the information provided by the source by way of the operation of discounting.

We are going to attempt to construct a model for such a degree, which will be applied to a set S of sources. The construction of such a degree based on the questioning of a human is the object of measurement, the essential elements of which – particularly the different types of scales – are recalled in section 5.2.3. The approach described here to quantify a degree of reliability consists of basing ourselves on a set of attributes, as in example 1. For a source $S \in S$, we use the notation $x(S) \in X$ for the values assumed by S on the basis of the n attributes. The degree of reliability d_F of the source S is then obtained by application of the model [5.2] to the vector $x(S)$:

$$d_F(S) = A(U(x(S)))$$ [5.7]

The aggregation function A may be composite, just as it was in section 5.2.7. The Choquet integral or integrals can be determined as described in section 5.2.6, and the determination of the utility functions $U = (u_1, \ldots, u_n)$ uses the approach detailed in section 5.2.3. Note that the hypothesis of commensurability implies that the utility functions and the different aggregation functions will produce evaluations on the same type of scale, which can indeed be interpreted as a degree of reliability. The degree $\mathbb{0}$ ($\mathbb{0}_i \in X_i$) corresponds to the lack of reliability, and results in the expert not taking the source into consideration. Conversely, the degree $\mathbb{1}$ ($\mathbb{1}_i \in X_i$) corresponds to maximum reliability, and expresses a decision-maker who takes account of the source's testimony without a moment's hesitation.

5.3. Reliability of sources on Twitter

In section 5.4, we illustrate the approach introduced in the previous section on a particular type of sources: Twitter accounts. First, though, we give a brief presentation of Twitter in section 5.3.1, followed in section 5.3.2 by a state of the art on the problem of evaluating the reliability of this type of sources.

5.3.1. *Twitter*

Twitter[2] is a micro-blogging platform which is somewhat like a social network. Since its launch in 2006, the service has rapidly become popular: in 2011, a hundred million users connected at least once a month, 230 million messages were sent every day [TAY 11] and 1.6 billion requests were handled daily [TWI 11]. In 2012, the total number of users registered on the platform was estimated at several hundred million [DUG 12].

Twitter allows its users to broadcast textual messages of 140 characters, known as *tweets*. These messages can be published by sending an e-mail, an SMS or *via* dedicated Web applications. The messages are time-stamped and may be geographically located. They may contain URLs and therefore link to images, videos and, more generally, Web pages. Twitter has a certain number of functionalities and a vocabulary which is entirely its own (although similar concepts can be found on other social networks). A user can explicitly address another user by prefixing the latter's name in his message with an @ symbol: this is known as a mention. He can also make explicit the topic or topics dealt with in his message by including *hashtags*, i.e. terms corresponding to those topics, preceded by a hash symbol (#). A user may also decide to *subscribe to* (or "follow") another user in order to be able to view the latter's tweets as soon as they are sent (tweeted). Another widely used function is the *retweet*: the sending of a tweet by a user comprising a copy of a tweet sent by another user, along with an explicit reference to that other user. Finally, any user registered on Twitter can make his profile more specific, with various different attributes associated with his account: a username, a short

---

2 http://www.twitter.com.

message, a photo, a geographical location and a URL linking to a personal or professional Website.

Generally, messages sent by Twitter users are public, as is all the other information associated with the users, such as profiles and followers. The Twitter service therefore provides a large amount of information which can be used for a variety of purposes, in a context going far beyond the simple exchange of information between individuals – e.g. the detection of a flu epidemic [CUL 10], the discovery of new information sources [DIA 12], the furthering of knowledge of the situation in the context of a terrorist attack [OH 11] or an accident [BEA 09; MUR 11]. Apart from the ease of collecting these data, it is the habits of publishing information on Twitter which account for the emergence of this type of applications. The brevity of the messages, the existence of numerous applications for publishing messages from mobile devices, telephones, tablets, etc., render this platform highly reactive.

5.3.2. *Reliability of sources on Twitter: state of the art*

However, a central problem which appears in a number of uses of Twitter is how to estimate the reliability of the Twitter accounts and of the information which they disseminate. Indeed, as demonstrated by the examples of the earthquake in Chile [MEN 10] and the post-election protests in Iran [ESF 10], Twitter can serve as a medium for the dissemination of false rumors. This problem is the subject of numerous publications. Below, we outline some of the most recent ones.

In [CAN 10], the authors propose a method to identify Twitter users who are reliable in a particular domain. The first step of their algorithm is to identify a set of users, called *candidates*, who may be relevant for a particular subject of interest. This step is performed by 1) representing a subject of interest in the form of a request, 2) entering that request into Twitter's standard search engine, 3) retrieving the list of users, known as *voters*, who wrote the tweets returned by the search engine, 4) establishing the list of candidates as being the users followed by at least one member of the voters.

The second step is to rank the candidates using measures reflecting their social status, these measures being based primarily on two numbers: the number of voters who follow a candidate and the total number of users on Twitter who follow that same candidate. We note that in an improved version of the algorithm, a third step is added, where the candidates are reordered using a measure reflecting the topical similarity between a user and a request (this measure is based on the content of the user's tweets). The performances of their algorithm are then evaluated by way of two protocols. In the first evaluation, it is noted that their algorithm is effective for identifying users who are relevant in a particular domain – at least as effective, in any case, as the commercial tool WeFollow[3], which is able to determine users who are influential in a given domain. In a second evaluation, it is shown that the list of Twitter users held up by their algorithm generally corresponds to a list of experts in the target field, i.e. reliable sources. It should be noted that the proposed algorithm does not suffer the weaknesses of some approaches dedicated to influential user identification, such as the need for access to the entire social graph or the dependency on information entered by users. Finally, let us state that the choice to base their algorithm on the content of tweets and on the social status of the users is supported by the study performed by the same authors and described in [CAN 11], which reveals that the reliability of a Twitter account in relation to a particular domain, as perceived by humans, depends in no small part on the strength of the association between the textual content of the account's tweets and the domain in question (in part it reflects that user's legitimacy to comment on the subject), and, to a lesser extent, on the social status of the account. For example, a user will be perceived as being more reliable in the automobile domain if his tweets deal mainly with that domain, and if he follows and is followed by a large number of other users.

In [ULI 11], the STANAG 2022 is applied to Twitter, and the reliability of the sources is estimated on the basis of a measure of centrality provided by TunkRank.[4] This measure is similar to PageRank, but takes account of the peculiarity of Twitter and

---

3 http://wefollow.com.
4 http://tunkrank.com.

particularly the use of retweets. Thus, a source is deemed to be more influential if he is followed by sources which are themselves influential, and is frequently retweeted. Here we see again the importance of a source's social status and integration into the social network in the estimation of his reliability. In addition to this measure, formal rules are applied to detect unreliable users – e.g. a rule which helps to detect users sending false retweets.

In [CAS 11], where the goal is to estimate the credibility of a piece of news rather than the reliability of a source, the authors propose a system which is capable of distinguishing, firstly, the topics relating to the news and therefore likely to convey informative content, from those relating to conversations. This system then automatically analyzes the topics identified as news and evaluates their credibility in a binary fashion: those reporting almost certainly true information, and those reporting almost certainly false information. This system is based on a decision-tree-type classifier, trained using a learning set labeled by humans, and whose characteristics can be divided into four types: characteristics based on the message (number of characters in the tweet, presence of a question mark, of a mention, number of URLs in the tweet, etc.); characteristics relating to the user (number of days since the user joined Twitter, tweets made since registering, number of accounts being followed by the user, number of his own followers, verified account or not, presence of a description, a URL linking to a personal Website); characteristics relating to the topic (number of tweets on the topic, average length of a tweet, number of different hashtags, etc.); and characteristics based on retweets of a message (the root degree in the propagation tree, the depth of the propagation tree, etc.). The authors report only a low error rate when the system is applied to their dataset. Qualitatively analyzing their results, they remark that the most active users tend to disseminate more credible information, alongside recently-registered users following and followed by many people.

An in-depth study of the factors influencing users' perception of the credibility of a tweet is conducted in [MOR 12]. The study is divided into a survey and a subsequent experiment. The study identifies 26 characteristics which Twitter users themselves say that they look at when assessing tweets, and then, for each of these characteristics, evaluates the extent to which it has an impact on the credibility and the level of attention received by that tweet. This survey reveals that the characteristics which most enhance the credibility of a tweet relate to its author. In particular, they include the author's influence (measured in numbers of followers, retweets and mentions, which are revealing of his social status), his expertise in the domain dealt with by the tweet (established by the number of tweets published in le domain, or indeed by the fact that the author's geographical location is relevant for the domain in question) and his reputation (dependent on whether or not the author is verified and whether the user is a follower of that author). The experiment, for its part, focuses on three characteristics which receive a high degree of attention from users (because they are easily accessible on the Twitter interface) and are deemed to be very important from the perspective of impact on credibility. These characteristics are the topic of the message, the username and the avatar used by the author of the tweet. The experiment shows that author usernames including a theme – e.g. the username *All Politics* – inspire the highest estimation of reliability of an author in the eyes of users; this is followed by conventional names, such as *Alex_Brown*, with (Internet) pseudonyms, such as *tenacious 27*, receiving the lowest scores. In terms of the image used as an avatar, it reduces the reliability rating of an author only if that image is the default image used for Twitter accounts. Hence, it is mainly factors which reflect significant involvement of a person in his account and in the network, alongside his legitimacy as a commentator in the domain dealt with by his remarks, which were evidentiated by this study. In conclusion, the authors also note the importance of grammar, spelling and richness of expression which, if they are of poor quality, have a significant negative impact on the perception of the reliability of the sources and of the credibility of their tweets.

The article [DIA 12] is also interesting, in that it provides a variety of indicators of reliability of sources on Twitter, in the particular context of events that have just happened. These indicators are then analyzed by journalists, who are specialists in the field of social media. The most basic information presented includes the user's full name, the name of his Twitter account, his avatar, joining date, number of "following" and "followers", description and URL. Then comes information derived from data gleaned from Twitter, such as the user's geographical location, the number of retweets he has obtained and a figure representing the users who are actively posting about the event in question and who are followers of the user under discussion. The highest-level information is calculated by way of classifiers. In particular, each source is placed in one of the three categories "journalist/blogger", "organization" or "ordinary person" by a first classifier developed by the same authors and described in [CHO 12], and the label of *eyewitness* is associated with a source by a second classifier if that source's tweets include words belonging to a dictionary of words unique to eyewitnesses. The analysis of these indicators by experienced journalists reveals that the labels "eyewitness", "journalist/blogger" and "organization", used in conjunction with the geographical information, can help to detect interesting information sources. Also, information such as the date a user registered, mentions, tweet history, number of following and followers, are all recognized as being useful in evaluating the reliability of sources. In addition, it is noted that sources who have friends close to an event are perceived as being more reliable. The proximity of the source to the event that he is reporting is, in this study, a key factor influencing the legitimacy of the source and ultimately his reliability.

The review of the different approaches in the existing body of literature to evaluate the reliability of Twitter accounts (directly or by way of the evaluation of the credibility of the tweets sent by those accounts) which we have presented in this section has helped to highlight a certain number of points which it is essential to take into account in order to make a pertinent estimation of this notion of reliability. To begin with, it is crucial not to consider reliability on an absolute level, but rather to evaluate it in a specific domain, on a particular topic. It must not be forgotten that the main advantage to estimating the reliability of a Twitter account is to be able to judge the credibility of a tweet sent by that account. Thus, it is primarily the reliability of the account in the domain corresponding to the topic discussed in the tweet which is important. Note that this remains true with regard to any medium for publishing information. Secondly, the various studies have demonstrated the importance of a number of factors specific to Twitter in being able to estimate that reliability:

– the involvement of a person in his account (presence of a photo, level of detail of the description associated with the account, volume and frequency of publication, integration in the social network);

– the legitimacy of the account in regard to a particular topic (proximity of that topic to the subjects of interest or to the geographical location displayed);

– the richness of expression (quality of spelling, grammar).

5.4. Multi-criteria model for the reliability of Twitter accounts

In this section, we describe a multi-criteria model for estimating the degree of reliability of a Twitter account. This model does not have a generalist outlook in the sense that it is not intended to be applied to any and all Twitter accounts and produce an absolute reliability rating for an account – a notion which would make little sense. On the contrary, the model detailed here is a function of a system analyzing only particular Twitter accounts which have recently provided information about a particular topic or event of interest. The implication of this is that the same account could possibly be attributed different reliability ratings if it communicates on more than one subject of interest. This also implies that accounts with non-informative content, i.e. accounts which are used primarily for the purpose of conversation, do not fall within the remit of application of our model. Note that in any case, the notion of reliability of this type of account is essentially meaningless. Our automated treatment also excludes verified accounts. Indeed, we can quite easily see that messages from the President, for instance, are in any case important enough to be processed manually by the user. Our function therefore applies to the very large number of more "anonymous" accounts of citizens spontaneously expressing their views on current affairs in the form of direct or indirect testimony. Add to this the less anonymous population of authors enjoying a loyal audience or numerous followers. In particular, here, we are thinking of journalists or experts, but the category also includes amateurs who have managed to create a community of followers around their account.

Like with any multi-criteria model, the different available and relevant attributes are aggregated to form higher-level concepts. On the other hand, we can also analyze the ingredients making up the notion of reliability for a user, and see which are the underlying concepts and the phenomena which are taken into account. From our study of the literature in this domain (see section 5.3), we have extracted three concepts which seem essential for the reliability evaluation of the Twitter accounts which we are interested in: the degree of involvement in the account, the legitimacy to comment on the subject, and the richness of expression.

The first concept stems from the observation that a person who has made a great personal investment in his Twitter account has a lot to lose by producing erroneous content. This is obviously true for journalists, who could eventually lose all credibility. It is also true of amateurs who have succeeded in amassing a large number of followers. Indeed, this is only possible if one has spent time on one's account, and produced a certain quantity of tweets, but also tweets of sufficient quality and veracity. Of course, heavy involvement in an account is not an infallible gage of reliability. In particular, we might think of the use of Twitter accounts devoted to self-promotion, publicity, but also propaganda and deliberate misleading. Our function does not deal with these cases. As these sources have existed for a long time, they are usually identified beforehand, and can therefore be excluded from our automated processing. On the other hand, accounts created specifically for the purpose of promulgating occasional disinformation are dealt with, and will be considered to be unreliable, as we shall see later on.

The notion of legitimacy to comment on the subject corresponds to the idea that in order to be relevant, a source must give testimony about an event to which that person was in physical proximity, or produce an analysis or summary about a subject in which he is specialized. The first case corresponds to a simple civil witness. The second corresponds to journalists or experts.

Finally, the richness of expression takes account of notions relating to the form rather than the content. This may seem confusing. Yet as can be seen, for instance, in [MOR 12; CAS 11], these aspects clearly constitute indicators about the reliability of sources. One explanation for this phenomenon probably lies in a supposed correlation between quality of expression and level of education, which may be associated with analytical capacity and critical thinking – qualities which are desirable for the production of reliable content. The three concepts introduced above are the essential elements in the multiple criteria model which we advance for the evaluation of the reliability of a Twitter account; they are to be found on the top level of Figure 5.1, which represents our model. For reasons of space, we cannot describe all the elements of our model. Thus, in what follows, we shall focus only on some of the most important elements, and describe in detail only certain parts of the model in order to illustrate its implementation.

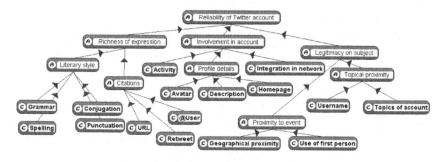

Figure 5.1. *Multi-criteria model to evaluate the reliability of a Twitter account*

Figure 5.1 shows a multi-level form of organization – see section 5.2.7. Nodes labeled with an "A" are aggregations such as the Choquet integral; those labeled with a "C" are the criteria with which the attributes of the Twitter accounts are associated. The overall evaluation corresponds to the root node, at the top of the graph. As we can see from this figure, the three concepts which we have identified are founded upon other, more specific notions. Certain concepts are easy to understand. For instance, richness of expression is based on literary style, which in turn is based on spelling, grammar, conjugation and punctuation. The idea is to quantify these criteria using a spell check such as those which are built into text processing software. Richness of expression is also based on the notion of citations, which represents the fact that a Twitter account cites its sources (by way of the use of URLs, mentions or retweets in their tweets). Other concepts present in the model are less easy to grasp at first glance. Such is the case of the notion of activity, which contributes to involvement in the account. This criterion is based on a set of indicators such as the age of the account, the number of messages published, the average frequency of publication, but also the number of messages published over the past month. They are all indicative of an abundance of energy on the part of the author and therefore contribute to the evaluation of his involvement in his Twitter account. This criterion is one of those which penalize sources created to disinform on a one-off basis. In other words, any recently-established account will have a poor score in terms of the criterion of *activity*, which includes accounts created specifically to mislead readers. The function which translates from the indicators mentioned above to the notion of activity is external to the multi-criteria analysis and is therefore not described here. The involvement in the account is also reflected by the presence of details on the account profile, such as the account's avatar being different to Twitter's default avatar, the account having a description or a link to a Web page. Finally, the involvement in the account is also evaluated on the basis of the notion of integration into the network, which is based on a set of indicators such as the number of subscriptions and followers. With regard to legitimacy to comment on the subject, it is determined on the basis of the concepts of proximity to the event and topical proximity. The proximity to the event is obtained on the basis of information about geographical proximity (based on knowledge of the user's geographical location) and whether the user of the Twitter account being analyzed is an eyewitness to the event. This can be estimated using a number of lexical and syntactical markers, including the use of the first person. Topical proximity, for its part, is established on the basis of the similarity of the username of the account and the tweets published by the account, with the topic of the event.

In this context, we shall illustrate the process of aggregation by the Choquet integral described in section 5.2, and particularly the construction of the reliability rating, interpreted as a degree of reliability (see section 5.2.8). The construction of the utility functions is based on the MACBETH method described in section 5.2.3. The construction of parameters of the Choquet integrals for all the aggregation functions in our model uses the approach outlined in section 5.2.6.

It is important to note that all the leaves of the tree correspond to attributes which will be quantified at the end. In addition, they need to be automatically quantified. This quantification can be performed by direct mining of information from Twitter, such as the Boolean describing the use of an avatar other than the default avatar. However, it can also be done by way of a more complex treatment such as in the case of activity. On the other hand, regardless of the way in which the attribute is obtained, the treatment to which it is subjected is of the same nature. It corresponds to the implementation of the results of the measurement theory described in section 5.2.3.

To illustrate this, let us take the simple example of number of spelling mistakes, which contributes to the evaluation of style, which in turn influences the score for richness of expression. In practice, using a spell check, we estimate the average number of spelling mistakes per 100 words written. In order to ensure commensurability between the criteria, let us begin by identifying the values of the average number of spelling mistakes, which correspond to the two reference levels 0_3 and 1_3 (supposing that this attribute corresponds to the label 3 criterion). Suppose that the expert says that the reliability is maximum only when the number of mistakes is 0 (i.e. $1_3 = 0$). The expert also finds that the reliability is zero when the number of mistakes is greater than or equal to 7, i.e. $0_3 = 7$. Finally, we ask the user of our model how he evaluates the difference in reliability between a source who writes flawless texts in comparison to another source who produces some, but only very few, mistakes (0.2 mistakes/100 words). This difference in reliability needs to be quantified by a level chosen from *very low, low, moderate, high, very high* and *extreme*. This questioning is repeated for a set of spelling mistake frequencies, as can be seen from Figure 5.2. The direction of preference is represented by the < or > signs. The levels *very low* to *extreme* are represented by two indicators ranging from 1 to 6, above and below on the right of each comparison sign. These intensities are represented by two levels rather than just one in order to take account of any potential uncertainty. For instance, the expert might judge the loss of reliability between 5 and 7 mistakes per 100 words as being between *high* and *extreme*: $5 >^6_4 7$.

	0.0	0.2	1.0	2.0	3.0	4.0	5.0	7.0
0.0		$>^2_2$	$>^6_6$					
0.2	$<^2_2$		$>^5_5$					
1.0	$<^6_6$	$<^5_5$		$>^2_2$				
2.0			$<^2_2$		$>^1_1$			
3.0				$<^1_1$		$>^3_3$		
4.0					$<^3_3$		$>^4_4$	
5.0						$<^4_4$		$>^6_4$
7.0							$<^6_4$	

Figure 5.2. *Creation of a utility function based on learning examples*

This type of question leads to the calculation of the utility function shown in Figure 5.3. As we can see, our user is very sensitive to the occurrence of even the slightest mistake: the reliability drops sharply between 0 and 1. It stabilizes a little between 1 and 3 before dropping fairly steeply beyond 3. It must be noted that the use of abbreviations is common on Twitter. Thus, it is common for a person with perfect mastery of spelling to produce texts with an error rate between 1 and 3 mistakes per 100 words. However, beyond 7 mistakes/100 words, our user judges that all the sources are to be evaluated on the spelling aspect and are evaluated very badly.

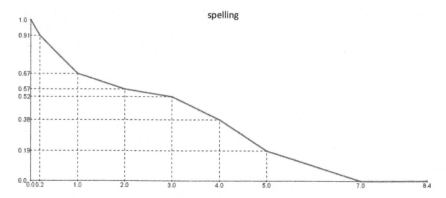

Figure 5.3. *Example of a utility function for criterion Spelling*

Of course, criterion *spelling* may be compensated by a very good evaluation on other criteria which are indicative of the reliability of the account. This type of compensation is specified at the aggregation level. Take the example of richness of expression, based on literary style and citations. In a similar manner to questioning the user with regard to the utility functions, we ask him to compare an account producing tweets with many mistakes and no citation, an account producing some mistakes with no citation, another producing citations without mistakes and finally an account free from mistakes with a great many citations. The two aggregations "Citations" and "Literary style" are supposed to bear the labels 1 and 2 respectively. Once again, these pairwise comparisons are quantified by a level on an interval scale, as illustrated in Figure 5.4. In this table, "{}", "Citations", "Citations & Literary style" and "Literary style" correspond respectively to the alternatives $\emptyset$, r^1, $r^{1,2}$, r^2. For instance, comparison $r^2 >_4^4 \emptyset$ means that the level of reliability increases greatly (intensity 4) when the "Literary style" changes from unreliable to reliable, in the absence of reliability on the basis of "Citations".

	{ }	Citations	Citations& Literary style	Literary style
{ }		$=$	$<\begin{smallmatrix}6\\6\end{smallmatrix}$	$<\begin{smallmatrix}4\\4\end{smallmatrix}$
Citations	$=$		$<\begin{smallmatrix}6\\6\end{smallmatrix}$	$<\begin{smallmatrix}4\\4\end{smallmatrix}$
Citations& Literary style	$>\begin{smallmatrix}6\\6\end{smallmatrix}$	$>\begin{smallmatrix}6\\6\end{smallmatrix}$		$>\begin{smallmatrix}6\\6\end{smallmatrix}$
Literary style	$>\begin{smallmatrix}4\\4\end{smallmatrix}$	$>\begin{smallmatrix}4\\4\end{smallmatrix}$	$<\begin{smallmatrix}6\\6\end{smallmatrix}$	

Figure 5.4. *Creation of an aggregation using learning examples*

After computation, we obtain the aggregation represented graphically in Figure 5.5, which is written as:

$$C_\mu(Rich.) = 0.3u_1(Cita.) + 0.7u_2(Style) - 0.6/2|u_1(Cita.)-u_2(Style)|$$

Using $\wedge$ to represent the operator *minimum*, the aggregation can be rewritten as:

$$C_\mu(Rich.) = 0.4u_2(Style) + 0.6(u_1(Cita.) \wedge u_2(Style))$$

According to this aggregation function, the citations alone are not indicative of a good richness of expression for our user:

$$\begin{cases} u_1(Cita.)=1 \\ u_2(Style)=0 \end{cases} \Rightarrow C_\mu(Rich.)=0$$

In addition, a good style is crucial in order for the richness of expression to be good:

$$C_\mu(Rich.) \leq u_2(Style)$$

However, a good style may be greatly penalized by a lack of citations:

$$\begin{cases} u_1(Cita.)=0 \\ u_2(Style)=1 \end{cases} \Rightarrow C_\mu(Rich.)=0.4$$

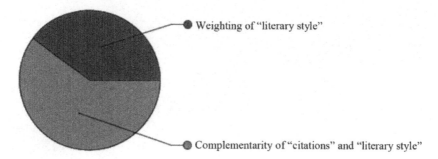

Figure 5.5. *Graphic representation of aggregation*

5.5. Conclusion

In this chapter, we have proposed a general approach for evaluating the reliability of information sources, based on the aggregation by the Choquet integral of dimensions indicative of reliability. Our approach was then applied to a particular type of sources: Twitter accounts.

However, this preliminary work needs further, more in-depth investigations. Indeed, the performances of our approach could be evaluated. For instance, experiments similar to those described in [CAN 10] could be performed. The genericity and relevance of the approach could also be verified, by producing multi-criteria models for other types of sources. A first step could be to look at other social networks, for which the models should be fairly similar to the one proposed for Twitter.

5.6. Bibliography

[BAN 94] BANA E., COSTA C., VANSNICK J., "A theoretical framework for measuring attractiveness by a categorical based evaluation technique (MACBETH)", *XIth Int. Conf. on MultiCriteria Decision Making*, Coimbra, Portugal, pp. 15–24, August 1994.

[BEA 09] BEAUMONT C., "New York plane crash: twitter breaks the news, again", *The Telegraph*, http://www.telegraph.co.uk/technology/twitter/4269765/New-Yorkplane-crash-Twitter-breaks-the-news-again.html, January 2009.

[CAN 10] CANINI K.R., SUH B., PIROLLI P.L., "Finding relevant sources in twitter based on content and social structure", *Workshop on Machine Learning for Social Computing, Neural Information Processing Systems (NIPS) conference*, Whistler, Canada, 2010.

[CAN 11] CANINI K.R., SUH B., PIROLLI P.L., "Finding credible information sources in social networks based on content and social structure", *third IEEE International Conference on Social Computing* (Social Com), Boston, United States, 2011.

[CAS 11] CASTILLO C., MENDOZA M., POBLETE B., "Information credibility on twitter", *20th international conference on World Wide Web, WWW'* ACM Press, New York, no. 11, pp. 675–684, 2011.

[CHA 08] CHATTERJEE K., DE ALFARO L., PYE I., "Robust content-driven Reputation", in BALFANZ D., STADDON J., (eds.), *First ACM Workshop on AISec*, ACM Press, New York, United States, pp. 33–42, 2008.

[CHO 12] DE CHOUDHURY M., DIAKOPOULOS N., NAAMAN M., "Unfolding the event landscape on twitter: classification and exploration of user categories", *ACM conference on Computer Supported Cooperative Work, CSCW'12*, New York, United States, pp. 241–244, 2012.

[CUL 10] CULOTTA A., "Towards detecting influenza epidemics by analyzing Twitter messages", *First Workshop on Social Media Analytics, SOMA'10*, New York, United States, pp. 115–122, 2010.

[DES 08] DESTERCKE S., CHOJNACKI E., "Methods for the evaluation and synthesis of multiple sources of information applied to nuclear computer codes", *Nuclear Engineering and Design*, vol. 238, no. 9, pp. 2 484–2 493, 2008.

[DES 11] DESTERCKE S., BUCHE P., CHARNOMORDIC B., "Evaluating data reliability: an evidential answer with application to a web-enabled data warehouse", *IEEE Transactions on Knowledge and Data Engineering*, vol. 25, no. 1, pp. 92–105, 2013.

[DIA 12] DIAKOPOULOS N., DE CHOUDHURY M., NAAMAN M., "Finding and assessing social media information sources in the context of journalism", *ACM annual conference on Human Factors in Computing Systems, CHI'12*, pp. 2 451–2 460, New York, United States, 2012.

[DUG 12] DUGAN L., "Twitter To Surpass 500 Million Registered Users On Wednesday", http://www.mediabistro.com/alltwitter/500-million-registered-users_b18842, February 2012.

[ELO 04] ELOUEDI Z., MELLOULI K., SMETS P., "Assessing sensor reliability for multisensor data fusion with the transferable belief model", *IEEE Transactions on System Man and Cybernatics B*, vol. 34, no. 1, pp. 782–787, 2004.

[ESF 10] ESFANDIARI G., "The Twitter Devolution", *Foreign Policy*, http://www.foreignpolicy.com/articles/2010/06/07/the_twitter_revolution_that_wasnt, June 2010.

[GRA 03] GRABISCH M., PERNY P., "Agrégation multicritère", in BOUCHON-MEUNIER B., MARSALA C. (eds.), *Logique floue, principes, aide à la décision*, Hermès, Paris, pp. 81–120, 2003.

[GRA 04] GRABISCH M., LABREUCHE C., "Fuzzy measures and integrals in MCDA", in FIGUEIRA J., GRECO S., EHRGOTT M. (eds.), *Multiple Criteria Decision Analysis*, Kluwer Academic Publishers, Dordrecht, pp. 563–608, 2004.

[GRA 09] GRABISCH M., MARICHAL J.L., MESIAR R., PAP E., "Aggregation functions", *Encyclopedia of Mathematics and its Applications*, vol. 127, 2009.

[GRA 10] GRABISCH M., LABREUCHE C., "A decade of application of the Choquet and Sugeno integrals in multi-criteria decision aid", *Annals of Operations Research*, vol. 175, pp. 247–286, 2010.

[KEE 76] KEENEY R.L., RAIFFA H., *Decision with Multiple Objectives*, Wiley, New York, 1976.

[KLE 10] KLEIN J., COLOT O., "Automatic discounting rate computation using a dissent criterion", *Workshop on the Theory of Belief Functions, BELIEF 2010*, Brest, April 2010.

[KRA 71] KRANTZ D., LUCE R., SUPPES P., *et al.*, *Foundations of measurement, vol. 1: Additive and Polynomial Representations*, Academic Press, London, 1971.

[MAY 10] MAYAG B., Elaboration d'une démarche constructive prenant en compte les interactions entre critères en aide multicritère à la décision, Doctoral thesis, Université Paris I Panthéon-Sorbonne, May 2010.

[MEN 10] MENDOZA M., POBLETE B., CASTILLO C., "Twitter under crisis: can we trust what we RT?", *1ˢᵗ Workshop on Social Media Analytics, SOMA'10*, Washington, USA, July 2010.

[MOR 12] MORRIS M.R., COUNTS S., ROSEWAY A., et al., "Tweeting is believing? understanding microblog credibility perceptions", *ACM conference on Computer Supported Cooperative Work, CSCW'12*, New York, United States, pp. 441–450, 2012.

[MUR 11] MURTHY D., "Twitter: microphone for the masses?", *Media, Culture & Society*, vol. 33, no. 5, pp. 779–789, July 2011.

[OH 11] OH O., AGRAWAL M., RAO H.R., "Information control and terrorism: tracking the mumbai terrorist attack through twitter", *Information Systems Frontiers*, Kluwer Academic Publishers, Dordrecht, vol. 13, no. 1, pp. 33–43, March 2011.

[RAM 04] RAMCHURN S.D., HUYNH D., JENNINGS N.R., "Trust in multi-agent systems", *The Knowledge Engineering Review*, vol. 19, pp. 1–25, 2004.

[SCH 11] SCHUBERT J., "Conflict management in dempster-shafer theory using the degree of falsity", *International Journal of Approximate. Reasoning*, vol. 52, pp. 449–460, 2011.

[SHA 76] SHAFER G., *A mathematical theory of evidence*, Princeton University Press, Princeton, 1976.

[SME 93] SMETS P., "Belief functions: the disjunctive rule of combination and the generalized Bayesian theorem", *International Journal of Approximate Reasoning*, vol. 9, no. 1, pp. 1–35, 1993.

[TAY 11] TAYLOR C., "Twitter has 100 million active users", http://mashable.com/2011/09/08/twitter-has-100-million-active-users/, September 2011.

[TWI 11] TWITTER SEARCH TEAM (TWITTER ENGINEERING BLOG), "The engineering behind twitter's new search experience", http://engineering.twitter.com/2011/05/engineering-behind-twitters-new-search.html, May 2011.

[ULI 11] ULICNY B., KOKAR M.M., "Toward formal reasoning with epistemic policies about information quality in the twittersphere", *International Conference on Information Fusion*, Chicago, USA, 2011.

[YU 02] YU B., SINGH M.P., "An evidential model of distributed reputation management", *First International Joint Conference on Autonomous Agents and Multiagent Systems*, ACM Press, New York, pp. 294–301, 2002.

Chapter 6

Uncertainty of an Event and its Markers in Natural Language Processing

6.1. Introduction

Supposing a given event is extracted by automated means from a textual document, how are we to determine the level of certainty which should be associated therewith? Has this event already happened or is it simply predicted? If it is described as having already happened, how much trust should we attach to its actual occurrence, on the basis not only of the reliability of the source, but also of the semantic and temporal markers in the text from which it is extracted?

The studies presented in this chapter use linguistic analysis to model the uncertainty linked to detected events. The first step was to create a theoretical model to reflect how uncertainty is expressed in written texts. The second step of implementation consisted of using a

Chapter written by Mouhamadou El Hady BA, Stéphanie BRIZARD, Tanneguy DULONG and Bénédicte GOUJON.

reference corpus of nearly 15,000 articles and 13 million words[1] to construct dictionaries and grammars covering all of uncertainty cases which might be expressed in the selected texts. These dictionaries and grammars match features, drawn from the model of uncertainty defined previously, to textual forms. Finally, uncertainty detection was combined with the detection of named entities and events from texts, in order to limit the detection and characterization of the different uncertainty forms to those relating to events only. The third and final step was technological implementation. A free-text analysis software module was developed. This module associates each word (or group of words) from the text with a linguistic resources entry. These resources include dictionaries, local grammars, thesauri and ontologies. All resources can use annotations produced upstream as input. The implementation of the model consists of rolling out an analysis procedure through linguistic resources which ultimately identify linguistic markers in the form of annotations that can be handled by the developed program.

In this chapter, after giving a brief state of the art on domains relevant for uncertainty management, we present the work which has enabled us to develop our own tool.

6.2. State of the art

Characterization of the certainty or uncertainty of events described in texts involves a number of stages: detection of named entities, detection of events reliant on named entities, and detection of the uncertainty expressed. Our state of the art presents these three steps.

6.2.1. Detection of named entities

The issue of automated detection of the names of persons, locations or dates in texts emerged in the mid-1990s, as attested by the holding of the MUC (*Message Understanding Conference*) series in

---

1 This reference corpus called "Europe's defense industry position" is the fruit of automated collection on the basis of many relevant sources subject to active monitoring on the Web: written and audiovisual press sites, think tanks, blogs of senators/members of congress, governmental sites, NGO sites or defense industry sites.

the US [EHR 08]. The objective at that point was to aid automatic understanding of military messages. The domains of application later evolved toward competitive or strategic intelligence or toward question-answering systems. Initially, named entities were grouped in to the following three categories (MUC 6) [CHI 97]:

– ENAMEX: for named entities such as persons, organizations and locations. Sub-types are: Person, Organization and Location;

– TIMEX: for temporal expressions. Sub-types are: Date and Time;

– NUMEX: for numerical expressions such as money and percentages. Sub-types are: Money and Percent.

Later, named entity categories were enriched and evolved to adapt to the intended applications. Today, the basic named entities are persons, organizations and locations, and numerous other named entities are used as and when needed. For example, applications in biology will primarily be interested in detecting the names of genes or proteins (in this case, the detection of persons' names is of little interest).

Two main methods can be used for detecting named entities: machine learning on the basis of corpora which were pre-annotated with named entities, and the use of linguistic patterns based on dictionaries. Other approaches have also been put forward, combining machine learning and linguistic patterns, in order to overcome the limitations of each method (the need for large corpora for machine learning, and the cost of manually-produced linguistic patterns) [POI 03].

Here are a few examples illustrating the use of linguistic patterns to detect person names. To detect the name "Jacques Chirac", it is possible to use a dictionary of first names and a grammar describing that a phrase formed by a first name followed by a word beginning with a capital letter (the surname) corresponds to a named entity of the type Person. A similar grammar might be based on a word introductory to a person's name, as in "Mr. Obama" or "President Obama" to detect other forms of persons' names. Many named entities can be automatically extracted in this way. Certain tricky cases require the use of more complex grammars, so as not to pick up on the name of a person in instances such as "Charles de

Gaulle Airport". Similarly, for certain applications, "the President of the United States" could be considered as a named entity if, in the applicative context, this phrase is not ambiguous and refers to a single and clearly identified person. For other applications, that expression would be anaphoric and would necessitate the finding of a surname for the purposes of disambiguation.

6.2.2. Detection of events

The detection of events involves finding relations between named entities. For example, in "YouTube was bought by Google in 2006", three named entities – the company being bought: "YouTube", the buyer company "Google" and the date "2006" –are linked by an event of the type PURCHASE. Thus, the initial step consists of detecting the named entities which might be in relation in the relevant events. Then, the objective is to find the expression of an event and markers enabling us to attribute roles (agent, patient or object, date, location, etc.) to the different entities in relation.

The initial requirements in event extraction were formalized in the MUC 3 (1991) and MUC 4 (1992) campaigns, where the objective was to identify locations, dates and victims associated with past terrorist events. During these campaigns, the notion of a named entity had not yet been defined (it emerged for MUC 6), but the need was certainly to detect events linking elements such as locations, dates and persons. More recently, the ACE (automated content extraction) campaigns have integrated the task of event extraction.

Various tools propose to extract events from texts, basing the process – similarly as with named-entity recognition – either on machine learning methods using annotated corpora (SIE [GIU 05], Grishman tool [ZHA 05]), or on linguistic patterns (Sem + [GOU 05], Zenon [HEC 08]).

6.2.3. Detection of uncertainty

The detection of uncertainty markers in texts is based on linguistic works relating to modalities, negation and reported speech. The identification of the uncertainty expressed in texts for intelligence, using linguistic knowledge, was proposed by Canadian intelligence specialists [AUG 08]; however they neither described a new model nor any form of implementation. Here we present two existing models to deal with issues similar to our current topic, and various works in linguistics regarding some points relating to uncertainty.

6.2.3.1. *Rubin's model*

Rubin *et al.* [RUB 05] put forward a model for categorizing certainty, based on four dimensions: "level", "perspective", "focus" and "time". Figure 6.1 elucidates these dimensions.

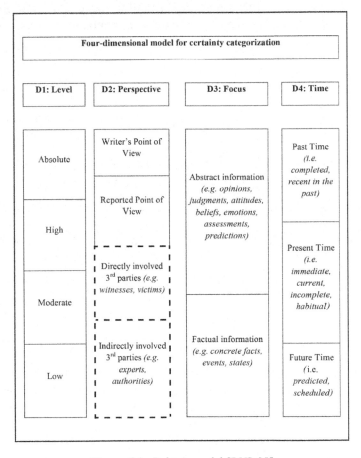

Figure 6.1. *Rubin's model [RUB 05]*

In this model, level (D1) corresponds to the reporter's level of certainty. Our model also uses a dimension "Level", but in our approach it represents the level of factuality associated with the event. We have also adapted our model for automated annotation, whereas Rubin's was developed for manually-annotated corpora.

6.2.3.2. Saurí's model

In Saurí [SAU 08], the authors propose a model for annotating the factuality of events in a corpus. This model is used for manual annotation of the Fact Bank corpus (208 documents, over 8,000 events), in addition to annotations produced using Time ML (a markup language for annotating temporal and event expressions). Table 6.1 illustrates the categories which are annotated to characterize the factuality of events.

	Positive	Negative	Underspecified
Certain	Fact:<CT, + >	Counterfact: <CT, ->	Certain but unknown output: <CT, u>
Probable	Probable:<PR, + >	Not probable:<PR, ->	(NA)
Possible	Possible:<PS, + >	Not certain:<PS, ->	(NA)
Under-specified	(NA)	(NA)	Unknown or uncommitted:<U, u>

Table 6.1. *Factuality values according to Saurí [SAU 08]*

In order to better understand this model, note that the certain/under specified scenario, represented as <CT, u>, is exemplified by "John knows whether Mary came." In the Time ML model, most verbs and predicative nouns express events, as demonstrated by the following sentence, containing 8 events, taken from the Time Bank corpus:

13   The move <u>seemed</u>$_{e83}$ <u>aimed</u>$_{e84}$ at <u>heading</u>$_{e85}$ off more <u>trouble</u>$_{e86}$ with Iran, which had <u>condemned</u>$_{e87}$ Iraq 's <u>invasion</u>$_{e88}$ of Kuwait on Aug. 2 but also <u>criticized</u>$_{e90}$ the multinational force <u>dispatched</u>$_{e91}$ to Saudi Arabia.

Figure 6.2. *Example of event annotation using Saurí's system*

In our approach, the notion of event is more restrictive, being limited to events which interest the end user. In addition, we felt the distinction between "probable" and "possible", which is at the heart of this model, was not helpful, as we are primarily wishing to find out whether or not an event has taken place, or the degree of certainty with which the author is presenting it.

6.2.3.3. *Work on reported speech, modalities and evidentiality*

Reported speech[2], which is one of the ways of expressing a certain detachment from the message, has often been studied, but for reasons different to ours. For instance, in Battistelli and Chagnoux [BAT 07], reported speech is used to represent the enunciative and modal dynamics of texts, i.e. to mark the discursive relations between different clauses in texts. A number of different referential frameworks are associated with the clauses: enunciative, possible and mental referential frameworks. The objective is to make explicit the hierarchical structure of a text, but not to attribute combined values of factuality or certainty to the source, as we wish to do.

Evidentiality, which is presented in detail by Dendale and Coltier [DEN 03], relates to the mode of access to a piece of information. In that article, three cases of evidentiality are presented: evidentiality by direct perception, which corresponds to situations where the speaker was in direct contact with what he is describing (for instance, he saw what happened); evidentiality by relay, which corresponds to reported speech; and finally, evidentiality by inference, based on clues or indicators – this might be introduced, for example, by the verb

---

2 Chapter 8 is devoted to an examination of uncertainty estimation models when a piece of information is reported by a string of successive sources, as is the case with reported speech.

"think". This notion is directly related with our topic, and can be seen from the values of many of the characteristics of our model (see the description of our model below).

6.3. Model for representing the uncertainty of an event

6.3.1. *Named entity model*

As the MUC proposition [CHI 97] is not sufficient to cover all domains of application, we have opted for our own classification of named entities. Our typology comprises eight categories: Person, Organization, Location, Temporal expression, Numerical expression, Contact information, Artifact and Event (entity). These classes are modularized into nearly a hundred sub-classes and sub-sub-classes in total, and also include attributes – particularly for persons (civil status, surname, forename, nationality and occupation, amongst others). These named entities are extracted using either linguistic patterns or predefined lists which may take the form of termino-ontological referentials (TORs) such as thesauri or ontologies.

6.3.2. *Event model*

Our event annotation model draws inspiration from the ACE directives [ACE 08]. The resources for event extraction were created specifically on the basis of the corpora being analyzed. By "events", sometimes referred to as "relations between named entities", we understand two notions:

– static relations, which remain true for a certain, and potentially long, period of time – e.g. "YouTube has been a subsidiary of Google since 2006". The link connecting the two named entities YouTube and Google (a binary relation) is stable;

– dynamic relations, expressing an action between participants, which occurs at a given moment – for instance, "the buying of YouTube by Google in 2006". The ACE specifies that the arguments invoked by the predicate are the participants in the event. Each of these participants has a specific role (agent, object, source, target, etc.)

[DOD 04], all within a non-essential spatio-temporal framework [EZZ 10].

In both cases, instances of relations are "n-ary": they can accommodate numerous different attributes (including dates and locations). The event annotation model shows the structuring of arguments (mandatory) and attributes (non-mandatory) around a predicate. Arguments and attributes also bear the hallmark of their role. An event is annotated in its entirety, and semantic sub-traits characterize arguments and attributes. Predicates, for their part, are not specifically annotated. Event recognition relies on correct prior identification of the named entities which, when associated with a given predicate, may represent arguments or attributes in a relation.

6.3.3. Uncertainty model

The uncertainty model presented here has been adapted for automated annotation of factuality in texts, in addition to automated annotation of events. This constraint of the combination of models and the implementation sets our approach apart from the work done on modeling by Rubin and Saurí, who put forward their models independently of their potential implementation. An initial version of the uncertainty model was presented in [GOU 10]. The model shown in Figure 6.3 is the updated version, which is based on six dimensions.

The dimensions of this model are presented in detail below.

Level	Absolute	High	Moderate	Low
Time	Past	Present		Future
Source	Writer		Source Name	
Negation				
Perspective	Secondary Source Perspective		Primary Source Perspective	
Commitment	Absolute	High	Moderate	Low

Figure 6.3. *Model for annotation of factuality*

6.3.3.1. *Level*

The dimension Level in our model corresponds to the level of factuality expressed. Here, the term "factuality" is used in the sense of "the reality of the fact as presented". What we are seeking to evaluate is the apparent level of reality of an event, based on what is expressed in the text by its writer. Thus, if no nuance at all is expressed, Level has the value Absolute which is its default value (we suppose that the writer is absolutely convinced of the reality of the event that he is reporting). If a high degree of certainty is expressed (definitely, without a doubt, affirm, etc.) with regard to the reality of the information, Level has the value High. If a low degree of certainty is expressed (improbable, uncertain, etc.), Level has the value Low. In other cases, where a relative uncertainty is expressed (by "perhaps", the use of the conditional, "it seems that", and so on), Level is associated with the value Moderate.

6.3.3.2. *Time*

The dimension Time not only corresponds to the tense of the verb which is at the heart of the event identification pattern. It corresponds, more specifically, to the moment when the event happened in relation to the time when the statement is made. Thus, "will go", "must go", "is going tomorrow" or "should go" correspond to the value Future. In order to mark the value Present, we use expressions such as "at the moment", "currently" or "to be doing…" The default value is Past.

6.3.3.3. *Source(s)*

The dimension Source(s) is used to mark reported speech by identifying the source of a piece of information. By default, its value is Writer, as it is the writer of the text who is the primary source. If a local source is specified: "The spokesman announced…", it is included in the dimension Source(s). The source does not necessarily have to be a person – it may also be a piece of media, a document, a political organization, etc. When the value of this dimension is not Writer, we are dealing with reported speech, which corresponds to evidentiality by relay in Dendale and Coltier's theory [DEN 03].

6.3.3.4. *Negation*

The dimension Negation is used to identify when an event is presented accompanied by a negative turn of phrase.

6.3.3.5. *Perspective*

The dimension Perspective enables us to specify whether the source has had direct contact with the event described (Primary Source Perspective), or indirect contact (Secondary Source Perspective), when it is explicit. If we have the sentence "Our special reporter saw Laurent Gbagbo in Rome", the value is Primary Source Perspective. If we have "Our special reporter believes Laurent Gbagbo to have been in Rome", the dimension has the value Secondary Source Perspective. This dimension is related to evidentiality by direct perception, in Dendale and Coltier's model.

6.3.3.6. *Commitment*

The degree of commitment of the source to what is being described is expressed in the dimension Commitment. When the source (here "Laurent Gbagbo") is not highly committed: "Laurent Gbagbo thinks that...", its value is Low. This case corresponds to evidentiality on the basis of clues, as described by Dendale and Coltier. When the source is very committed: "Laurent Gbagbo affirms that...", its value is High. By default, its value is Absolute.

6.3.3.7. *Additional models*

In our model for annotating factuality, we do not seek to characterize the source's opinions, sentiments, judgments or emotions in relation to what he is reporting. These elements are not usually expressed by the writer of the press article, but are undeniably present in cases of indirect speech, such as in "'The scene is just as harrowing as one might imagine', commented the Lord Mayor of the city", or "Even the daily paper *Le National*... has condemned this raid". In the context of aiding the evaluation of open-source information, we have chosen to center our model on the reality, or lack thereof, of an event which is described in a text.

6.4. Linguistic resources

6.4.1. *Technological context*

The information extraction module (see section 6.1.2.3) is based on the HST[3] environment and a linguistico-symbolic approach[4]. HST uses, either together or separately, free formats (DELA[5] [COU 90], Unitex local grammars [PAU 08]) and proprietary formats such as pattern dictionaries[6] (PDs). HST is distinguished by its capacity to also handle termino-ontological resources expressed in accordance with the standards of the W3C (SKOS[7], OWL[8]). Regardless of their nature, extraction resources are intended to describe language structures ranging from a simple dictionary entry to the reproduction of complex linguistic patterns (local grammars [GRO 95]). All the resources are able to draw upon annotations generated upstream.

6.4.2. *Development and test corpora*

The linguistic and semantic resources implement the model defined previously. These resources were developed as part of the corpus study mentioned in the chapter introduction.

The linguistic resources were constructed (and tested) thanks to the study of the development corpus. Their performance was also verified using a test corpus comprising articles from the French newspaper *Le Monde* (year 2007)[9]. These iterative tests enabled us to check the

---

3 High Speed Transducer.
4 Approach based on the description of linguistic patterns.
5 *Dictionnaire électronique du Laboratoire d'automatique documentaire et linguistique* (Electronic Dictionary of the LADL – Documentary and Linguistic Automation Engineering Lab).
6 The pattern dictionaries (PDs) are intermediary resources between a grammar and a dictionary. They can accommodate extended syntax, relying on semantic and morpho-syntactic annotations drawn from the dictionaries or grammars processed upstream.
7 Simple Knowledge Organization System, http://www.w3.org/2004/02/skos/.
8 Rearranged acronym for Web Ontology Language, http://www.w3.org/2004/OWL/.
9 The test corpus is far smaller than the development corpus. It includes 210 articles and almost 130,000 words.

behavior of the resources on a different type of corpus (written press only) and on far more wide-ranging topics than those in the reference corpus. The analyzed results led us to improve the resources to tend toward a generalization of the patterns described, particularly for event annotation.

6.4.3. Linguistic resources for named entity recognition

Named entity annotation relies on local grammars, and on an ontology created specifically for this purpose.[10] The grammar shown in Figure 6.4 is used for recognizing named entities of the type "Political Institutions". The following extract shows a call to lists of known named entities {Political Org} (acronyms or full forms), possibly preceded by a left-hand context {Org Trigger L} (a trigger element such as "movement", "organization", etc.), which may or may not be followed by a right-hand context of appearance (a word beginning with a capital letter <PRE> or an acronym, called by the sub-graph "abbrev-org-EN").

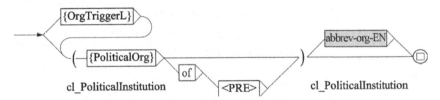

Figure 6.4. *Extract from a local grammar for detecting Political Institutions*

For example, this grammar could detect "Free Resistance of Dagbas" in the sentence "The organization *Free Resistance of Dagbas* (FRD) has not claimed responsibility for the attack on 31 May", where "organization" would be a trigger {Org Trigger L}, "Free Resistance of Dagbas" a known element in the list {Political Org} and "FRD" an abbreviation recognized by the graph "abbrev-org-EN". The structures, however, may be far more complex and need not be based

10 A thesaurus for the domain was also created. The concepts are used as triggers for the relation extraction grammars.

on any previously known element. Thus, linguistic patterns involve describing noun phrases such as "movement of Ektimostan nationalist forces".

The ontology includes over 1,900 instances distributed into 52 named entity classes, the most densely populated being "Defense industry company", with 1,084 individuals. The ontology has been enriched manually and automatically. The class "Defense industry company" is an exploitation of the online directory Ixarm.[11] This ontology models named entities specific to the domain being analyzed. It uses a proprietary meta-model which has been enriched with 36 sub-classes specific to the domain and to the reference corpus. For the class "Person", for instance, we have:

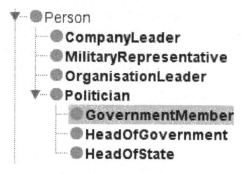

Figure 6.5. *Extract from the typology of the Defense ontology, class: Person*

6.4.4. *Linguistic resources for event extraction*

Eight types of events were considered in our study: Contact, Movement, Merge, Acquisition, Leadership, Appointment to an executive position, Partnership and Contract signature. For each of these events, a linguistic diagnostic of the patterns needing to be extracted was performed, in order to create a semantico-logical model (arity, arguments, attributes, predicates) and to determine which types of arguments and attributes need to be annotated: named entities

---

11 Ixarm is an armament portal set up by the French Ministry of Defense so as to facilitate suppliers' access to the defense markets: http://www.ixarm.com/index_fr.

and/or personal pronouns and/or definite descriptions. The semantico-logical model enables us to define certain constraints in order to extract from the corpus those segments which indicate the different linguistic constructions in a relation. From this, regularities were identified and used to create a model with five grammars:

– predicate noun at the beginning of the segment before the two arguments;

– predicate verb at the beginning of the segment before the two arguments;

– predicate noun in the middle of the segment between the two arguments;

– predicate verb in the middle of the segment between the two arguments;

– predicate verb at the end of the segment after the two arguments.

Figure 6.6 is an example of annotation using the grammar Contract signature, exhibiting a segment with a nominal predicate placed before the two arguments: "On 21 March, an agreement signed between Colonel al-Adel and Captain Ixil".

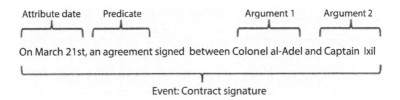

Attribute date   Predicate   Argument 1   Argument 2

On March 21st, an agreement signed between Colonel al-Adel and Captain Ixil

Event: Contract signature

Figure 6.6. *Example of a segment extracted by the grammar "Contract signature"*

In this version of the event extraction resources, only constructions in the active voice have been developed. Pronominal anaphora and definite descriptions are taken into account by the patterns described above. However, they are not exploited by the information extraction module as they cannot be associated with a module for resolution of anaphora and co-references.

6.4.5. *Linguistic resources for uncertainty extraction*

6.4.5.1. *List creation*

The corpus "Europe's defense industry position" was used to manually create a list of words likely to provide indications about the uncertainty associated with an event. Based on automatic extractions from a sub-corpus of 4,800 articles drawn from the reference corpus, we created lists of verbs, adverbs and adjectives, and associated levels of uncertainty with each of them. For instance, as shown by the extract from the table of verbs (see Table 6.2), we have classified the verbs in terms of the dimensions Level, Time and Commitment. We have done the same thing for adverbs and adjectives.

		Level	**Time**	**Commitment**
	Verbs			
1	to learn, to assure that, to attest, to warn	High		High
2	to announce, to indicate, to precede, to prefigure	Absolute	Future	Moderate
	Adverbs			
3	currently, at present, today		Present	
4	previously, before, beforehand		Past	
5	certainly, absolutely, assuredly	High		High
	Adjectives			
6	probable, admissible, possible	Moderate		Moderate
7	absolute, sure, proven, convinced, true	High		High
8	doubtful, random, ambiguous, dubitable	Low		Low

Table 6.2. *Extract from the lists of verbs, adverbs and adjectives selected from the corpus "Europe's defense industry position"*

An extracted event containing one of the verbs in row 1 of the table has a high level of factuality (Level = High) and the speaker exhibits strong commitment to that event (Commitment = High). Note that there is sometimes a certain heterogeneity between factuality and commitment, i.e. no systematic correlation (see row 2 of the table). The verbs can also give us information about the time attached to the event. Thus, certain verbs such as "announce" or "precede" indicate an event which has not yet taken place, so it is classified as a future event. Because the level of certainty of an event depends on whether or not it has been completed, this information gives us an initial indication of the level of certainty even before any evaluation takes place. The lists of adverbs and adjectives also enabled us to extract information about the other relevant dimensions for calculating the level of uncertainty. Thus, although few of the extracted verbs enable us to define the perspective on the event adopted by the speaker, or the source of the information, certain adverbs (e.g. apparently, possibly) and adjectives (e.g. doubtful, supposed) necessarily indicate a secondary, reputed perspective, which is less reliable than a first-person perspective.

6.4.5.2. *Verb tense and modes, uncertainty*

Using the lists thus extracted, we were able to study the relationships between the different components of the sentence and draw up compositional rules to calculate the overall uncertainty of the event on the basis of the uncertainty associated with the different words (verbs, adjectives and adverbs) employed to speak about that event. The verbs have a twofold impact on Commitment and Level by way of two criteria: their semantic charge (for example, "assure that" is not the same as "estimate that") and the verbal tense in which they are conjugated. In our implementation, we lent greater weight to the dimension Level, exploiting the verb tense used rather than the semantic charge (Commitment). For instance, in the following sentence, a possible proof of innocence is announced:

"The dissident Usbek is believed to have proven his lack of involvement".

The unconfirmed existence of proof, manifested by the use of the conditional verbal mode, wins out in this instance over the semantic charge associated with the verb "prove".

We developed a carefully-considered theory about the interaction between the verb tense and the temporality (situation in time) of the event extracted, showing that the tense in which the verb is conjugated not only sometimes modifies the situation of the event on the timeline, but also sometimes introduces a degree of uncertainty which cannot be modeled using grammars. Table 6.3 recaps our results in this domain.

Tense and grammatical modes	Level	Time	Perspective
Present		Present	Primary
Imperfect		Past	Primary
Simple past	Absolute	Past	
Future	Moderate	Future	
Present conditional	Low		Secondary
Pluperfect	Absolute	Past	
Future perfect	Moderate		
Past conditional	Low	Past	Primary

Table 6.3. *Table summarizing markers of uncertainty in verb tenses and verbal modes*

In order to analyze the impact of verb tense on the uncertainty attached to the event, we have represented the situation by way of timelines, which can be used to situate the moment of the actual observation (the event itself observed by a direct witness); the moment of collection (contact between the writer of the article and his source), and the moment of writing, when the writer signs off his article.

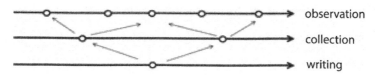

Figure 6.7. *Diagram of timelines*

Collection may either take place before writing, or afterward in the case of anticipation. The observation may itself be prior to collection, or later in the case of all sorts of promises or anticipations made *via* an official announcement. For example: "Usbek is expected to announce this evening that he has proved his lack of involvement" corresponds to a situation where collection is after writing, and observation before collection. Hence, theoretically, we have three situations for observation: when the writer is, has been or expects to be a direct witness to the event (or he deems his sources to be sufficiently reliable to have a factual discourse). When the observation is made by a source, the writer relates his collection of that observation, and that collection may be accomplished (past) or expected (anticipation), which leaves us with at least six *theoretical* possibilities, which are not all equally represented in practice.

The expressiveness of the language (modalities of conjugation, adverbs, lexical meaning) can be used to clearly identify these possibilities, by including in the announcement of the event the expression of trust in the source being cited.

6.4.5.3. *Dictionaries and grammars*

On the basis of the lists defined previously, and of the study of the relationships between verb tenseand event temporality, pattern dictionaries were automatically generated for each syntactic category (adjectives, adverbs) and verb tense (simple and compound tenses – see Figure 6.11). These dictionaries associate lexical entries and conjugated verbs with the dimensions of the uncertainty model *via* typed semantic traits, which can be re-used in grammars.

```
<accredit.V:F> -> ms_Level_Moderate + ms_Time_Future + MsVerb

<aim.V:F> -> ms_Level_Moderate + ms_Time_Future + MsVerb

<assure.V:F> < + CONJS> -> ms_Level_Moderate + ms_Time_Future + MsVerb
```

Figure 6.8. *Extract from simple future dictionary*

```
definitely -> ms_Level_High + ms_Commitment_High + MsAdv

at present -> ms_Time_Present + MsAdv

in the future -> ms_Time_Future + MsAdv
```

Figure 6.9. *Extract from dictionary of adverbs*

```
absolute -> ms_Level_High + ms_Commitment_High + MsAdj

absurd -> ms_Commitment_Low + MsAdj

acceptable -> ms_Level_Moderate + ms_Commitment_Moderate + MsAdj
```

Figure 6.10. *Extract from dictionary of adjectives*

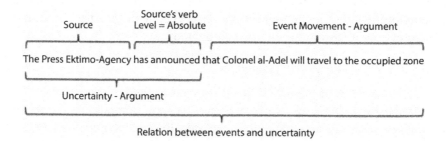

Figure 6.11. *Extract from annotated corpus*

Beyond the isolated annotation of uncertainty dimensions, a "super grammar" was developed to make evident the connection between the source, the level of uncertainty and the events, in order to cater for the needs of information evaluation processing. This grammar was constructed on the same principle as the event extraction grammars, where the source, its verb and the event are arguments in the overarching relation.

In the example below, three grammars come into play:

– the grammar to extract the Movement event on the basis of the predicative verb "travel" and the arguments Person "Colonel al-Adel" and Location "occupied zone";

– the source extraction grammar: here it is the verb "announce" which enables us to identify the source "Press Ektimo-Agency" on the basis of a simple pattern of the type "uncertainty verb drawn from the dictionaries, immediately followed or preceded by a named entity";

– and finally the "super grammar" for extraction of the relation between events and uncertainty.

Note that in this example, the verb "announce" gives the segment its Level value. Only verbs appearing in the uncertainty dictionaries generate scores for the Level criterion, which explains the lack of annotation on "will travel" in the given example. Furthermore, as previously explained, the adverbs and adjectives are also taken into account to evaluate uncertainty in texts. If more than one Level annotation is present in the same segment, they are aggregated by processing prior to information extraction.

6.5. Realization

The prerequisites for evaluating our model are: a voluminous corpus, different from the development corpus, annotated manually (following the requisites of the uncertainty and event extraction model), and the possibility to perform a comparison with the annotations produced automatically. The implementation of the presented model has not yet been evaluated in terms of recall, precision or f-measure.

However, the construction of linguistic resources necessitates that a methodology and quality process be followed, which notably involve iterative tests to verify the coverage and relevance of the annotations. In addition to "hot" tests, we have also put in place automated non-regression tests, verifying the match between an extraction currently under way and a reference validation.

Volumes of specific resources			
Named entities	1 ontology	1,904 instances	52 classes and sub-classes
	1 thesaurus	7 head concepts	129 hyponyms
Events	43 dictionaries 1,552 entries	8 main grammars	139 sub-graphs
Uncertainty	18 dictionaries 1,868 entries	2 main grammars	58 sub-graphs

Table 6.4. *Table summarizing the volumes of specific linguistic resources*

At the end of the phase of resource construction, it appears that the uncertainty markers are autonomous and have no direct link with a particular domain. The event extraction resources, on the other hand, are heavily dependent on the reference corpus, and on the dominant theme. Event annotation is also based on proper preliminary identification of the attributes and arguments, i.e. the named entities or co-reference noun phrases.

6.6. Conclusions and perspectives

In this chapter, we have presented the implementation of a model used to detect and extract the uncertainty in events. This uncertainty model draws on [RUB 05] and [SAU 08] for inspiration. The simultaneous treatment of named entities, events and uncertainty markers ensures precise extraction of the factuality of events in large corpora.

We have focused on the development of linguistic resources such as electronic dictionaries, local grammars and termino-ontological referentials which, firstly, form an autonomous set of linguistic resources for extraction and semantic analysis and, secondly, feed into a chain of computerized processing.

The development of these resources followed a number of axes:

– construction of termino-ontological referentials in the domain of Defense, and constant improvement of the existing named entity recognition resources;

– description and production of grammars and lexicons for event extraction;

– implementation of the uncertainty model by way of formalization through the grammatical categories (verbs, adverbs, adjectives) associated with five dimensions ("Level", "Time", "Source(s)", "Commitment", "Perspective");

– and finally, tracing of the connections between the sources, the uncertainty markers and the events in relation to which they appear.

The uncertainty resources constitute an autonomous set which can be reused independently of event extraction and of any application domain. This is a fairly significant result which opens up the possibility of evaluating these resources for industrial usage. Indeed, the evaluation cost of a linguistic function is relatively high, which is one of the reasons why industrial evaluation is beyond the scope of the current project. It is therefore very helpful, or crucial even, to have been able to identify a resource which, relatively independently, serves a specific informative function. This reduces the complexity of the evaluation. It is also useful if the function can be put to use on a literary genre which touches on all industrial domains and is an intrinsic vector for event-related information: journalist reports. Event annotation, for its part, seems to be very closely linked to the domain and to the corpus being used. Nevertheless, an effort has been made to generalize the patterns described by testing the resources on the *Le Monde* corpus, which is different from the development corpus. However, an innovation appears to be necessary to modularize event annotation, e.g. distinguishing between a phase of statement syntactic analysis, which is generic and independent of the classes of events being annotated, and a phase of inference of events on the basis of a target model and the syntactic elements raised by the statement analysis.

6.7. Bibliography

[ACE 08] LDC ACE, "English annotation guidelines for relations, V 6.2", *Linguistic Data Consortium* (LDC), Pennsylvania, United States, 2008.

[AUG 08] AUGER A., ROY J., "Expression of uncertainty in linguistic data", Fusion 2008, Cologne, Germany, 2008.

[BAT 07] BATTISTELLI D., CHAGNOUX M., "Représenter la dynamique énonciative et modale de textes", *TALN 2007*, Toulouse, pp. 23–32, 2007.

[CHI 97] CHINCHOR N., "MUC-7 Named entity task definition", *7th Message Understanding Conference (MUC-7)*, Fairfax, Virginia, United States, 1997.

[COU 90] COURTOIS B., "Un système de dictionnaires électroniques pour les mots simples du français", *Langue française*, no. 87, pp. 11–22, 1990.

[DEN 03] DENDALE P., COLTIER D., "Point de vue et évidentialité", *Cahiers de praxématique*, no. 41, pp. 105–129. 2003.

[DOD 04] DODINGTON G., MITCHELLE A., PRZYBOCHKI M., *et al.*, "The Automatic Content Extraction Tasks, Data, and Evaluations", *4th International on Language Resources and Evaluation (LREC 2004)*, Lisbon, Portugal, 2004.

[EHR 08] EHRMANN M., Les entités nommées, de la linguistique au TAL : statut théorique et méthodes de désambiguïsation, Doctoral thesis, Université Paris 7 Denis Diderot, 2008.

[EZZ 10] EZZAT M., "Acquisition de grammaires locales pour l'extraction de relations entre entités nommées", *17e Conférence sur le traitement automatique des langues naturelles (TALN 2010)*, Montreal, Canada, July 2010.

[GIU 05] GIULIANO C., LAVELLI A., ROMANO L., "Simple Information Extraction (SIE)", *ITC-irst, Istituto per la Ricerca Scientifica e Tecnologica*, Trento, Italy, 2005.

[GOU 05] GOUJON B., FRIGIÈRE J., "Extraction of relations between entities from texts by learning methods", *IST-055 Specialists Meeting on "Information Fusion for Command Support"*, The Netherlands, 2005.

[GOU 10] GOUJON B., "Annotation de la factualité d'événements exprimés dans les textes", *VSST 2010*, Toulouse, 2010.

[GRO 95] GROSS M., "Une grammaire locale de l'expression des sentiments", *Langue française*, no. 105(1), pp. 70–87, 1995.

[HEC 08] HECKING M., "System ZENON. Semantic Analysis of Intelligence Reports", *LangTech 2008*, Rome, 2008.

[PAU 08] PAUMIER S., *Unitex 2.1 User Manual*, available online at http://www-igm.univ-mlv.fr/~unitex/index.php?page=4, 2008.

[POI 03] POIBEAU T., *Extraction automatique d'information. Du texte brut au web sémantique*, Hermès, Paris, 2003.

[RUB 05] RUBIN V.L., LIDDY E.D., KANDO N., "Certainty identification in texts: categorization model and manual tagging results", *Computing Attitude and Affect in Text: Theory and Applications, The Information Retrieval Series*, Springer Netherlands, vol. 20, pp. 61–76, 2005.

[SAU 08] SAURI R., PUSTEJOVSKY J., "From structure to interpretation: a double-layered annotation for event factuality", *LREC 2008*, Marrakech, Morocco, 2008.

[ZHA 05] ZHAO S., GRISHMAN R., "Extracting relations with integrated information using kernel methods", *43rd Annual Meeting of the ACL*, pp. 419–426, Ann Arbor, Michigan, United States, June 2005.

Chapter 7

Quantitative Information Evaluation: Modeling and Experimental Evaluation

7.1. Introduction

As part of the process of information watch, information evaluation, such as it is defined in the military doctrinal corpus, aims to evaluate a piece of information using two ratings: the reliability of the source and the credibility of the informational content. As discussed in Chapter 4, the rules and good practices set out in the doctrine to quantify these ratings suffer from certain shortcomings. For instance, we can point to the independence between the reliability of a source and the credibility of the informational content, or the lack of consideration given to relations between sources reporting the same information.

The problem of evaluating the quality of information is by no means limited to the military domain. In the civilian domain, it is accorded great importance in sectors such as competitive intelligence or health, as demonstrated by the setting up of projects such as Net Scoring.[1] The approaches developed are usually based on manual, rather than automated, procedures to judge the quality of information

Chapter written by Marie-Jeanne LESOT, Frédéric PICHON and Thomas DELAVALLADE.
1 http://www.chu-rouen.fr/netscoring/.

available on the Web. As this type of approach is very costly to implement, projects drawing on the collaborative aspect of an increasing number of publication platforms have emerged. The study by [SET 10] or the Web of Trust[2] project are examples of this. The general idea in such a case is to exploit the relations between the users of a social network and the ratings that they give to other users or to content published by others to propagate trust ratings throughout the network.

More recently, work grounded in machine learning has been carried out, with the aim of automating the estimation of the trust that can be afforded to a piece of information published on the Internet. Thus, a certain number of metrics have been defined to estimate different aspects of the credibility of texts published on blogs [WEE 12]. These metrics are applied directly by a search engine, with the aim of being able to reorder the results on the basis of these criteria, so that spammers have more difficulty in skewing results than with search parameters based only on the connectivity of the blogs. With this type of approach, automation is total, but there is no absolute rating reflecting the credibility of a blog article, as this is dependent upon the query. Closer to what concerns us here are, e.g., the works of [CAS 11]. Using metrics similar to those set out in [WEE 12], and a set of tweets labeled on the basis of their truthfulness, the authors train a model to determine automatically whether or not a message published on Twitter is credible.

Yet we feel this complete automation is undesirable. Indeed, it is essential for users to be able to simply understand and alter the set of computations performed. It is also very important for a user to be able to enrich the evaluation process with elements of which he is aware from sources other than the Internet (e.g. links between sources or conflicts of interest for a source on a given subject). For that reason, in this chapter we put forward a semi-automated method to carry out the process of information evaluation. In addition, we wish to preserve the guiding ideas in the doctrine of intelligence, but with the aim of overcoming the limitations mentioned above. Thus, in keeping with the doctrine's indication that filtering of non-factual information needs

---

2 http://www.mywot.com/.

to be carried out, we have considered that only those events[3] reported in the documents collected could be subject to scoring for evaluation. However, if we take account of the reliability of a source to judge the degree of exactness of the event which that source reports, the output from the process of information evaluation is not a bigram, but rather an estimation of the trust that we can invest in the fact that the event did or did not happen. The user still has access, though, to the reliability ratings for the sources, particularly through the elements making up the final rating. Note that here, we shall not discuss how to estimate the reliability of a source, as that question is dealt with in Chapter 5.

The method of quantitative information evaluation which we advocate in this chapter, to overcome the limitations of the doctrines mentioned above, has been developed with the following in mind: given a particular event to examine, to answer the question "Did that event take place?", but supplement the binary response (Yes/No) with a degree of confidence. This is a numerical value which quantifies the certainty attached to the response given. In order to provide this enriched response, the procedure exploits the information extracted from a corpus of textual documents relating to the event, which provide partial – and sometimes contradictory – responses to the question at hand. The proposed model is based on a two-stage process: first a degree of confidence is associated with each relevant piece of information, individually; then those ratings are combined in order to calculate the overall degree of confidence. At each level, aggregation operators chosen by the user lend the process its flexibility, meaning it can implement diverse configurations and, thereby, diverse stances towards the evaluation depending on the level of caution he may wish to adopt before considering a piece of information to be credible.

This chapter also discusses the task of experimental evaluation of such a procedure: the complexity of that task stems from the difficulty in obtaining real-world labeled data, i.e. data relating to events which we know to have, or not to have, taken place. In the absence of such

---

3 For our purposes, we use the term "event" for any relation between two named entities. Thus, an event is characterized by its type and its arguments (the named entities interrelating with one another) and its possible attributes: date, place, etc.

data, we have no reference against which to compare the result obtained. The necessity of turning to artificial data then raises the problem of generation of realistic data. This chapter describes a procedure generating such data, which are representative of real-world cases.

The chapter is organized as follows: section 7.2 presents the formal framework used to represent uncertainty: possibility theory. Section 7.3 then describes the proposed architecture for our evaluation support tool, and section 7.4 the experimental context of evaluation, presenting the problem of the generation of realistic data, the proposed protocol and the experimental study carried out.

7.2. Formal framework used: possibility theory

This section presents the formal framework used to model the uncertainty associated with the response to a question such as "Did this event take place?" After justifying the choice of possibility theory as the uncertainty management framework (section 7.2.1), we recap its basic principles, and particularly the concept of possibility distribution (section 7.2.2), as well as the aggregation operators which can be applied to these distributions (section 7.2.3). Finally, in section 7.2.4, we detail the peculiar points of possibility distributions in the context of information evaluation.

7.2.1. Reasons for using possibility theory

The degree of confidence associated with the result of information evaluation needs to reflect that uncertainty attached to the response given: the truthfulness cannot be judged absolutely, so our knowledge remains incomplete. Indeed, the response is constructed by contrasting textual documents which provide partial responses and whose information is also generally *imperfect* in that it can be imprecise or ambiguous, uncertain or indeed conflicting.

The choice of the formal frame work in which this uncertainty is modeled is of crucial importance, and influences the richness of expression and flexibility of the resulting model (e.g. see [BLO 94] for a discussion in the case of image processing). There are many uncertainty management theories which can be used. For instance, we can distinguish ordinal models such as the many-valued logics formalism (see [RES 69; GOT 01] and, for their application to information evaluation [REV 07; REV 11]), numerical models, such as probability theory, belief-function theory [SHA 76] or possibility theory [ZAD 78]. Here we consider the second category: numerical uncertainty.

Probability theory imposes stringent axiomatic constraints which, for instance, restrict the aggregation operators which it is possible to use. In addition, it cannot be used to model ignorance, which is indistinguishable from a purely random phenomenon, as illustrated by the following example [GEL 06]: in ignorance of whether the boxing world champion would beat the wrestling world champion, each option is given a probability of 0.5, but there is no discernible difference here with a case of pure, random chance – e.g. a coin flip – where, on the contrary, it is known that both options are equally probable. In addition, the modeling of ignorance when faced with an alternative depends on the number of options that are presented (each option being associated with the probability $1/c$ if c is the number of options), although the size of the universe in question does not appear to be a relevant parameter. Finally, probability theory usually requires us to define *a priori* probabilities, which may be tricky to obtain. In the context of information evaluation, for example, we would need to have a numerical value representing the *a priori* probability that a given source is reliable.

Belief-function theory [SHA 76] generalizes probability theory and possibility theory, and has already been applied to the problem of information evaluation (see [CHO 10; PIC 12], for instance). It has a great richness of expression, which enables it to avoid the limitations mentioned for probability theory. Yet hand in hand with this richness of expression comes a greater complexity than probability - or possibility theory in terms of uncertainty representation. A fairly advanced level of expertise is therefore needed to ensure the end user is able to properly grasp the outputs from an information evaluation procedure based on this theory.

Unlike probability theory, possibility theory [ZAD 78] is capable of representing ignorance, and also offers a greater range of aggregation operators (see section 7.2.3), and therefore a greater flexibility in terms of fusing different pieces of information relating to the same event and provided by different sources. In addition, the representation of uncertainty with this theory is simpler than with belief-function theory. Finally, possibility theory is compatible with fuzzy set theory [ZAD 65], which can be exploited to model the imprecisions inherent to natural language.

7.2.2. Recap of possibility theory

Possibility theory was initially introduced by Zadeh [ZAD 78], and then largely developed – particularly in the area of logical reasoning (see [DUB 90], for instance). This section recaps its essential principles; the reader can refer to [DUB 88; BOU 95] for a detailed presentation.

7.2.2.1. Measure and distribution of possibility

Given a reference universe X, the principle of possibility theory is to assign each event defined in X, i.e. each subset of X, a coefficient between 0 and 1, which evaluates the point at which that event is possible. Formally, a *measure of possibility* Π is defined as follows:

$$\Pi: P(X) \rightarrow [0.1]$$

such that:

$$\Pi(\varnothing) = 0$$

$$\Pi(X) = 1$$

$$\Pi\left(\bigcup_{i=1}^{n} A_i\right) = sup_{i=1-n} \, \Pi(A_i) \text{ for all } A_i \in P(X)$$

where P(X) denotes all of the parts of X. In particular it satisfies max $(\Pi(A), \Pi(A^c)) = 1$ for any $A \in P(X)$, where A^c denotes the complement of A in X.

A *possibility distribution* π is defined for each singleton in the universe, rather than for its subsets:

$$\pi: X \rightarrow [0,1]$$

such that:

$$sup_{x \in X} \pi(x) = 1$$

$\pi(x) = 0$ means that x is impossible, $\pi(x) = 1$ that x is entirely possible. Ignorance is represented by a distribution measuring 1 for all values of x, indicating that everything is possible.

Because of the third property of the measures of possibility discussed above, and because a subset of X is the union of the singletons which make it up, the measures of possibility are entirely defined by the coefficients associated with the singletons of X – that is to say that they are defined by the possibility distribution. More specifically, for any A ∈ P(X), we have $\Pi(A) = sup_{x \in A} \pi(x)$.

7.2.2.2. *Measure of necessity*

A measure of possibility is not sufficient to describe the uncertainty associated with an event $A \subseteq X$. Thus, $\Pi(A) = 1$ indicates that A is entirely possible, but we must distinguish between the cases $\Pi(A^c) = 1$ and $\Pi(A^c) = 0$. Indeed, in the first case, the complement of A is also entirely possible, which indicates absolute ignorance, whereas in the second case, only A can be true, so A is certain.

Therefore, a measure of possibility is dually associated with a *measure of necessity*, which can be formally defined thus:

$$N: P(X) \rightarrow [0,1]$$

such that:

$$N(\varnothing) = 0$$

$$N(X) = 1$$

$$N(\cap_{i=1}^{n} A_i) = inf_{i=1..n} N(A_i) \text{ for any value of } A_i \in P(X)$$

In particular, any measure of possibility induces a measure of necessity defined for any $A \in P(X)$ by

$$N(A) = 1 - \Pi(A^c)$$

Note that we then have $\max(\Pi(A), 1-N(A))=1$. Thus, if A is not entirely possible ($\Pi(A) \neq 1$), then its necessity, i.e. the certainty attached to it, is zero. On the other hand, if the degree of certainty of A is non-null – i.e. informally, if A is at least a little certain, written as $N(A) \neq 0$, then A is entirely possible.

7.2.3. Aggregation operators for possibility distributions

Generally speaking, an aggregation operator is a function φ: $[0,1] \rightarrow [0,1]$ which reduces a set of n numerical values to a single value, in order to provide a summary. There are a great many aggregation operators and various axes of classification can be envisaged. Readers can usefully refer to [BOU 98; DET 00], for instance, for detailed presentations, and to [DUB 00] for a discussion of the case of possibility distributions. Aggregation can therefore be viewed as a problem of combination of pieces of information from heterogeneous sources, with each one representing its knowledge by a possibility distribution. Here we present a number of operators that are relevant for the problem of information evaluation, classifying them by their semantics, i.e. by their behaviors; more specifically, we distinguish four types of logical attitudes. These behaviors can be matched with any knowledge about the reliabilities of the sources who provide the possibility distributions to be aggregated [DUB 00]. Table 7.1 shows the representatives of each family used in the rest of the chapter. For clarity's sake, we only give the details for each operator for the case of aggregation of two values. As these operators are all associative[4], it is not particularly problematic to expand these examples for the aggregation of n criteria.

---

4 Clearly this is not the case with the arithmetic average, but its formulation for n values is sufficiently well known so as not to have to be explicitly given here.

Attitude	Name	Formula
Conjunctive operators	Zadeh's t-norm	$\varphi(x,y) = \min(x,y)$
	Probabilistic t-norm	$\varphi(x,y) = xy$
Disjunctive operators	Zadeh's t-conorm	$\varphi(x,y) = \max(x,y)$
	Probabilistic t-conorm	$\varphi(x,y) = x + y\text{-}xy$
Compromise operator	Arithmetic average	$\varphi(x,y) = \dfrac{1}{2}(x + y)$
Variable operator	Minimal uninorm with a threshold of 0.5	$\varphi(x,y) =$ $$\begin{cases} \dfrac{1}{2}\min(2x,2y)\, if\, x,y \le \dfrac{1}{2} \\ \dfrac{1}{2}+\dfrac{1}{2}\max(2x-1,2y-1)\ if\ x,y \ge \dfrac{1}{2} \\ \min(x,y)\, else \end{cases}$$

Table 7.1. *Examples of aggregation operators for the four types of attitudes*

The so-called *conjunctive* operators, e.g. those in the family of t-norms, are "cautious" operators, whose result does not go beyond the minimum of the arguments. More specifically, they have the property called negative reinforcement: the aggregation of small values yields an even smaller value.

On the other hand, *disjunctive* operators, illustrated by t-conorms, are optimistic, giving a result that is greater to or equal to the maximum of the values: they have the property of positive reinforcement.

Compromise operators are between the previous two forms of behavior, and give intermediary results, situated in the same range of values as the arguments themselves. Thus, they offer the property of compensation: a low value may be counterbalanced by a high value, and *vice versa*. For instance, compromise operators include the arithmetic, geometric or harmonic means, or OWA (*Ordered Weighted Averaging*) operators [YAG 88].

It should be noted that the classification of conjunction/ compromise/disjunction is not a strict one; rather it is an axis upon which we can situate the operators [EUD 98]. For example, certain compromise operators are more cautious than others, and therefore exhibit a behavior similar to that of conjunctive operators.

Finally, the last category encapsulates *variable attitude* operators, whose behavior changes depending on their arguments: they are conjunctive for low values, disjunctive for high values and compromising in intermediary cases. Thus, they possess the property of total reinforcement: low values penalize one another, giving an even lower value; high values reinforce one another, yielding an even higher value; if one of the aggregated values is low and the other high, it yields an intermediary result. This family can be illustrated by uninorms [FOD 97] or symmetric sums [SIL 79]. Their parameters are determined by a threshold which indicates when the values should be considered to be low or high.

Given a set of possibility distributions defined for the same discrete universe, the use of such aggregation operators consists of applying the operator to the values corresponding to each element in the universe, and then normalizing the results obtained. Indeed, the operator provides no guarantee of obtaining a possibility distribution, because the property of a maximum value of 1 may not be satisfied [DUB 00]. Therefore, a step of normalization is performed.

The aggregation operators discussed above are symmetrical and attach the same degree of importance to the aggregated distributions. In order to be able to take account of the concept of priority, a *discounting operation* can be applied to a possibility distribution: in cases where each distribution represents, e.g., the information provided by a source, this operation enables us to take account of the reliability of the source to decrease the importance of information provided by unreliable sources. The above aggregation operators are then applied to the distributions obtained after discounting [DUB 00].

Yager [YAG 84] proposes two discounting operators, respectively based on the minimum and on the product, which associate with a distribution π the distributions π' respectively defined as shown below, for any value of u in the universe in question:

$$\pi'(u) = \min(1, 1 - \alpha + \pi(u))$$

$$\pi'(u) = \alpha \, \pi(u) + 1 - \alpha$$

α is a parameter between 0 and 1 which expresses the extent of the discounting performed. It is greater (we come closer to the situation of ignorance) when the value of α is small. In our context, α corresponds to the reliability of a source, which enables us to consequently reduce the credibility of the information that source has delivered. It should be noted that in both cases, if $\pi(u) = 1$, we also have $\pi'(u) = 1$: only the values different to 1 are affected. In addition, it is worth noting that the discounting operation based on the minimum is more effective than that based on the product, in the sense that it leads to a distribution which is more heavily discounted for the same value of the parameter α.

7.2.4. *Application to information evaluation*

As posited above, the result of the information evaluation is the response, weighted with a degree of confidence, to the question "Did the event take place?" Formally, we propose to model it by way of a possibility distribution defined in a binary universe $E = \{e, \neg e\}$, with e indicating that the event did indeed take place, and $\neg e$ indicating the opposite.[5]

The quantification of the uncertainty attached to an event is then modeled by a possibility distribution π defined in E: the model of information evaluation must provide an estimation of the values $\pi(e)$ and $\pi(\neg e)$. The result of the information evaluation is therefore a vector with two components $(\pi(e) \; \pi(\neg e))$, at least one of which being equal to 1.

If $\pi(e) = 1$, i.e. for a vector of the form (1 a), the event is considered to have taken place; the associated level of confidence

---

5 The symbol $\neg$ represents negation: $\neg e$ should be read as "non-e".

corresponds to the degree of necessity of e. We have $N(\{e\}) = 1-\Pi(\{\neg e\}) = 1\text{-}a$. If, on the other hand, $\pi(\neg e) = 1$, i.e. for a vector of the form (b 1), we can consider with a degree of confidence 1-b that the event did not take place.

7.3. Proposed architecture

In order to construct the possibility distribution which formalizes the weighted response to the question "Did the event take place?", the process of information evaluation is based on a set – a corpus – of textual documents relating to the event, which provide partial and sometimes contradictory responses to the question. Hence, prior to the evaluation itself, the following tasks need to be performed:

– automated document collection;

– filtering, to find the informational textual content (in the case of documents taken from the Web, for instance, deletion of advertising or navigational links).

The texts thus obtained, which serve as input for the process of information evaluation, first undergo two pre processing stages, which are described in greater detail in section 7.3.2.1:

– structuring of the information to extract the events which are being reported in the documents. This involves a refined linguistic analysis of the filtered textual contents.[6] The result of this structuring is known as an SIR, for *Structured Informational Resource;*

– identification of those SIRs which are sufficiently similar to the event to which the evaluation applies to be able to provide some elements of a response.

In this section, we detail the process of evaluation applied, using this corpus of documents, presenting in turn its general principle, its inputs and then the two main steps, highlighting their flexibility and the various configurations to which they lead. We illustrate this

---

6 This analysis is detailed in Chapter 6 of this book.

process throughout the section using the fictitious example presented in the introduction to the book.

7.3.1. *General principle*

Each of the SIRs extracted from the different documents collected may potentially provide a partial response to the question at hand: "Did the event take place?" The approach, illustrated in Figure 7.1 and detailed below, consists of evaluating the confidence inspired by each SIR individually, and then combining them in a procedure of aggregation to define the overall rating.

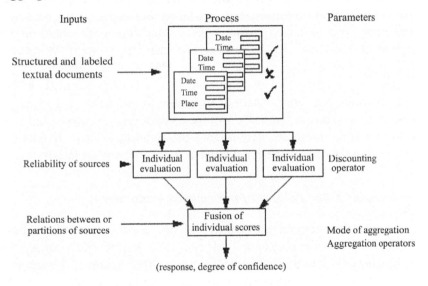

Figure 7.1. *General architecture of the evaluation support tool*

Each individual rating evaluates the confidence inspired by an SIR taken in isolation. As discussed in the previous chapters of this book, we deem it to be dependent upon the source expressing the information, and on the way in which he expresses himself. More specifically, the confidence varies on the basis of the reliability of the source: a piece of information given by a reliable source enjoys a higher level of trust than another. The reliability of the source may itself be the result of multiple aspects, such as his legitimacy or his involvement with respect to the reported event (see Chapter 5). In addition, the way in which the source expresses himself, i.e. the terms he chooses to transmit his knowledge, also influences the level of trust afforded to him: the use of the conditional, for instance, indicates the doubts of the source himself.

The final rating is then obtained by aggregation of the ratings of the SIRs considered individually – particularly in order to take account of the effect of corroboration, which is of crucial importance in the initial models of information evaluation [NAT 03]: pieces of information which confirm one another increase the confidence associated with the overall response, whereas contradictions decrease that confidence. In addition, we can take other aspects into account, and carry out nuanced fusion. Thus, any potential relation of dependency between the sources can alter the notion of corroboration: a confirmation by sources which have a relation of affinity ought, for instance, to have less of an influence than a confirmation given by sources which are independent of or hostile to one another. Indeed, it is to be expected that "friendly" sources will be in agreement with one another, and produce redundant information. This redundant information should not be considered as a genuine confirmation.

7.3.2. Inputs to the process of information evaluation

As per the general principles set out above, the information evaluation process takes several types of inputs: the structured informational resources extracted from the textual documents collected, and information about the sources, indicating their reliability and the relations between them, amongst other things. These inputs are detailed in turn below.

7.3.2.1. Structured informational resources

The evaluation process does not take account of the texts provided directly; rather, those texts are preprocessed. Firstly we need to structure them so as to extract the useable informational elements; then we need to identify those SIRs from among that corpus which provide elements of a response to the question at hand; finally we need to determine whether they favor a positive or negative response to the question posed, i.e. whether they provide a confirmation or an invalidation to one of the responses to the question. Note that the last two stages of preprocessing are not universal; they depend on the question under discussion. These preprocessing steps are illustrated in Figure 7.2 and detailed in the following sections.

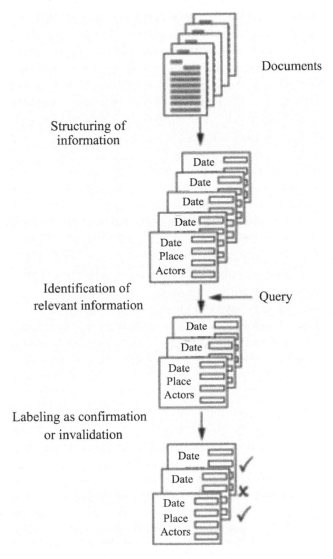

Figure 7.2. *Preprocessing of texts*

7.3.2.1.1. Structuring of information

The first processing step is intended to extract from the text in natural language a set of pertinent fields – e.g. to identify the type of event which it discusses, those who are involved, the date or place, and more generally the properties of the event, which depend on its type. In the case of a bomb attack, for instance, the structuring should identify, if they are mentioned in the text, the date, the place, the assumed perpetrator, and possibly the number of victims. Note that this step may make use of a model based on the fuzzy sets theory, so as best to represent the imprecisions of natural language [LES 11]. Here we can see the advantage in choosing a possibilistic uncertainty management framework. The interfacing between fuzzy sets and possibility distributions is indeed natural and is grounded in theory.

The structuring must also extract meta-information about the document itself, such as the publication date, the source and the certainty which it expresses. Indeed, the linguistic formulations chosen by the sources indicate their own certainties about the events which they report, or the caution that they display. These linguistic indicators include adjectives and adverbs, such as "likely", "certain" or "possibly", modes of speech – particularly the conditional – or more complex idiomatic structures. Modifiers such as "very" or "slightly" can also be used to strengthen or weaken these terms. The overall level of certainty can be determined by aggregation of the levels of various linguistic indicators [GOU 09], e.g. into four values: "low", "moderate", "high" and "absolute". This process is detailed in Chapter 6.

The type and collection of the properties of an event reported in a document constitute the SIR. The SIRs extracted from all the collected documents are stored in a database which can be used for evaluation purposes.

Table 7.2 details the different SIRs extracted using the process described above for the illustrative example, concerning an attack in Dagbas on 31 May and the possible involvement of the factious combatants of the *Free Resistance of Dagbas* (FRD). Thus, in his remarks, quoted in the first dispatch considered, the Minister Balldar uses a conditional, to mark a certain degree of caution. The certainty which he is expressing is therefore indicated as being low.

ID	Meta-information about the document			Information about the event			
	Publication date	Source	Certainty expressed	Type	Perpetrator	Place	Date
c_1	31/05	Minister Balldar	low	attack	FRD	Dagbas	31/05
c_2	01/06	Captain Ixil	absolute	attack	Not (FRD)	Dagbas	31/05
c_3	02/06	Colonel al-Adel	absolute	attack	FRD	Dagbas	31/05
c_4	03/06	Colonel al-Adel	absolute	attack	?	Dagbas	31/05
c_5	21/06	General Quieto	absolute	attack	General San-Gerio	Capital of Realleo	10/10

Table 7.2. *Example of structured informational resources*

7.3.2.1.2. Identification of relevant SIRs

The process of information evaluation does not take account of all the information available in the database, but only those pieces of information which provide elements of a response to the question posed. This phase of identification of the relevant pieces of information can be carried out manually by the user, but is then painstaking and tedious. Automated processing tools may also be used [LES 11]: these tools calculate the similarity between the SIRs and the query, by aggregating the measures of similarity calculated for each of the fields describing the events.

The SIRs can then be ordered by decreasing similarity to the query, and thresholding – either manual or automated – is used to identify the relevant elements.

In the example at hand, where the query poses the question "Are the insurgents of the *Free Resistance of Dagbas* responsible for the attack in Dagbas on 31 May?", we ought, for instance, to eliminate the element c_5, which relates to a different attack than the one in question, and the element c_4, which provides no information as to the perpetrator of the attack.

7.3.2.1.3. Status of confirmation/invalidation

Finally, the relevant structured informational resources need to be associated with a status indicating whether they give a positive or negative response to the user's question. This step requires semantic understanding of the information, which automated tools may fail to provide. Indeed, although explicit terms characteristic of negations ("not", "never", or verbs such as "deny" or "protest") can be processed, the negation is often expressed subtly and is difficult to recognize for an automaton. Hence, an expert has to label the relevant informational elements selected during the previous step, as to whether they constitute a confirmation or an invalidation of the evaluated piece of information.

Thus, in the example under discussion here, the two elements c_1 and c_3 should be indicated as confirmations and the element c_2 as an invalidation of the response that the insurgents are in fact the perpetrators of the attack.

7.3.2.2. *A priori characteristics of the sources*

The process of evaluation also requires information about the sources – particularly their reliability ratings and the relations between them.

7.3.2.2.1. Contextual reliability

The reliability of a source, sometimes also called the value of that source, reflects is ability to deliver quality information. A variety of methods for estimating this notion of reliability can be envisaged, ranging from the most manual, based solely on the accumulation of expertise, to the most automated, using machine learning techniques. Interested readers can refer to Chapter 5 of this book which constructs a state of the art in this domain, and advances a semi-automated method of estimation based on multi-criterion aggregation.

We propose to model a contextual form of reliability, which depends on the topic at hand: this contextualization expresses the fact that a source may be competent regarding a particular topic, for which he can be trusted, and less competent in other domains, wherein his statements must be considered with a greater degree of caution.

In our possibilistic framework, for a given topic T, we model the reliability of a source by way of a possibility distribution over the binary universe $F = \{f_T, \neg f_T\}$, where f_T denotes the event "The source is reliable for the topic T". Usually, we consider that a source is reliable with a greater or lesser degree of certainty; in this case, the possibility distribution is of the form $(1 r_T)$. The quantity $N(f) = 1 - r_T$, i.e. the necessity for reliability, then represents the degree of certainty that the source is reliable.

In the case of our illustrative example, we can consider that for Minister Balldar, the head of Ektimostan's secret police, and for the Head of State al-Adel, the certainty of reliability is 0.5 in the context of relations with the anti-regime insurgents, and that Captain Ixil, the leader of the insurgents, ratings 0.3. These values can be obtained by subjective analysis – e.g. by considering that whilst Captain Ixil may be competent to speak about an attack, his objectivity may be slight. The possibility distributions in the universe F are therefore (1 0.5) for Minister Balldar and Colonel al-Adel, and (1 0.7) for Captain Ixil.

7.3.2.2.2. Relations of affinity or hostility

Finally, the evaluation also depends on the relations between the sources. These relations influence the notion of corroboration, as suggested in section 7.3.1 and detailed in section 7.3.4.2. In order to take account of these relations between sources, but with a view to limiting the complexity of our model, we have chosen to consider only the relations of affinity, hostility and independence between sources. More specifically, in our model, the evaluation may depend on a division of the sources into sub-groups, so that inside the same group, the sources tend to have a relation of affinity, whereas sources in different sub-groups tend to have a relation of hostility or independence. Such a division may be given by an expert, directly, or by looking at the relations between the sources on a pair-by-pair basis. In the latter case, we then have a graph of relations between sources to which we can apply graph-partitioning algorithms [BAE 11].

In the case of our illustrative example, an expert may indicate that the head of the secret police and the Head of State of Ektimostan have a relation of affinity, and that both of them have a relation of hostility with the head of the insurgents. A graph-partitioning algorithm then constructs two groups, as illustrated in Figure 7.3. It is also possible for an expert to directly indicate that two groups need to be considered: the first containing Minister Balldar and Colonel al-Adel, and the second containing only Captain Ixil.

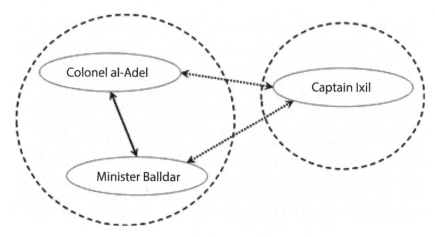

Figure 7.3. *Breakdown of the network of sources in the illustrative example. The dotted arrows indicate relations of hostility; the solid arrow shows the relation of affinity*

7.3.3. *Evaluation of individual elements*

The first step in the process of evaluation is applied to each structured informational resource c: the aim of this step is to calculate the confidence relating to the event e upon which the evaluation is focused, which can be deduced from that element taken in isolation. Formally, this confidence is modeled as a possibility distribution in the universe $E = \{e, \neg e\}$, and should therefore enable us to calculate the values $\pi_c(e)$ and $\pi_c(\neg e)$. It should be noted that this procedure is not applied to all of the informational elements available, but only to those which have been identified as relevant. Also, their status as a confirmation or invalidation needs to have been specified.

If a given element is a confirmation, the event is considered to be borne out by the source, so $\pi_c(e) = 1$, and only $\pi_c(\neg e)$ needs to be determined. Conversely, when we have an invalidation, then $\pi_c(\neg e) = 1$, and $\pi_c(e)$ needs to be calculated.

As previously indicated, we consider two indicators: the certainty expressed by the source and his reliability. Indeed, the confidence attached to the occurrence of an event is maximal if a reliable source reports it as being certain.

7.3.3.1. Expressed certainty

Structured informational resources include a field representing the level of certainty expressed by the source. This is subdivided into four levels: *low*, *moderate*, *high* and *absolute*. These levels must be expressed as numerical values. We propose to assign them a value η, which respectively assumes the values $\eta = 0.3, 0.5, 0.7$ and 1.

The possibility distribution generated by the linguistic indicator of the expressed certainty is then $\pi_{ling} = (1 \; 1 - \eta)$ for a confirmation, and $\pi_{ling} = (1 - \eta \; 1)$ for an invalidation.

These values are indicated in the third column in Table 7.2 for the illustrative example under discussion here. In this table, the column *Status* indicates whether the element has been marked as a confirmation or an in validation. π_{ling} gives the possibility distribution generated by the uncertainty linguistically expressed by the source, r_T the degree of certainty about the reliability of the source on this particular topic and π_c the resulting individual rating.

ID	Status	π_{ling}	r_T	π_c
c_1	confirmation	(1 0.7)	0.5	(1 0.85)
c_2	invalidation	(0 1)	0.3	(0.7 1)
c_3	confirmation	(1 0)	0.5	(1 0.5)

Table 7.3. *Rating for the individual elements*

7.3.3.2. *Combination with reliability*

The confidence which a user can attach to an informational element is therefore the result of the combination of this certainty with the reliability of the source, which also influences the confidence that can be attached to his assertions. The reliability can be considered to be meta-knowledge, which needs to be used to correct the confidence expressed by the source: even if the source is very confident, if he is not reliable, it is probably wise not to attach too much importance to his assertion.

As indicated in section 7.2.3, numerous operators can be envisaged. The desired semantics is as follows: if the source is perfectly reliable, i.e. given the possibility distribution (1 0) in the universe F, then the final certainty is equal to the certainty expressed by the source himself. If, however, there is no certainty as to the reliability of the source, associated with the distribution (1 1), then the assertion should not be taken into account, and the confidence should be null. Generally, the reliability of a source cannot increase the certainty expressed by that source; it can only decrease it.

We propose to exploit these two pieces of information by using the discounting operators put forward by Yager [YAG 84], to reduce the possibility distribution expressed by the source on the basis of his reliability. Thus, the discounting parameter we use is the certainty of reliability of the source, notated $N(r) = 1 - r_T$. Using the discounting operator based on the product, for instance, we then have:

$$\pi_c(e) = N(r)\, \pi_{ling}(e) + 1 - N(r)$$

$$\pi_c(\neg e) = N(r)\, \pi_{ling}(\neg e) + 1 - N(r)$$

The values obtained for the illustrative example are shown in the last column in Table 7.3. We can see that, because of the lack of reliability of the sources involved, for each of them the degree of possibility of the opposite of their assertions increases, with a concomitant decrease in the associated confidence. This is particularly true for the assertion of Captain Ixil, with the ID c_2: his absolute confidence is transformed into a piece of information of only 0.3 certainty.

7.3.4. *Fusion of individual ratings*

The last step in the evaluation process corresponds to the phase of corroboration, which plays an essential role in the initial models of information evaluation [NAT 97]. The objective is to aggregate the individual results obtained by the structured informational resources considered independently of one another, to exploit the effects of confirmation or invalidations as to increase or decrease the overall confidence.

Formally, the problem can be formulated as a problem of aggregation of possibility distributions: the distributions associated with the relevant informational elements by the individual evaluation described in the previous section.

7.3.4.1. *Direct aggregation*

The simplest approach to fusion is to perform a direct aggregation of the individual possibility distributions. As discussed in section 7.2.3, the choice of operator implies that of the semantics.

If we consider, say, a compromise operator, defining the overall possibility distribution as the normalized average of the distributions of all the informational elements, then for the present example we obtain (1 0.87): the group of insurgents led by Captain Ixil is considered to be a possible perpetrator of the attack, with only a low level of certainty.

7.3.4.2. *Exploitation of relations between sources*

We can also take account of the complementary dimensions, which enable us to carry out more nuanced fusions. In particular, we can take account of a degree of corroboration of the information provided by the different informational elements. This may depend, for instance, on the temporal dimension of the elements being fused, on the basis of how old they are, to decrease the influence of potentially obsolete information [LES 11]. The notion of corroboration may also be nuanced on the basis of any relations of dependency between the sources providing the information. Indeed, the confidence in a piece of information should increase with confirmation by additional parties;

however, if the confirmations are given by "friendly" sources, they should have less of an influence than confirmations given by independent or hostile sources. Thus, it is expected that sources who have a relation of affinity will provide redundant informational elements, but this does not indicate a true corroboration of the information. In particular, such modeling helps to avoid the phenomenon of self-intoxication, whereby the veracity of a piece of information is perceived as increasing even if it is only a repetition of an identical, already-rated piece of information.

Therefore, given a division of sources into affinity-based sub-groups (see section 7.3.2.2.2), fusion includes two stages: first partial fusion within each friendly group, and then fusion of the results provided by the different groups. Two aggregation operators, respectively said to be internal and external, therefore need to be chosen. They lend flexibility to the method by enabling us to model multiple stances of trust.

7.3.4.2.1. Partial fusion

In order to limit the weight of redundant information, we propose to use compromise operators, such as the average, to carry out partial fusion of the pieces of information delivered by friendly sources. These operators return a value situated within the range of the values to be aggregated: if all the sources are in agreement, whether with high or low confidence values, the result lies within that same range. If the group contains contradictions, i.e. if one of the sources gives a greatly different value from the other sources, this may be compensated.

Another, more severe possibility is to reject and penalize such internal contradictions, i.e. discord and dissension. This second approach imposes the condition that sources with a relation of affinity must be consistent in order for us to trust their assertions. In such a case, a conjunctive operator, such as the minimum, must be considered: therefore, a single source in disagreement with its group is sufficient to largely decrease the overall confidence rating.

7.3.4.2.2. Overall fusion

The last step combines the results provided by the different groups, which are mainly independent or hostile to one another. Therefore, in this step, the redundancy of the pieces of information given may itself be interpreted as a reinforcement: if independent or hostile sources accord a high degree of confidence to an event, their unanimity may be considered to be significant. Thus, the groups mutually reinforce one another's information, leading to a higher level of confidence. Similarly, an overall agreement with regard to a low level of confidence may lead to an even lower overall level of confidence. Finally, in the expected scenario where a disagreement is observed, a simple compromise behavior can be considered. We propose to use operators with variable behaviors for total reinforcement, such as uninorms (see section 7.2.3).

Yet a compromise operator may also be considered if a more neutral attitude is desired. Finally, disjunctive operators, such as the probabilistic t-norm, can be used to model cautious behaviors, thus preventing the taking of rash decisions.

It also seems appropriate to take account of the size of the groups in question. Indeed, a group comprising numerous sources could play a more important role than a smaller group, but without its contribution to the final result eclipsing that of the second group. Therefore, we propose to give each group of sources a weight defined on the basis of its cardinal. As a linear function would cause a behavior of domination, so that the influence of small groups is negligible in the aggregation, we propose to use the square root of the cardinals, which attenuates the effect of the larger groups without ignoring the smaller ones.

7.3.4.2.3. Illustrative example

For the example under consideration, Minister Balldar and Colonel al-Adel, assigned to the same group, provide the same information, as expected. Thus, their respective certainties about the perpetrator of the bombing are not enhanced. If the average is applied as a compromise operator, the possibility distribution obtained after normalization is (1 0.68). The second group contains only one source, providing only one informational element, whose possibility distribution is therefore unchanged (0.7 1).

These two distributions are then amalgamated: two hostile groups provide contradictory information, as expected. Therefore, the fusion creates a compromise, weighted by the size of the sub-groups. After normalization, we then get the distribution (1 0.92).

This result displays a very high degree of uncertainty, because the necessity is only 0.08: it is entirely possible that the Free Resistance of Dagbas is behind the attack, but it is almost just as possible that another, unknown, perpetrator is responsible.

The uncertainty increases greatly compared to the case of fusion without account taken of the relations. This result stems from the reduced role assigned to the sources proclaiming the responsibility of Captain Ixil, because they are considered to be similar and therefore do not provide mutually complementary information.

7.4. Experimental study

In this section, we make an experimental study of the performances of our evaluation support tool and compare various configurations (discounting operation and fusion modes).

This experimental study involves considering a set of events, where we know that they did actually happen, the sources which expressed themselves and what they said about those events, and more specifically the degree of uncertainty they expressed on the subject. We can therefore compare the possibility distributions computed by our tool against the expected values, using appropriate quality measures which will be discussed later on.

Ideally, such a study should be based on real-world data. However, this strategy is very costly because it requires a substantial effort in terms of data collection and manual annotation in order to determine, from the reported events, those which really did take place. To our knowledge, no such corpus exists. In order to get around the problem, we have chosen to evaluate the performances of our tool using simulated data. This approach also poses problems – due mainly to the generation of the data, and to the constraints of realism that those data have to respect: the data simulation must indeed be representative of a real-world process and compatible with its biases.

In this section, we describe a method to realistically simulate the uncertainty of a source regarding an event, given his reliability or the pronouncements of his allied sources about the same event. This method is the cornerstone of the experiments which we have conducted: it is used to construct different simulated datasets on which we test the performances of our tool. These datasets and the different configurations of the tool tested are detailed in section 7.4.2. Section 7.4.3 presents the quality measures chosen when comparing the tool's output against the target values. Finally, in section 7.4.4, we analyze the results of the conducted experiments.

7.4.1. *Realistic generation of the uncertainty of a source*

In order to validate the architecture of our tool, as described in section 7.3, the simulation needs to provide realistic data, which are representative of real-life data. Otherwise, the comparison with the expected result is meaningless; in particular, we cannot expect the evaluation support tool to be able to find the expected result– e.g. the fact that a particular event did take place – if all the informational elements provided contradict that result. At a finer level, similarly, the reliable sources must have a high probability of providing information in line with the expected result. In addition, if friendly sources are constantly contradicting one another, it is unrealistic to expect the tool to provide a quality result.

The source's uncertainty about the information is expressed, at a linguistic level, by the terms that he chooses, and at a formal level, by the possibility distribution $(\pi_{ling}(e)\,\pi_{ling}(\neg e))$. As set out in section 7.3, the switch from the linguistic terms to the possibility distribution is done in part during the preprocessing (section 7.3.2.1.1) and in part during the modeling of the different levels of uncertainty (section 7.3.3.1). With simulated data, we can simply generate the distribution itself directly, rather than linguistic terms.

As we can see, the issue of simulation of the uncertainty expressed by the sources boils down to the generation of distributions $(\pi(e)\pi(\neg e))$. However, in such a couple, at least one of the two values is equal to 1, as one of the two events is entirely possible. The other value then indicates the uncertainty of the source about this occurrence. Hence, the simulation divides the generation of the couple into two steps:

1) choice of the value to set as 1;

2) generation of the second value.

In what follows, we examine these two points in turn and, without sacrificing generality, we consider only the scenario where the event about which the source is speaking proves to have occurred.[7] We begin by examining the constraints imposed by the reliabilities of the sources on such a couple, before discussing those imposed by the relations between the sources.

7.4.1.1. *Realism in terms of the reliabilities of the sources*

To a certain extent, knowledge about the reliability of the source imposes a constraint in terms of the associated possibility distribution. Indeed, when an event is known to have happened, represented by the distribution $(\pi(e)\ \pi(\neg e)) = (1\ 0)$, a source whose reliability is certain should not often be associated with a distribution of the form $(0\ 1)$: this indicates that the source is certain that $\neg e$ occurred – i.e. that he is sure of the opposite of reality. Such a phenomenon must remain possible, to represent the fact that even a reliable source can make mistakes, but it should be unlikely. In case of a source whose reliability is less certain, such a phenomenon may have a higher probability. The realism of the generated possibility values thus requires a correlation with the reliabilities of the sources with which they are associated.

---

7 The case $(0\ 1)$, i.e. when $\neg e$ has happened, can be dealt with using the same procedure: we only need to invert the two values generated by the procedure, e.g. consider the couple (b a) if the procedure gives us the couple (a b).

The first step in the generation of the couple ($\pi(e)$ $\pi(\neg e)$) consists of choosing which of the two values to set as 1, i.e. choosing whether e or $\neg e$ is entirely possible according to the source. As previously highlighted, the more certain we are that the source is reliable, the more likely it should be that he will indicate that e is possible, meaning that the probability that $\pi(e) = 1$ should be higher. However, making it impossible for a reliable source to make mistakes would seem to be too strict a definition of reliability: the probability that he will give a maximal possibility to $\neg e$ must not be null. We can interpret such errors as being due to the fact that the source is not omniscient (with sources who are not totally reliable, the error may be due to the lack of reliability).

Thus, we propose to define the probability $p(\pi(e) = 1)$ as an increasing function of the certainty about the reliability of the source, i.e. N(r). The maximum for this function is not 1, but a value γ, interpreted as a degree of *omniscience*, enabling us to model the fact that a reliable source may not consider an event which has actually happened to be totally possible, unlike an entirely omniscient source. In order to preserve the simplicity of the simulation model, we propose to use a linear function such that:

– if N(r) = 0 –that is, if no knowledge about the reliability of the source is available –then $p(\pi(e) = 1) = 0.5$. Indeed, in this case, the reliability provides no information, and the source must have the same probability of thinking that e and that $\neg e$ have taken place. Therefore a uniform distribution, free of *a priori* knowledge or bias, is applicable;

– if N(r) = 1, the source is certified reliable, then $p(\pi(e) = 1)$ needs to be maximal. We therefore propose to set this maximum value at the threshold $\gamma < 1$.

This modeling gives us $p(\pi(e) = 1) = 0.5 + (\gamma - 0.5) N(r)$.

After having selected the value at 1 in the possibility distribution, the second value has to be generated. It corresponds to the uncertainty associated with the decision, and it too may depend on our knowledge of the source's reliability. We can distinguish two cases, depending on the result of the previous step:

– if $\pi(e) = 1$, we can generate $\pi(\neg e)$ using a uniform law in the interval $[0, 1]$, which is tantamount to supposing that there is no expected correlation between the certainty expressed by the source and his reliability;

– if $\pi(\neg e) = 1$, we are witnessing a "mistake" on the part of the source, and we can therefore expect him to express a low degree of certainty. More specifically, the more certain the reliability of the source, the lower his certainty that $\neg e$ has occurred should be, in probability, meaning that $\pi(e)$ should be higher. We therefore propose to generate $\pi(e)$ using a probability law which is biased toward high values, with the bias depending on $N(r)$. With this in mind, we propose to generate the value using a uniform law in an interval $[x, 1]$, where the threshold x depends on the reliability of the source: the greater the certainty about the source's reliability, the higher the value of x must be, leading to significant uncertainties about whether $\neg e$ has taken place. We define x as $x = \min(N(r), \gamma)$. As the degree γ tends in our experience to be high, this mainly enables us to ensure that a totally reliable source can express non-null certainty with regard to $\neg e$.

7.4.1.2. *Realism in terms of friendly sources*

The procedure described in the previous section is based on the reliability and omniscience of the source. However, these two criteria, which are attributes unique to the source himself, are not sufficient if we wish to reproduce what actually happens in reality: it is also helpful to use the context in which the source is expressing himself, and in particular the fact that a source may be influenced by the other sources in his affinity group expressing views on the event. In this section we outline two strategies to generate the uncertainty of a source regarding an event, taking account of the sources in a relation of affinity with the first source.

These two strategies are in fact variants of the following principle: the uncertainty expressed by a source regarding an event is the result of his own knowledge about the event and that which his friendly sources (the sources in the same sub-group as him) are saying. Let π_{SExp} be the possibility distribution representing the uncertainty expressed by a source S. The above principle leads us to posit $\pi_{SExp} = f(\pi_S, \pi_C)$, where:

$-\pi_S$ is the uncertainty of the source S resulting from his own knowledge (in a misuse of language, we shall speak of the source's "own uncertainty") regarding the event. We propose to approximate π_S by the procedure described in section 7.4.1.2;

$-\pi_C$ is the overall uncertainty of all the sources in the same affinity group.

The fusion operator f and π_C still need to be determined. For f, we propose to use the weighted average, with a weight equal to the reliability of S, so as to reflect the following idea: the more reliable a source is, the less he tends to be influenced by other sources. For π_C, we suggest two strategies:

– strategy 1 (S1): π_C = average of the "own uncertainties" of each of the sources (except the source S) in the sub-group. Using this strategy involves considering that firstly, a consensus is established between the different sources in the group with regard to the event to be reported, and then the source reports the event by combining the result of that consensus with his own beliefs;

– strategy 2 (S2): taking account of the fact that the sources are not expressing themselves at the same time. π_C = uncertainty expressed about the event by the last source before source S to have expressed a view. This strategy, unlike S1, does not assume that the members of a group of friendly sources must first have discussed the situation amongst themselves and arrived at a consensus regarding the event that is to be reported. What it does suppose is that each source needing to express himself about an event has knowledge of, and is influenced by, the declarations on the same subject by the sources in his own group, once these declarations become available. In order to avoid lending too much weight to those sources within a group who express themselves first, we have supposed with this strategy that only the last declaration by another member of the group was taken into account.

7.4.2. Description of the experiments

In this section we describe the set of experiments conducted to evaluate the proposed evaluation support tool. First, in section 7.4.2.1, we present the experimental datasets, and then in section 7.4.2.2, the different configurations of the tool which we tested.

7.4.2.1. *Data simulation*

The approach chosen to evaluate the information evaluation chain requires a set of events, for each of which we need to know whether it did actually occur, and have, firstly, the reliability ratings for the various sources having expressed a view about it and, secondly, the uncertainties of those sources on the subject. In this section we describe the method which we used to generate these datasets, and then detail those which we actually constructed and used to assess our evaluation support tool.

The first thing which needs to be decided is the number of events (NE) about which the various sources in the simulation can express a view. Then, we need to create a set of sources. For this purpose, we choose a number of sources (NS), a minimum degree of reliability (R) and a degree of omniscience γ: each of the NS sources is randomly assigned a degree of reliability in the interval [R,1]; the degree of omniscience is the same for all the sources. The next step is to partition the set of sources into affinity groups. In order to do so, we choose a vector $G = (G_1, ..., G_N)$ where N determines the number of groups and G_i denotes the number of sources in the i-th group; the distribution of the sources into the groups is done at random. Finally, for each of the NE events (which are all considered to be proven events, without loss of generality), we need to generate possibility distributions simulating what the sources would have reported about that event. The number of possibility distributions for each event is drawn randomly between two numbers *NDP m in* and *NDP max*. Each of the possibility distributions is then randomly associated with one of the NS sources (for the same event, multiple possibility distributions may therefore be associated with the same source) and generated by way of the procedure described in section 7.4.1, after having chosen one of the two strategies *S1* or *S2* (described in section 7.4.1.2); the strategy is the same for all of the sources in the dataset.

Test in gall of the different combinations of these parameters would be misguided. Hence, we opted for the following strategy: we constructed a reference dataset and then constructed different datasets by varying only one parameter with respect to the reference, so as to be able to look at the influence of that parameter alone on the tool's behavior. The reference set of parameters is as follows: $NE = 100$, $NS = 60$, $NDP\ min = 5$, $NDP\ max = 20$, $G=(20,20,20)$, $F = 0.3$, $\gamma = 0.9$, Strategy $S1$.

Around this reference set, nine other datasets (labeled 2–10) were constructed. They are detailed in Table 7.4. For each dataset, we have specified only the parameters which differ from the reference set. We also constructed ten additional datasets similar to the first ten, changing the strategy for taking account of the network of sources ($S2$ rather than $S1$).

	NE	NS	NDP min	NDP max	G	F	γ
Reference	100	60	5	20	(20,20,20)	0.3	0.9
Set 2							0.7
Set 3						0.5	
Set 4					(15,15,15,15)		
Set 5					(10,10,10,10,10,10)		
Set 6			20	30			
Set 7		180			(60,60,60)		
Set 8		180			(30,30,30,10,80)		
Set 9		180	40	50	(30,30,30,10,80)		
Set 10	500	1000	5	70	(40,200,10,100,20, 75,25,30)		

Table 7.4. *Parameter configurations tested for the simulation of the 10 datasets being evaluated*

7.4.2.2. *Configurations of the tool tested*

As described in section 7.3, the proposed architecture is flexible, and means that our tool can be configured in a number of different ways. In particular, for the evaluation of the individual elements, different discounting operations can be used; similarly, different modes of fusion of the individual ratings are possible. We detail the different configurations tested below.

We considered the two discounting operations in the family of operations introduced by Yager, respectively based on the minimum and on the product. For fusion, two modes were studied: overall aggregation of the individual ratings and aggregation exploiting the partition of the sources into sub-groups, which requires the choice of two operators (see section 7.3.4.2): one internal for the partial fusion in to each group, and one external for the overall fusion between the groups. The complete list of the fusion configurations tested is given in Table 7.5.

Partition-based aggregation			
No.	Name	Internal operator	External operator
1	AvgAvg	Arithmetic average	Arithmetic average
2	AvgUni	Arithmetic average	Uninorm
3	AvgCoP	Arithmetic average	Probabilistic T-conorm
4	MinAvg	Minimum	Arithmetic average
5	MinUni	Minimum	Uninorm
6	MinCoP	Minimum	Probabilistic T-conorm
Overall aggregation			
No.	Name	Operator	
7	Avg	Arithmetic average	
8	Uni	Uninorm	
9	CoP	Probabilistic T-conorm	
10	Max	Zadeh's T-conorm (maximum)	
11	Tprob	Probabilistic T-norm	
12	Min	Zadeh's T-norm (minimum)	

Table 7.5. *List of aggregation configurations tested*

7.4.3. Measures of quality

The evaluation of the performances of the proposed tool necessitates the introduction of specific measures to quantify the quality of its output. This can be seen as a possibilistic information source in that, for a given event, it provides a measure of uncertainty in the form of a possibility distribution. Thus, it is possible to use methods for evaluating the quality of sources, or possibilistic classifiers, similar to those used in [DRU 06] and [DES 08], based on the criteria known as *informativeness* and *calibration*. These criteria rely on the comparison of the distribution in question, π, with two reference distributions – respectively the expected distribution and the distribution representing ignorance.

The criterion of informativeness, notated as In $f(\pi)$, measures the accuracy of the information π provided by the source, comparing it to the situation of total ignorance, in which all the options are equally possible. In the particular case of information evaluation, where the universes in question are binary, informativeness is defined by:

$$\text{In } f(\pi) = |\pi(e) - \pi(\neg e)|$$

Calibration, notated as $\text{Cal}(\pi)$, measures the consistency between the information provided and the distribution representing the expected result. In the case of information evaluation, for an expected result, represented by the distribution (1 0), we have:

$$\text{Cal}(\pi) = \pi(e).$$

Besides informativeness and calibration, we propose a new measure, based on the normalized Manhattan distance between a distribution π to be evaluated and the expected result, to evaluate the validity of π. More specifically, we consider a similarity $S = 1 - D$, where D represents the Manhattan distance, i.e. the expected possibility distribution is considered to be (1 0):

$$S(\pi) = 1 - 0.5 * \left(|\pi(e) - 1| + |\pi(\neg e) - 0| \right)$$
$$= 1 - 0.5 * \left(1 - \pi(e) + \pi(\neg e) \right)$$

This measure enables us to model the preference we wish to attach to calibration over informativeness. For instance, an obtained distribution (1 1) is preferable to an obtained distribution (0 1) for an expected distribution (1 0): the second distribution corresponds to the worst case scenario, because it totally contradicts the expected result. The first distribution is still unsatisfactory, because it represents total ignorance, but nevertheless it remains compatible with the expected result.

Table 7.6 illustrates the process for calculating the three measures of quality defined above, for an expected distribution of (1 0) and for various possibility distributions, from the distribution obtained to the contradictory distribution, with the uncertainty gradually increasing to the point of ignorance and then gradually decreasing once more. Note that the measure of similarity is strictly monotonic decreasing, whereas the calibration has less of a capacity for discrimination. The informativeness is not monotonic.

Distribution	(1 0)	(1 0.5)	(1 0.9)	(1 1)	(0.5 1)	(0 1)
Inf(π)	1	0.5	0.1	0	0.5	1
Cal(π)	1	1	1	1	0.5	0
S(π)	1	0.75	0.55	0.5	0.25	0

Table 7.6. *Measures of quality of a possibility distribution compared with the expected distribution (1 0)*

7.4.4. *Results*

We shall comment on the results obtained first from an overall point of view, then by detailing the comparisons between the configurations tested, particularly in terms of measuring the similarity with the expected possibility distribution.

7.4.4.1. *Overall performance*

The observed values of calibration and informativeness, which have been omitted for reasons of space, show that in all cases – i.e. whatever the datasets, strategies and events considered, and whatever the discounting- and fusion operators examined – the calibration is equal to 1. This means that in all cases, it is the event e which is assigned the degree of possibility 1, in accordance with the expected distribution: only the certainty associated there with and which, in this case, is given directly by the informativeness value, changes. The Manhattan similarity values, discussed in detail in section 7.4.2.2, also exhibit variations from case to case, but they are always greater than 0.5, which might be considered to be a high value.

This observation corresponds to an unsurprising result: the input data upon which the experiments are based are "of good quality", in the sense that – on the one hand – the confirmation-to-invalidation ratio is greater than 1 (it is 2.5 in the "worst case", obtained for dataset 2 with strategy $S2$, and reaches up to a value of 31 for dataset 9 with strategy $S1$), and – on the other – the invalidations are skewed so as to be uncertain in the case of reliable sources. Therefore, for the most part, they are in accordance with the expected distribution and are unambiguous.

These unsurprising results do, however, indicate that the discounting operators and fusion operators are all compatible, *a priori*, with the expectations about the behavior of the evaluation tool, and that none of them throw up a contradictory result. In addition, the computation times were measured for all the experiments: there is no significant difference between the computation times for all of the configurations examined.

7.4.4.2. *Comparative study*

The two graphs in Figure 7.4 indicate, for dataset 3 and for both strategies, the average and standard deviation of the Manhattan similarity between the possibility distribution produced by our tool and the binary possibility distribution expected (1 0). The horizontal axis indicates the identifier of the operator in question (using the identifiers shown in Table 7.5), ordered by decreasing values of the average similarity; the vertical axis shows the average Manhattan similarity. For reasons of space we have omitted the graphs corresponding to the other datasets, but it is important to stress that for these other sets, very similar graphs were obtained.

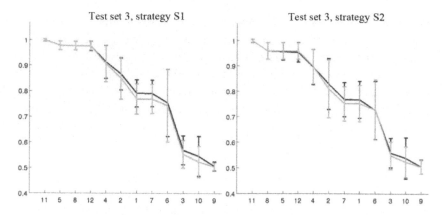

Figure 7.4. *Average Manhattan similarity on the events in dataset 3.*
Left: strategy S1; right: strategy S2[8]

We can see overall that the differences between the datasets, and between strategies *S1* and *S2*, are slight. The comparative study which follows therefore focuses on the differences between the discounting operators and aggregation methods.

With regard to the two discounting operations, we note that the differences between them are slight and meaningless: on the graphs for all the datasets, and for both strategies *S1* and *S2*, the averages of the two curves show differences less than the standard deviations with which they are associated.

With regard to the fusion operators, we observe that it is possible to distinguish three levels of similarity values, defining three groups of operators, here classified in decreasing order of average Manhattan similarity values. Within each of these groups, the operators also share common semantics (see section 7.2.3), which we touch upon below:

– operators with a conjunctive overall behavior: the *t*-norms (operators 11 and 12), the uninorm (operator 8 – this operator is

---

8 The numbers for the configurations tested are given on the horizontal axis (see Table 7.5 for the corresponding configurations). The dark and light curves respectively correspond to the discounting operation based on the product and based on the minimum.

globally conjunctive, and the zone of positive reinforcement is rarely used), and the combination by partition Min Uni (operator 5);

– operators with a compromise behavior: these are the operators which make use of the arithmetic average, either alone or with account taken of the partition (operators 1, 2, 4, and 7);

– operators with a disjunctive overall behavior: the t-conorms (operators 9 and 10), and the combination Avg CoP (operator 3).

The operator Min CoP (operator 6), for its part, oscillates between the last two groups.

It may be remarked upon that this global characterization into three groups does not exploit the distinction between fusion methods which take account of the partition of the sources and those which do not: these results show that the choice of fusion method must depend more on its overall semantics than on the elements on which that semantics is based.

7.4.4.3. *Optimal operator*

The results obtained lead us to conclude that in the context of the experiments carried out, operators with a conjunctive overall behavior are preferable.

The best results obtained with this group of operators can be explained by the remark made above: the experiments are based on good-quality data, i.e. data which are largely consistent with the expected distribution. However, operators with conjunctive behavior have the property of revealing the zone of agreement between sources: if the sources are mainly in agreement as to the occurrence of the event e, it is clear that these operators exhibit better performances than the others, which in the case of these experiments means that the event e is assigned the highest degrees of certainty.

In order to decide definitively on the use of a configuration based on a conjunctive operator, it is helpful to validate the hypothesis that the input data are generally of good quality. If this hypothesis is not realistic, we need to carry out an evaluation with low-quality data in order to see whether the conclusions obtained remain the same.

7.5. Conclusions

In this chapter, we have put forward a semi-automated approach to assist in the evaluation of information drawn from textual documents, based on a possibilistic framework of uncertainty management. The objective is to help an analyst to answer a factual question relating to the veracity of a particular piece of information and to estimate the confidence which he can reasonably attach to the response suggested to him in view of the mass of available information.

This process of information evaluation can be divided into three main stages. The first consists of identifying, within the body of information collected, those pieces which are relevant in answering the question at hand. The second consists of estimating the elementary uncertainty associated with each piece of relevant information, considered independently of the others. Finally, the third stage is the fusion of these elementary uncertainties.

These three stages are applied sequentially, which enables us to adopt a modular, flexible approach. This is a definite asset when we want to adapt the process to the peculiarities of the data being processed. For instance, we can easily alter the fusion process to take account or not to take account of the relations between the information sources depending on whether or not this information is available.

Our approach presents a twofold advantage. On the one hand, it automates a large part of this confidence estimation. On the other, it affords the analyst a central role in the process of evaluation. Indeed, it is to him that the task falls of validating the information automatically extracted from the texts and the divisions between pieces of information. This semi-automated nature is essential for being able to process large volumes of data, and indispensable in order for the approach to be able to be implemented practically, whilst ensuring the analyst has total control over every step of the information evaluation process.

In order to judge the performances of this process, we developed a simulator capable of generating data as realistic as possible. Firstly this enabled us to forego the difficult and costly construction of a reference baseline for the evaluation, which would have necessitated the manual labeling of a large number of texts. Secondly, as we have a simulator, we have total control over the process of data generation which means that by adjusting the parameters, we can quickly and simply construct evaluation datasets appropriate for the use context we have in mind. Without such a simulator, we would have to construct a new labeled dataset teach time the application context changes, which is unrealistic.

The data which we simulated correspond to a context in which the information is of good quality, provided by relatively reliable sources. In this context, we have been able to demonstrate the good performances of the proposed approach and identify an optimal configuration, with the determining factor being the choice of an aggregation operator with a conjunctive behavior to carry out the last step – fusion.

These performances are very promising, but it would be helpful to perform evaluations of this information evaluation chain using a broader range of application contexts. This is crucial in order to get closer to an evaluation in real conditions. Indeed, we need to be able to judge the quality of the evaluation made in the overall chain of processing, i.e. estimate the influence of the linguistic information extraction processing on the evaluation. Depending on whether we are working with texts taken from blogs, for a, social networks, mail exchanges or institutional sites, it is certain that the quality of the information extracted from these documents, which serves as the input to the process of evaluation, will be very different.

In addition, given the importance of the human operator in the information evaluation process, in the medium term we need our approach to be assessed by specialists in the domain. In order to give the analysts context and gather their impressions and criticisms of the process and the results obtained, we have implemented this process via a Web interface which offers easy navigation of the different documents collected and the information extracted from those documents, and also enables the users to launch queries in order to evaluate a particular piece of information and view the elements contributing to the final score.

Finally, one interesting aspect of our approach relates to its proximity to a method commonly used by analysts – analysis of competing hypotheses (ACH) [HEU 99]. This technique aims to evaluate the likelihoods of different hypotheses with regard to a list of information confirming or invalidating these hypotheses. Our evaluation chain enables us, at least, to serve certain stages of this method. It also provides a formal framework for calculating the likelihoods.

7.6. Bibliography

[BAE 11] BAERECKE T., LESOT M.J., AKDAG H., *et al.*, "Stratégie de fusion d'informations exploitant le réseau des sources", *Atelier Fouille de données complexes, journées francophones extraction et gestion des connaissances, (EGC'11)*, 2011.

[BLO 94] BLOCH I., MAITRE H., "Fusion de données en traitement d'images : modèles d'information et décisions", *Traitement du signal*, no. 11, pp. 435–446, 1994.

[BOU 95] BOUCHON-MEUNIER B., *La logique floue et ses applications*, Addison-Wesley, Reading, MA, 1995.

[BOU 98] BOUCHON-MEUNIER B., *Aggregation and Fusion of Imperfect Information*, Physica-Verlag, Heidelberg, Germany, 1998.

[CAS 11] CASTILLO C., MENDOZA M., POBLETE B., "Information credibility on twitter", *20th International Conference on World Wide Web (WWW)*, pp. 675–684, 2011.

[CHO 10] CHOLVY L., "Evaluation of information reported: a model in the theory of evidence", in HÜLLERMEIER E., KRUSE R., HOFFMAN F. (eds.), *International conference on Information Processing and Management of Uncertainty in knowledge-based systems(IPMU'10)*, pp. 258–267, 2010.

[DES 08] DESTERCKE S., CHOJNACKI E., "Methods for the evaluation and synthesis of multiple sources of information applied to nuclear computer codes", *Nuclear Engineering and Design*, vol. 238, no. 9, pp. 2484–2493, 2008.

[DET 00] DETYNIECKI M., Mathematical aggregation operators and their application to video querying, Doctoral Thesis, Université Pierre et Marie Curie, Paris 6, 2000.

[DRU 06] DRUMMOND I., MELENDEZ J., SANDRI S., "Assessing the aggregation of parametrized imprecise classification", *Frontiers in Artificial Intelligence and Applications*, vol. 146, pp. 227–235, 2006.

[DUB 00] DUBOIS D., PRADE H., "Possibility theory in information fusion", *3rd International conference on Information Fusion, (FUSION'00)*, Paris, France, 2000.

[DUB 88] DUBOIS D., PRADE H., *Possibility Theory*, Plenum, New York, NY, 1988.

[DUB 90] DUBOIS D., PRADE H., "An introduction to possibilistic and fuzzy logics", in SHAFER G., PEARL J. (eds.), *Readings in Uncertain Reasoning*, Morgan Kaufmann Publishers Inc, Burlington, MA, pp. 742–761, 1990.

[EUD 98] EUDE V., Modélisation spatio-temporelle floue pour la reconnaissance d'activités militaires, Doctoral thesis, Université Pierre et Marie Curie, Paris 6, 1998.

[FOD 97] FODOR J.C., YAGER R., RYBALOV A., "A structure of uninorms", *Journal of Uncertainty, Fuzziness and Knowledge-Based Systems*, no. 5, pp. 411–427, 1997.

[GEL 06] GELMAN A., "The boxer, the wrestler and the coin flip: a paradox of robust bayesian inference and belief functions", *The American Statistician*, no 60, pp. 146–150, 2006.

[GOT 01] GOTTWALD S., "A Treatise on many-valued logics", *Studies in Logic and Computation*, Research Studies Press, Baldock, United Kingdom, vol. 9, 2001.

[GOU 09] GOUJON B., "Uncertainty detection for information extraction", *International conference on recent advances in natural language processing*, Borovets, Bulgaria, 2009.

[HEU 99] HEUER R.J., Psychology of intelligence analysis, Center for the Study of Intelligence, Central Intelligence Agency, 1999.

[LES 11] LESOT M.J., DELAVALLADE T., PICHON F., *et al.*, "Proposition of a semi-automatic possibilistic information scoring process", *7th Conf. of the European Society for Fuzzy Logic and Technology (EUSFLAT-2011)*, 2011.

[NAT 97] NATO, STANAG 2511, Intelligence Reports, 2003.

[PIC 12] PICHON F., DUBOIS D. DENOEUX T., "Relevance and truthfulness in information correction and fusion", *International Journal of Approximate Reasoning*, no. 53, pp. 159–175, 2012.

[RES 69] RESCHER N., *Many-Valued Logic*, McGraw Hill, New York, 1969.

[REV 07] REVAULT D'ALLONNES A., AKDAG H., POIREL O., "Trust-moderated information-likelihood. A multi-valued logics approach", *3rd Conf. on Computability in Europe, (CiE 2007)*, pp. 1–6, 2007.

[REV 11] REVAULTD' ALLONNES A., Evaluation sémantique d'informations symboliques : la cotation, Doctoral thesis, Université Pierre et Marie Curie, Paris 6, 2011.

[SET 10] SETH A., ZHANG J., COHEN R., "Bayesian credibility modeling for personalized recommendation in participatory media", User Modeling, Adaptation, and Personalization, *Lecture Notes in Computer Science*, vol. 6 075, pp. 279–290, 2010.

[SHA 76] SHAFER G., *A mathematical theory of evidence*, Princeton University Press, Princeton, 1976.

[SIL 79] SILVERT W., "Symmetric summation: a class of operations on fuzzy sets", *IEEE Trans. on Systems, Man and Cybernetics*, no. 9, pp. 659–667, 1979.

[WEE 12] WEERKAMP W., DE RIJKE M., "Credibility-inspired ranking for blog post retrieval", *Information Retrieval*, vol. 15, no. 3-4, pp. 243–277, 2012.

[YAG 84] YAGER R., "Approximate reasoning as a basis for rule-based expert systems", *IEEE Trans. on Systems, Man and Cybernetics*, no. 14, pp. 636–643, 1984.

[YAG 88] YAGER R., "On ordered weighted averaging aggregation operators in multi-criteria decision making", *IEEE Trans. on Systems, Man and Cybernetics*, no. 18, pp. 183–190, 1988.

[ZAD 65] ZADEH L., "Fuzzy sets", *Information and control*, no. 8, pp. 338–353, 1965.

[ZAD 78] ZADEH L., "Fuzzy sets as the basis for a theory of possibility", *Fuzzy Sets and Systems*, no. 1, pp. 3–28, 1978.

Chapter 8

When Reported Information Is Second Hand

8.1. Introduction

In order to estimate the current state of the world, a rational agent seeks to acquire information about that state, using sources of various types: physical sensors, human observers, Websites, newspapers, etc.

The agent receiving this information then asks himself the question of whether to accept it as new beliefs or to reject it. Obviously, he can accept a piece of information as a new belief if he knows that the source providing it always gives information which is true. Similarly, if the agent knows that a source systematically provides false information, then he can accept as a belief the opposite of any information produced by that source.

For example, suppose I am interested in the flow rate of a river fed only by melt water from a glacier. In order to estimate the flow rate of that river, I telephone a friend who lives near the glacier. That friend tells me that the temperature around the glacier has increased dramatically in the past few months. If I trust that friend to give accurate climatic information, then I can accept the fact that the

Chapter written by Laurence CHOLVY.

temperature in the environs of the glacier has increased, and conclude from this that the flow of the river has also increased. Now suppose that instead of phoning my friend, I read the weather report in my newspaper, which says that the temperature in the mountains has risen. If I know that the weather reports in that newspaper are always wrong, then I can conclude that the temperature near to the glacier has not increased, and therefore that the flow of the river has not increased either.

In [DEM 04], the author looks at a variety of properties which an information source may have, of which *validity* and *completeness* are particularly interesting. For Demolombe, an agent's validity and completeness depend on the information he is communicating and on the agent to whom he is communicating that information. More specifically, an agent who is *valid* for a given piece of information in relation to another agent informs that other agent of the information *only* if it is true; an agent who is *complete* for a given piece of information in relation to another agent informs that other agent of the information if it is true. Validity and completeness are very important properties for the issue in which we are interested here. Indeed, if the agent receiving a piece of information from another agent trusts him to be valid, then he can conclude that the information is true. Similarly, if the agent does not receive a certain piece of information from an agent whom he trusts to be complete, then he can conclude that the information is false.

The article [DEM 04] focuses on information produced directly by a source. However, in many cases, the information source does not exactly provide the information which we need, but rather cites another source who is providing it. Such is the case, for instance, when I am informed by my neighbor that one of his friends who lives near the glacier has told him that the local temperature has risen. In this case, my neighbor is reporting that one of his friends has said that the temperature has risen near to the glacier, but he is not telling me himself that the temperature there has risen. In this case, it is immaterial whether I trust my neighbor to give me accurate weather information. However, trusting him to tell me the truth, and trusting my neighbor's friend to provide accurate weather information enables me to conclude that the temperature near the glacier has indeed increased. Note here that the information which is of interest to me (has the temperature in the vicinity of the glacier increased?) is reported *via* two agents: my neighbor's friend, and my neighbor, with the second citing the first. In other words, the information of interest to me is second hand.

The question of estimating whether or not an agent can believe a piece of information when it is reported *via* agents successively citing one another is the subject of the present research.

In order to solve this question, we have put forward a variety of models in the past [CHO 10; CHO 11a; CHO 11b; CHO 12], which highlight the importance of taking account of the properties of validity and completeness of sources, and which also introduce their dual properties. The dual property of validity characterizes agents whom we refer to as *misinformers*. An agent who is a misinformer for a given piece of information communicates it *only* if it is false. The dual property of completeness characterizes agents whom we call *falsifiers*. An agent who is a falsifier for a given piece of information communicates it if it is false. We have proposed versions of these models in modal logic. Then, in order to take account of a certain type of uncertainty, we proposed versions of these models in the context of the theory of evidence (or Dempster–Shafer theory) [SHA 76].

The primary objective of this chapter is to summarize the most advanced models and illustrate them using the example running through all the chapters of this book. We shall therefore demonstrate two types of models: one logical, the other numerical, to determine the credibility of a piece of information. The second objective of this chapter is to show that the logical model can also be used to generate plausible hypotheses about the properties of the information sources which, if they are verified, ensure that the information given in credible.

More specifically, this chapter is organized as follows. Section 8.2 briefly presents a number of works which are relevant for our study. Section 8.3 presents the most advanced logical model which we have defined, and formally introduces the four properties of information sources which we consider. Section 8.4 considers a certain form of uncertainty and presents a second model which we have put forward. We show that this model is an extension of the previous one. Section 8.5 returns to the logical model and shows how it can be used to generate hypotheses about the properties of the sources, guaranteeing that the information provided is credible. Section 8.6 draws conclusions from this chapter.

Additional material at the end of the chapter summarizes the main notions and notations of the formalisms of logic and theory of evidence used here.

8.2. Domains involved and related works

Let us now briefly present some of the domains where the question of reported information evaluation may become crucial but sometimes does not arise at all. We shall also present a number of related works which are interesting for this topic.

8.2.1. *Document mining on the Web*

In the context of document mining on the Web, the question of whether we can accept a piece of information as a new belief is of crucial importance. It is commonly considered that the factors which influence our belief in the information contained on a Web page relate to the writer of the document (e.g. his status, his area of expertise, his reputation, etc.), the objective of the document (e.g. production of information, militancy, publicity, etc.), the position adopted in the document (objective or not), the date the document was created, and so on.

8.2.2. *Military intelligence*

Similarly, in the context of military intelligence, the question of information evaluation is central, and a standard is defined by NATO to enable intelligence officers to evaluate information. According to this standard [NAT 03], all information is associated with a letter and a number, respectively representing the reliability of the source and the credibility of the information. We say that the letter and number form the rating of the information, and the process of attributing that value is information evaluation.

This method of information evaluation is open to criticism. In particular, it has been shown that the two criteria are not independent of one another. In addition, it cannot cope with a scenario where information is reported by numerous sources, citing one another in turn – the case with which we are dealing here. The doctrinal corpus relevant for information evaluation is discussed in Chapter 3 and its main shortcomings and weaknesses are demonstrated in Chapter 4.

8.2.3. Analysis of press reports

The work described in [JAC 07] focuses on the analysis of press reports and is the only work, to our knowledge, to look at the case of second-hand information. In this article, a report is represented by a single sentence. This report may have sources citing other sources. Returning to the scenario running through this book, such is the case with the report supposedly emitted by the *Press Ektimo-Agency*:

"Minister Balldar, chief of the secret police, declares that the so-called *Free Resistance of Dagbas* might be implicated in this morning's attack."

Here, the *Press Ektimo-Agency* reported the suggestion made by the minister Balldar, whereby the *Free Resistance of Dagbas* might be implicated in the attack. The factors held up in the article for the evaluation of such a report are the reliability of the source, the source's own opinion about the information he is giving, and the relations between the different actors in the discourse. To specify:

1) the reliability of the source may, if we already know the source, be a function of the history of his declarations and the reliability of those declarations. Alternatively, we can classify the source into different categories, each associated with a level of *a priori* reliability.

These categories are, in order of decreasing reliability: organizations, named people, anonymous representatives, texts and unknowns;

2) the source's opinion about his discourse is found by analysis of the text, where it is present in the form of a subjective modality. This may be epistemic (degree of certainty) or appreciative (appreciation of the speaker). The players in the discourse are the entities presented therein, whether they are secondary or involved in the fundamental piece of information;

3) the relations between the different players in the discourse are: hostility, neutrality or alliance. In the case of a non-neutral relation, the source may be giving an insincere report, propagating a piece of information which he knows to be false or exaggerated.

In [JAC 07], information evaluation is based on a multi-criteria aggregation method.

8.2.4. *Modal logic, validity and completeness of information sources*

In his work on the modeling of trust, [DEM 04], Demolombe focused on the relations between the statements communicated, truth and epistemic attitudes of the agents. The modal logic (see [CHE 80]) employed in this work uses the following operators: B_i ($B_i\,p$ means "the agent i believe sp"), K_i ($K_i\,p$ means "the agent i strongly believe sp"), I_i^j ($I_i^j p$ means "the agent i informs j that p"), and conventionally $\neg p$ means "p is false".

The operator B_i obeys the axiomatic of the KD logic:

– (D_B) $B_i \neg\, p \rightarrow \neg\, B_i\,p$;

– (K_B) $B_i\,p \wedge B_i\,(p \rightarrow q) \rightarrow B_i\,q$;

– (Nec_B) If p is a theorem then B_i pis too.

The operator I_i^j obeys only the rule of substitutivity of equivalents:

– (Sub_I) If $p \leftrightarrow q$ is a theorem then $I_i^j p \leftrightarrow I_i^j q$ is too.

The operator K_i obeys the following axiomatic:

$-(D_K)\ K_i \neg\, p \rightarrow \neg\, K_i\, p;$

$-(K_B)\ K_i\, p \wedge K_i\, (p \rightarrow q) \rightarrow K_i\, q;$

$-(KT)\ K_i\,(K_i\, p \rightarrow p);$

$-(Nec_K)$ If p is a theorem then $K_i\, p$ is too.

In addition, we accept that:

$-K_i\, p \rightarrow B_i\, p;$

$-I_i^j\, p \rightarrow K_j\, I_i^j\, p;$

$-I_i^j\, p \rightarrow K_j\, \neg I_i^j\, p.$

For Demolombe, an agent providing information may have numerous properties – notably that of being valid or being complete.

Thus, the agent i is valid regarding j for p if and only if (iff), when i informs that p, p is true. This is defined by:[1]

$\quad$ valid(i,j,p) $\equiv I_i^j\, p \rightarrow p$

The agent i is complete regarding j for p iff, if p is true then i informs that p. This is defined by:

$\quad$ complete(i,j,p) $\equiv p \rightarrow I_i^j\, p$

These notions are then used to derive the beliefs of an agent who receives an item of information. For instance, the formula:

I_{AL}^i attack-lethal$\wedge\, K_i$ valid(AL,i, attack-lethal) $\rightarrow K_i$ attack-lethal

is a theorem of this logic. It means that if Colonel al-Adel (AL) said during a radio broadcast that the attack in Dagbas was lethal, and if I strongly believe that al-Adel is valid for that information, then I strongly believe that the attack was lethal. Similarly, the formula:

$-I_{AL}^i$ attack-lethal$\wedge\, K_i$ complete (AL,i, attack-lethal) $\rightarrow K_i \neg$ attack-lethal

---

1 The symbol $\equiv$ means "is by definition".

is a theorem which means that if al-Adel did not say that the attack had killed anyone, and if I strongly believe that al-Adel is complete for that information, then I strongly believe that the attack was not lethal.

8.2.5. *Modal logic and modeling of lying*

The final piece of work which we wish to cite here is that of Philippe Capet [CAP 07] which focuses on the modeling of the notion of lying, and uses a modal logic to do so. Numerous definitions of lying are put forward, and are gradually enriched as the work progresses. In addition to the operator belief B_i, the author considers an operator of intention Int_i (where $Int_i\ \varphi$ means that the agent I intends for φ to be true). Finally, he considers an operator of announcement I_i^j (the author uses the notation $A_i^j\ p$, but for our purposes here it is preferable to conserve the same notation as before), and $I_i^j\ \varphi$ means that agent i tells φ to agent j. Three of the definitions successively put forward in the article are:

(1) $lies(i,p) \equiv I_i^j\, p \wedge \neg\, p$

According to this definition, an agent i is lying when he expresses to an agent j a fact contrary to the truth.

(2) $lies(i,p) \equiv I_i^j\, p \wedge B_i \neg\, p$

According to this definition, an agent i is lying when he states a fact which is contrary to his beliefs.

(3) $lies(i,p) \equiv I_i^j\, p \wedge B_i \neg\, p \wedge Int_i B_j\, p$

According to this definition, a lie is the statement of a fact contrary to the beliefs of the agent making the statement, and who has made it with the intention for his interlocutor to believe that fact. This definition, called elementary lying, can be refined by imagining an inference mechanism in the interlocutor:

(3') *lies(i,p)* ≡ $I_i^j p \land B_i \neg p \land Int_i B_j f(p)$ where $f(p)$ is a fact which depends on *p*, such as $p \land q, \neg p$, etc. This is the case, for example, when specialists announce, although they think the opposite, that the leak from a nuclear power plant will have no effect on water pollution, so that the public will believe that the nuclear plants in the country are safe.

Definition (1), whereby the transmitter is lying if he states something false, characterizes the notion of counter truth more than lying: we are dealing with an inaccurate statement, but there is no judgment saying that the speaker knows the statement to be false. For instance, when the weather forecast on a spoof Website proves to be inaccurate, the site can scarcely be accused of lying.

Definition (2), whereby the transmitter is lying when he states something which he believes to be false, does not prejudge the intention that the speaker has when he says this.

Definition (3), though, adds the intention on the part of the transmitter to make the receiver believe something other than what he himself believes. This final definition is in line with the "most commonly accepted" definition of lying, whereby to lie is to say something which we believe to be false to another person, with the intention for that person to believe it to be true.

8.3. A logical model to decide whether reported information is credible

This section presents the most elaborate logical model which we have hitherto defined to help a user to decide whether or not the reported information is credible.

We consider an agent *i*, information sources and an item of information φ. We shall show that *i* can use his beliefs about the information sources in order to be able to accept φ as a new belief. We shall first examine the case where φ is reported to *i* directly by an information source. Then we shall look at the case where *i* is informed by one source that φ is reported by a second source. In this section, the question which the proposed method should enable us to answer will be:

(Q): can agent i believe φ?

8.3.1. *Logical formalism*

We have taken Demolombe's work as the basis for our study, because *validity* and *completeness* are positive properties in an information acquisition context. Indeed, an information source who is both valid and complete for a piece of information and regarding a given agent communicates to him that information iff the information is true.

However, not all information sources are so perfect, and it is for this reason that we also look at the ("negative") counterparts to these properties, considering that the agents may also be *misinformers* or *falsifiers*. By definition, a misinformer will be an agent who only provides false information. A falsifier will be an agent who reports any false information.

In order to give formal definitions for these properties, we consider a modal logic which is a simplified version of that used in [DEM 04]. The first operators are used to represent the beliefs of the agents. More specifically, if i is an agent and φ is a piece of information, $B_i \varphi$ means that the agent i believes φ. The modalities B_i satisfy (K_B), (D_B) and (Nec_B) mentioned above.

The second operators are used to represent the fact that an agent has reported a piece of information. If i is an agent and φ is a piece of information, $R_i \varphi$ means that the agent i has reported the information φ. The modalities R_i will satisfy the axiomatic:

$$R_i(\varphi \wedge \psi) \leftrightarrow R_i \varphi \wedge R_i \psi$$

(Sub_R) if $p \leftrightarrow q$ then $R_i p \leftrightarrow R_i q$

The operator R_i is unary, and cannot be used to take account of the addressee, unlike the operator I_i^j mentioned earlier on, which is perfectly appropriate for modeling acts of communication such as public announcements.

The four properties of sources which we shall consider are therefore defined by:

$$\text{valid}(i,\varphi) \equiv R_i\,\varphi \to \varphi$$

$$\text{misinformer}(i,\varphi) \equiv R_i\,\varphi \to \neg\,\varphi$$

$$\text{complete}(i,\varphi) \equiv \varphi \to R_i\varphi$$

$$\text{falsifier}\ (i,\varphi) \equiv \neg\varphi \to R_i\,\varphi$$

It is noteworthy that the properties which we are considering here are all in the form of conditionals. Each property is conditioned by the fact that the agent reports (or does not report) a piece of information.

In addition, note that:

$$R_i\,\varphi \wedge (R_i\,\varphi \to \neg\varphi) \text{ is equivalent to } R_i\,\varphi \wedge \neg\varphi$$

We can conclude from this that a misinformer for φ is a liar (according to the first definition given in section 8.2.5) when he reports φ. A misinformer for φ is therefore a potential liar.

Note also that:

$$\neg R_i\,\varphi \wedge (\neg R_i\,\varphi \to \varphi) \text{ is equivalent to } \neg R_i\,\varphi \wedge \varphi$$

The behavior of a falsifier for φ is therefore similar to the behavior of the liar by omission, because he does not say that which is true.

8.3.2. *One level of imbrication*

In this section, the agent i is in direct contact with the information source, here denoted as j, who does or does not deliver the information. There are therefore two cases.

First case

Assume $B_i R_j \varphi$. That is, j has reported the information φ and i is informed of it. The following proposition answers the question *(Q)*.

PROPOSITION 8.1.– The following formulae are theorems and their premises are exclusive.

$$B_i R_j \varphi \wedge B_i \text{ valid } (j,\varphi) \rightarrow B_i \varphi$$

$$B_i R_j \varphi \wedge B_i \text{ misinformer } (j,\varphi) \rightarrow B_i \neg \varphi$$

This means that if i believes that j has reported φ and if i believes j to be valid (or respectively a misinformer) for φ, then i can conclude that φ is true (or respectively false). In addition, if i believes that j has reported φ, then he cannot believe that j is both valid and a misinformer for φ.

Second case

Assume $B_i \neg R_j \varphi$. That is, i believes that j has not reported the piece of information φ. The following proposition answers the question *(Q)*.

PROPOSITION 8.2.– The following formulae are theorems and their premises are exclusive.

$$B_i \neg R_j \varphi \wedge B_i \text{ complete}(j,\varphi) \rightarrow B_i \neg \varphi$$

$$B_i \neg R_j \varphi \wedge B_i \text{ falsifier}(j,\varphi) \rightarrow B_i \varphi$$

This means that if i believes that j has not reported φ, but he considers j to be complete (or respectively a falsifier) for φ, then he can conclude that φ is false (or respectively true). Furthermore, if i believes that j has not reported φ, then he cannot believe that j is both complete and is a falsifier for φ.

8.3.3. *Two levels of imbrication*

In this section we consider that the agent is not in direct contact with the information source, whom we denote as k here, but rather that he only receives information through an intermediary source whom we shall call j. There are four cases.

First case

Assume $B_i R_j R_k \varphi$. That is, i believes that j has reported that k had reported φ. The following proposition answers the question *(Q)*.

PROPOSITION 8.3.– The following formulae are theorems and their premises are exclusive.

– $B_i R_j R_k \varphi \land B_i \text{valid}(j, R_k \varphi) \land B_i \text{valid}(k,\varphi) \rightarrow B_i \varphi$

– $B_i R_j R_k \varphi \land B_i \text{valid}(j, R_k \varphi) \land B_i \text{misinformer}(k,\varphi) \rightarrow B_i \neg\varphi$

– $B_i R_j R_k \varphi \land B_i \text{misinformer}(j, R_k \varphi) \land B_i \text{complete}(k,\varphi) \rightarrow B_i \neg\varphi$

– $B_i R_j R_k \varphi \land B_i \text{misinformer}(j, R_k \varphi) \land B_i \text{falsifier}(k,\varphi) \rightarrow B_i \varphi$

In order to illustrate the second point of this proposition, let us return to the example of the report issued by the *Press Ektimo-Agency*: "Minister Balldar declares that 'the so-called Free Resistance of Dagbas could be implicated in this morning's attack'".

If I consider the *Press Ektimo-Agency* to be valid, then I can infer that Balldar has indeed affirmed that the *Free Resistance of Dagbas* was implicated in the attack. However, if I believe the minister to be a misinformer, then I can conclude that the *Free Resistance of Dagbas* was not implicated in the attack.

Second case

Assume $B_i \neg R_j R_k \varphi$. That is, i believes that j has not reported that k had reported φ. The following proposition answers the question *(Q)*.

PROPOSITION 8.4.– The following formulae are theorems and their premises are exclusive.

– $B_i \neg R_j R_k \varphi \wedge B_i$ complete(j, $R_k \varphi$)$\wedge$ B_i complete(k,φ)$\rightarrow B_i \neg\varphi$

– $B_i \neg R_j R_k \varphi \wedge B_i$ complete(j, $R_k \varphi$)$\wedge$ $B_i$falsifier (k,φ)$\rightarrow B_i \varphi$

– $B_i \neg R_j R_k \varphi \wedge B_i$ falsifier(j, $R_k \varphi$)$\wedge$ B_i valid(k,φ)$\rightarrow B_i \varphi$

– $B_i \neg R_j R_k \varphi \wedge B_i$ falsifier(j, $R_k \varphi$)$\wedge$ B_i misinformer (k,φ)$\rightarrow B_{i-}\varphi$

Third case

Assume $B_i R_j \neg R_k \varphi$. That is, *i* believes that *j* has reported that *k* had not reported φ. The following proposition answers the question *(Q)*.

PROPOSITION 8.5.– The following formulae are theorems and their premises are exclusive.

– $B_i R_j \neg R_k\varphi \wedge B_i$ valid(j,$\neg R_k \varphi$)$\wedge$ B_i complete(k,φ)$\rightarrow B_i \neg\varphi$

– $B_i R_j \neg R_k \varphi \wedge B_i$ misinformer (j, $\neg R_k \varphi$)$\wedge$ $B_i$valid (k,φ)$\rightarrow B_i \varphi$

– $B_i R_j \neg R_k \varphi \wedge B_i$ misinformer (j, $\neg R_k \varphi$)$\wedge$ B_i – misinformer (k,φ)$\rightarrow B_i \neg\varphi$

– $B_i R_j \neg R_k \varphi \wedge B_i$ valid(j, $\neg R_k \varphi$)$\wedge$ B_i falsifier(k,φ)$\rightarrow B_i \varphi$

Fourth case

Assume $B_i \neg R_j \neg R_k \varphi$. Put differently, *i* believes that *j* has not reported that *k* had not reported φ. The following proposition answers the question *(Q)*.

PROPOSITION 8.6.– The following formulae are theorems and their premises are exclusive.

– $B_i \neg R_j \neg R_k \varphi \wedge B_i$ complete (j,$\neg R_k \varphi$)$\wedge$ B_i valid(k,φ)$\rightarrow B_i\varphi$

– $B_i \neg R_j \neg R_k \varphi \wedge B_i$ complete (j,$\neg R_k \varphi$)$\wedge$ B_i misinformer (k,φ)$\rightarrow B_i \neg\varphi$

– $B_i \neg R_j \neg R_k \varphi \wedge B_i$ falsifier (j,$\neg R_k \varphi$)$\wedge$ B_i complete(k,φ)$\rightarrow B_i \neg\varphi$

– $B_i \neg R_j \neg R_k \varphi \wedge B_i$ falsifier (j,$\neg R_k \varphi$)$\wedge$ B_i falsifier(k,φ)$\rightarrow B_i \varphi$

8.3.4. *Conclusion about the logical model*

The logical model presented in this section demonstrates the fact that our trust in a reported piece of information depends on our belief about the properties of the information sources reporting it. This model considers four major properties of sources: two "positive" (validity, completeness) and two "negative" (the fact of being a misinformer and the fact of being a falsifier).

The above results also show that even supposing negative properties about the information sources may enable us, in certain cases, to trust the information provided (or trust the contrary).

We can show that the four properties considered here are the only conditional properties which link the act of reporting (or not reporting) a piece of information and the fact of that information being true (or false).

However, this model says nothing about how the agent receiving the information can determine the properties of the sources. This central question, although it is outside of the domain of the model, could begin to be answered if we take account of the sources' past behavior, their reputation, etc.

8.4. Taking account of uncertainty. A model for estimating the degree of credibility of a reported piece of information

The aforementioned model, based on a modal logic, enables an agent to reason in a binary manner with the beliefs that he has in relation to the various sources. No form of uncertainty can be taken into account. However, we would like an agent to be able to have graduated beliefs and possibly even ignorance, about the fact that a source is valid, a misinformer, complete and a falsifier. This is why we shall consider another type of formalism – the theory of evidence – which will enable us to take account of a certain form of degrees of belief and ignorance.

In section 8.7, the reader will find the main notions and notations in this theory.

Once again, we shall consider an agent i, information sources and an item of information φ. The question we shall attempt to answer this time is:

(Q): to what degree is it possible for i to believe φ?

8.4.1. *The numerical model*

We consider a classical propositional language, whereby the two letters φ and $R_j\,\varphi$ respectively represent the fact "the information φ is true" and "the agent j has reported φ".

DEFINITION 8.1.– *Consider two agents i and j and an item of information φ. Let $d_j \in [0,1]$ and $d'_j \in [0,1]$ be two real numbers such that $0 \le d_j + d'_j \le 1$. d_j is the degree to which i thinks that j is valid for φ and d'_j is the degree to which i thinks that j is a misinformer for φ iff i's beliefs are modeled by the mass function $m^{VD(i, j, \varphi, dj, d'j)}$ defined by:*

$$- m^{VD(i, j, \varphi, dj, d'j)} (R_j\,\varphi \rightarrow \varphi) = d_j$$

$$- m^{VD(i, j, \varphi, dj, d'j)} (R_j\,\varphi \rightarrow \neg\varphi) = d'_j$$

$$- m^{VD(i, j, \varphi, dj, d'j)} (True) = 1\text{-} (d_j + d'_j)$$

According to this definition, if i believes to the degree d_j that j is valid for φ and believes to the degree d'_j that j is a misinformer for φ, then his degree of belief in the fact "if j reports φ *then* φ is true" is d_j and his degree of belief in the fact "if j reports φ then φ is false" *is d'_j.* His degree of ignorance is *$1\text{-} (d_j + d'_j)$.*

NOTATION 8.1.– To simplify, we shall say that we have *VD(i, j, φ, d_j, d'_j))* to say that *i* believes to the degree d_j that j is valid for φ *and* believes to the degree d'_j that j is a misinformer for φ.

DEFINITION 8.2.– *Consider two agents i and j and an item of information φ. Let $c_j \in [0,1]$ and $c'_j \in [0,1]$ be two real numbers such that $0 \le c_j + c'_j \le 1$. c_j is the degree to which i thinks that j is complete* *for φ and c'_j is the degree to which i believes that j is a falsifier for φ if fi's beliefs are modeled by the mass function* $m^{CF(i, j, \varphi, cj, c'j)}$ *defined by:*

$$- m^{CF(i, j, \varphi, cj, c'j)} (\varphi \to R_j\varphi) = c_j$$

$$- m^{CF(i, j, \varphi, cj, c'j)} (\neg\varphi \to R_j\varphi) = c'_j$$

$$- m^{CF(i, j, \varphi, cj, c'j)} (True) = 1 - (c_j + c'_j)$$

According to this definition, if i believes to the degree c_j that j is complete for φ and believes to the degree c'_j that j is a falsifier for φ, then his degree of belief in the fact "if φ is true then j reports φ" is c_j and his degree of belief in the fact "if φ is false then j reports φ" is c'_j. His degree of ignorance is $1 - (c_j + c'_j)$.

NOTATION 8.2.– For simplicity's sake, we shall say that we have $CF(i, j, \varphi, c_j, c'_j)$) to say that i believes to the degree c_j that j is complete for φ and believes to the degree c'_j that j is a falsifier for φ.

8.4.2. *One level of imbrication*

Let us first give a number of preliminary definitions.

DEFINITION 8.3.– m^{VDCF} *is the mass function defined by:*[2]

$$- m^{VDCF} = m^{VD(i, j, \varphi, dj, d'j)} \oplus m^{CF(i, j, \varphi, cj, c'j)}$$

This mass function represents i's beliefs in the fact that j is valid, a misinformer, complete or a falsifier.

DEFINITION 8.4.– m^{ψ} *is the mass function defined by:* $m^{\psi} (\psi) = 1$.

In particular, $m_i^{Rj\varphi}$ represents the fact that the agent i is certain that j has reported φ and $m_i^{\neg Rj\varphi}$ *represents the fact that the agent* i is certain that j *has not* reported φ.

---

2 See section 8.7.2 for the explanation of the symbol $\oplus$.

First case

Assume that the agent i is certain that j has reported φ. In this case, i's beliefs are modeled by: $m = m^{VDCF} \oplus m_i^{Rj\varphi}$

PROPOSITION 8.7.– Let Bel be the belief function associated with the mass function m. Then: $Bel(\varphi) = d_j$ and $Bel(\neg\varphi) = d'_j$

Consequently, when we have *VD(i, j, φ, d_j, d'_j) and CF(i, j, φ, c_j, c'_j)* and when i knows that j has reported φ then we can conclude that i believes φ more than $\neg\varphi$ iff $d_j > d'_j$, i.e. if his degree of belief in the validity of j is greater than his degree of belief in the fact that j is a misinformer.

Let us highlight the following two particular cases:

1) When $d_j=1$ and $d'_j=0$ then $Bel(\varphi)=1$ and $Bel(\neg\varphi) = 0$. That is to say, i believes φ.

2) When $d_j=0$ and $d'_j=1$ then $Bel(\varphi)=0$ and $Bel(\neg\varphi) = 1$. That is to say, i believes $\neg\varphi$.

The results are therefore the same as those for proposition 1.

Second case

Assume that the agent i is certain that j has not reported φ. In this case, i's beliefs are modeled by: $m = m^{VDCF} \oplus m_i^{\neg Rj\varphi}$

PROPOSITION 8.8.– Let Bel be the belief function associated with the mass function m. Therefore: $Bel(\varphi) = c'_j$ and $Bel(\neg\varphi) = c_j$

Consequently, when we have *VD(i, j, φ, d_j, d'_j) and CF(i, j, φ, c_j, c'_j)* and when i knows that j has not reported φ then we can conclude that i believes φ *more than* $\neg\varphi$ iff $c'_j > c_j$, i.e. if his degree of belief in j's completeness is lesser than his degree of belief in the fact that j is a falsifier.

Let us highlight the following two particular cases:

1) When $c_j=1$ and $c'_j=0$ then $\text{Bel}(\varphi)=0$ and $\text{Bel}(\neg\varphi)=1$. That is to say, i believes $\neg\varphi$;

2) When $c_j=0$ and $c'_j=1$ then $\text{Bel}(\varphi)=1$ and $\text{Bel}(\neg\varphi)=0$. That is, i believes φ.

The results are therefore the same as those for proposition 2.

8.4.3. *Two levels of imbrication*

Similarly to in section 8.3.2, we consider that the agent i is not in direct contact with the information source whom we shall call k, but that he only receives information through an intermediary source, j.

In order to answer the question *(Q)*, we consider a propositional language, whose letters are : φ, $R_k\,\varphi$, $R_jR_k\,\varphi$, $R_j\,\neg R_k\,\varphi$, respectively representing "the information φ is true", "the agent k has reported φ", "the agent j has reported that the agent k had reported φ" and "the agent j has reported that agent k had not reported φ".

There are still four cases. We shall detail only the first.

Note that in this section, we shall use the following mass function VDCF:

$$m^{VDCF} = m^{VD(i,\,j,Rk\varphi,\,dj,\,d'j)} \oplus m^{CF(i,\,j,\,Rk\varphi,\,cj,\,c'j)} \oplus m^{VD(i,\,k,\,\varphi,\,dk,\,d'k)} \oplus m^{CF(i,\,k,\,\varphi,\,ck,\,c'k)}$$

This mass function represents the beliefs that i has about the fact that j is valid/complete/a misinformer or falsifier on the subject of the information "k has reported φ" and his beliefs about the fact that k is valid/complete/a misinformer or falsifier on the subject of the information φ.

First case

Assume that i believes that j has reported that k reported φ. In other words, i's beliefs are modeled by the mass function: $m = m^{VDCF} \oplus m_i^{RjRk\varphi}$.

PROPOSITION 8.9.– Let Bel represent the belief function associated with m. We have:

– $Bel(\varphi) = d_k.c'_k + d_k.d_j - d_k.c_k.d_j - d_k.c'_k.d'_j + c'_k.d_j$

– $Bel(\neg\varphi) = d'_k.c_k + d'_k.d_j - d'_k.c_k.d_j + c_k.d'_j - d'_k.c_k.d'_j$

In order to illustrate this proposition, let us return to the example of the report published by the *Press Ektimo-Agency*:

"Minister Balldar declares that the *Free Resistance of Dagbas* is implicated in this morning's attack".

If my degree of belief in the fact that the *Press Ektimo-Agency* is valid (or respectively complete) is 0.8, if my degree of belief in the fact that it is a misinformer (or respectively a falsifier) is 0.1, if my degree of belief in the fact that Balldar is valid (or respectively complete) is 0.1 and if my degree of belief in the fact that he is a misinformer (or respectively a falsifier) is 0.8, then we can verify that my degree of belief in the information the "the *Free Resistance of Dagbas* is implicated in the attack" is lower than my degree of belief in the contrary. I will therefore tend to conclude that the *Free Resistance of Dagbas* is not implicated in the attack.

PROPOSITION 8.10.–

1) If VD(i, j, Rk φ, 1, 0) and VD(i, k, φ, 1, 0) then Bel(φ) = 1 and Bel($\neg\varphi$) = 0

2) If VD(i, j, Rk φ, 1, 0) and VD(i, k, φ, 0, 1) then Bel(φ) = 0 and Bel($\neg\varphi$) = 1

3) If VD(i, j, Rk φ, 0, 1) and CF(i, k, φ, 1, 0) then Bel(φ) = 0 and Bel($\neg\varphi$) = 1

4) If VD(i, j, Rk φ, 0, 1) and CF(i, k, φ, 0, 1) then Bel(φ) = 1 and Bel($\neg\varphi$) = 0

The results are the same as those yielded by proposition 3 in the case with no uncertainty.

8.4.4. *Conclusion about the numerical model*

The above results show that the numerical model suggested in this section is a generalization of the logical model. Being richer, thanks to the mass functions, it enables us to quantify the belief that the receiving agent has in the fact that a particular source has a specific property, and also to quantify his ignorance.

The main limitation to this model lies in the choice of those masses. Put differently, what enables the user to quantify his degrees of belief? The validation of this model on applicative cases should be based on this question.

8.5. Use of the logical model to generate hypotheses about the information sources

8.5.1. *Motivation*

Let us return to the logical model described in section 8.3. We have shown that this model enables a user to decide, on the basis of hypotheses made about the properties of the information sources, whether or not to accept a piece of information reported to him as a new belief. In this section, we wish to show that the same model can be used by the user to determine the hypotheses which he can make about the properties of the sources in order to accept a piece of reported information as a new belief.

We shall illustrate this by way of an example, and consider that an agent, *a*, receives the following two pieces of information:

– according to the Press Ektimo Agency, the minister Balldar has stated that the Free Resistance of Dagbas is implicated in the attack;

– according to the Ektimostan Free Press, the Free Resistance of Dagbas is not implicated in the attack.

The new problem which we deal with in this section is that of finding the properties which the agent *a* can suppose about the different sources – the Press Ektimo Agency (PEA), the minister

Balldar (B), the Ektimostan Free Press (EFP) – to conclude that the *Free Resistance of Dagbas* is implicated in the attack.

This problem is formalized as follows. Consider Σ, φ_0, BB_a defined by:

- $\Sigma = \{ \text{valid}(i,\varphi) \leftrightarrow (R_i\,\varphi \rightarrow \varphi),$

  $\text{misinformer}(i,\varphi) \leftrightarrow (R_i\,\varphi \rightarrow \neg\,\varphi),$

  $\text{complete}(i,\varphi) \leftrightarrow (\varphi \rightarrow R_i\,\varphi),$

  $\text{falsifier}\,(i,\varphi) \leftrightarrow (\neg\varphi \rightarrow R_i\,\varphi)\ \}$

- φ_0 the proposition: the Free Resistance of Dagbas is implicated in the attack.

- $BB_a = \{ B_a\,R_{PEA}R_B\varphi_0,\ B_a\,R_{EFP}\neg\varphi_0 \}$

Finding the properties that the agent a can suppose the various sources to have, in order to reach the conclusion that the *Free Resistance of Dagbas* is implicated in the attack, involves seeking formulae H in the form $B_a\ valid(PEA, ...)$, $B_a\ valid(B, ...)$, $B_a valid(EFP, ...)$ $B_a misinformer(PEA, ...)$, etc. such that:

- $(\alpha)\ \Sigma \cup BB_a \cup \{H\} \models B_a\,\varphi_0$

Our goal here, then, is to seek out the missing premises for a given conclusion. This approach is known as abductive reasoning.[3]

However, certain formulae H which satisfy *(α)* are not "interesting" answers. For instance, any formula H which contradicts $\Sigma \cup BB_a$, satisfies *(α)* but is of no interest, because it characterizes a hypothesis which is impossible (given the agent's beliefs). Similarly,

---

3 *Abductive* reasoning – a term introduced by Peirce [BUC 55] – consists of seeking plausible explanations for observations. The study of this problem in artificial intelligence was introduced by Morgan [MOR 71] and Pople [POP 73] and numerous works have been devoted to the complexity of this reasoning, or to ways of automating it.

if H_1 and H_2 are two hypotheses which satisfy *(a)* and which are such that $|=H_1 \rightarrow H_2$, then it not helpful to consider H_1 in addition to H_2, because H_1 is a weaker hypothesis than H_2.

8.5.2. *An algorithm to generate responses*

We are therefore dealing with a problem of abduction, in the context of a modal logic. Rather than adapt an algorithm of abductive reasoning in modal logic to our particular modal logic [CIA 94], we preferred to translate the problem in to the context of classical logic and re-use a well-known algorithm, which is valid and complete to perform abductive reasoning [INO 92]. This algorithm is based on an inference rule, SOL-Resolution. It is capable of generating all logical consequences of a set of clauses which satisfy a certain property (for example, belonging to a certain language) and therefore all the lacking interesting premises for a given conclusion. Indeed, the link between abduction and generation of consequences is evident when we note that:

$$(\alpha)\ \Sigma \cup BB_a \cup H |= B_a \varphi_0$$

is equivalent to

$$(\beta)\ \Sigma \cup BB_a \cup \neg B_a \varphi_0 |= \neg H$$

We shall not go into detail about this algorithm here. However, we shall illustrate its application below.

8.5.3. *Illustration*

We return now to the two pieces of information stated in section 8.5.1.

BBa is coded in first-order logic by the two clauses:

1) believe(a, reports(PEA, reports(B, φ_0)));

2) believe(a, reports(EFP, nonφ_0)).

$B_a \varphi_0$ is coded by:

1) believe(a, φ_0).

The results produced by the algorithm are:

1) believe(a, misinformer (EFP, nonφ_0));

2) believe(a, valid(B, φ_0)) and believe(a, valid(PEA, reports(B, φ_0)));

3) believe(a, falsifier(B, nonφ_0)) and believe(a, misinformer (PEA, reports(B, φ_0))).

In other words, the agent *a* can conclude that the *Free Resistance of Dagbas* is implicated in the attack if one of the following conditions is satisfied:

1) *a* thinks that the *EFP* is lying;

2) *a* thinks that the *PEA* and B are both telling the truth;

3) *a* thinks that the *PEA* is lying (i.e. that Balldar did not say φ_0) and that B is a falsifier for not(φ_0) (Balldar would have said φ_0 if φ_0 were false).

8.5.4. *Conclusion about the generation of hypotheses*

The process described in this section, based on abductive reasoning, can be used to find plausible hypotheses about the properties of the sources to accept a reported piece of information as a new belief.

Once these hypotheses have been obtained, the user can attempt to confirm or invalidate them. In other words, this process is at the heart of a mechanism for seeking information about the sources.

In the above example, the user has three options: he can seek to verify that the EFP is lying, or that PEA and B are both telling the truth, or indeed that the PEA is lying and B is a falsifier. It is sufficient for one of his checks to return a positive result for him to conclude that the *Free Resistance of Dagbas is implicated in the attack.*

8.6. Conclusion

Any rational agent acquiring information must carefully consider whether to accept that information as a new belief or whether to reject it.

The issue is all the more tricky because the information sources may be imperfect, and may not tell the truth or indeed lie. In addition, the sources may not directly give the information of interest, but rather cite other sources.

It is in this complex context which we touch upon the question of information evaluation. The logical model presented in this chapter enables the agent to infer, on the basis of a certain number of hypotheses about the sources, whether he can accept a reported piece of information. It is also able to provide the agent, by abductive reasoning, with the hypotheses which he can make about the information sources in order to accept a reported piece of information as a new belief.

The numerical extension of this model which we elaborated enables us to introduce a certain form of uncertainty. More specifically, it enables the agent acquiring the information to quantify his belief about the properties of the sources.

Yet this model could benefit from being extended to take account of the uncertainty which the sources have about the information which they are delivering. This would enable us to use it to deal with more realistic cases, such as the report:

"Minister Balldar has affirmed that the Free Resistance of Dagbas could be implicated in the attack"

or the report:

"Minister Balldar is believed to have stated that the Free Resistance of Dagbas is implicated in the attack"

In the first report, the uncertainty is Balldar's uncertainty about who is responsible for the attack. In the second, the uncertainty is that of the press agency about Balldar's remarks.

Modeling this type of uncertainty and adding it into the existing model is one of our next activities. One possible solution would be to combine the model proposed here with the model proposed in Chapter 7.

Another task would be to compare our solution to the expression of uncertainty about the sources, against the model defined in [DUB 97] in possibilistic logic, and also with the model defined in [DEM 09], which advanced a qualitative approach to graded beliefs, although neither of these works deals with reported information.

8.7. Supplements

8.7.1. *Main notions of logic*

Mathematical logic provides us with formal tools to describe statements and reason about those statements. The choice of which type of logic to use depends on the complexity of the statements being handled and on the complexity of the reasoning needing to be done. We shall limit ourselves to propositional logic here.

8.7.1.1. *Language and formulae*

In the simplest case, it is sufficient to use conventional propositional logic, whose *language* is propositional, and comprises:

– an enumerable set of propositional letters;

– connectors: $\neg$ (negation), $\wedge$ (conjunction), $\vee$ (disjunction), $\rightarrow$ (implication), $\leftrightarrow$ (equivalence);

– parentheses ().

In certain cases, in order to be accurate, we have to use a modal propositional logic, whose language also contains one or more modalities (in the successive sections of the article we are introduced to the modalities B_i, K_i, I_i^j, R_i). In what follows, for simplicity's sake, we shall consider only one modality, represented by the box symbol $\square$.

The set of properly-formed formulas (or formulae) is the smallest set such that: if a is a letter, a is a formula; $\neg A$ is a formula if A is a formula; $A \wedge B$ is a formula if A and B are formulae. $\square A$ is a formula if A is a formula. Other formulae are defined by abbreviation: $A \vee B$ denotes $\neg(\neg A \wedge \neg B)$; $A \rightarrow B$ denotes $\neg A \vee B$; $A \leftrightarrow B$ denotes $((A \rightarrow B) \wedge (B \rightarrow A))$.

8.7.1.2. Interpretation

In the case of classical propositional logic, *an interpretation* i is a function which associates, with any propositional letter, a truth value in the set $\{0,1\}$. An interpretation i can be extended to the set of formulae by: $i(\neg A) = 1 - i(A)$; $i(A \wedge B) = 1$ iff $i(A) = 1$ and $i(B) = 1$. Consequently, $i(A \vee B) = 1$ iff $i(A) = 1$ or $i(B) = 1$; $i(A \rightarrow B) = 1$ iff $i(A) = 0$ or $i(B) = 1$; $i(A \leftrightarrow B) = 1$ iff $i(A) = i(B)$.

In the case of modal logic, or of predicate logic, the notion of interpretation is slightly more complex, but does not warrant going into detail here.

8.7.1.3. Logical consequence

Let E be a set of formulae and A a formula. We say that A *is a logical consequence* of E iff any interpretation which satisfies the formulae of E also satisfies A. This is represented as $E \models A$.

8.7.1.4. Deduction theorem

An important property which is used in that article (in section 8.5) is the deduction theorem, valid for classical (non-modal) logic recapped below:

Let A and B be two formulae and E a set of formulae:

$$E \cup \{A\} \models B \text{ iff } E \cup \{\neg B\} \models \neg A$$

8.7.2. *Main notions from the Theory of Evidence*

This theory offers formal tools to quantify the uncertainty that an agent may have about particular hypotheses. The peculiarity of this theory in comparison to probability theory is that it does not satisfy the property of additivity (the degree of belief in a set of hypotheses is not dependent upon the degrees of belief in those hypotheses individually), and that it can therefore be used to model ignorance (we can attribute a degree of belief in the union of all the hypotheses independently of the degrees of belief in those hypotheses).

This theory considers a *frame of discernment* $\Theta = \{\theta_1..., \theta_n\}$ whose elements are called *hypotheses* and are supposed to be exhaustive and exclusive.

A *mass function* is a function m: $2^\Theta \rightarrow [0,1]$ such that: $m(\emptyset) = 0$ and $\Sigma_{A \subseteq \Theta}$ $m(A)=1$. Based on a mass function, we can define:

– a *belief function*: Bel: $2^\Theta \rightarrow [0,1]$ by: $Bel(A) = \Sigma_{B \subseteq A}$ m(B);

– a *plausibility function*: Pl: $2^\Theta \rightarrow [0,1]$ by: Pl $(A) = 1 - Bel(\Theta - A)$.

In this theory, various *rules of combination* have been constructed, to combine two mass functions and produce a new one. The first of these rules to be defined is *Dempster's rule of combination*, notated as $\oplus$. It is as follows.

Consider m_1 and m_2 to be two mass functions on the frame of discernment Θ. The mass function obtained by combining m_1 and m_2 by applying the rule $\oplus$ is notated as $m_1 \oplus m_2$ and is defined by:

$$m_1 \oplus m_2 (\emptyset) = 0;$$

$$m_1 \oplus m_2 (C) = \Sigma_{A \cap B = C}\, m_1(A).m_2(B)/N \text{ for all values of } C \neq \emptyset;$$

where N is the normalization factor: $N = \Sigma_{A \cap B \neq \emptyset}\, m_1(A).m_2(B)$.

A logical version of the Theory of Evidence has recently been proposed [CHO 13] in which masses can be assigned to propositional formulas rather than to exclusive and exhaustive hypotheses.

Combination rule is redefined accordingly. This logical version is not more powerful than the initial version of the theory, but it enables us to assign masses to more compact expressions. This is the logical version which has been applied in this paper.

8.8. Bibliography

[BUC 55] BUCHLER J., *Philosophical writings of Peirce*, Dover, New York 1955.

[CAP 06] CAPET P., Logique du mensonge, Doctoral thesis, Université Paris 3, 2006.

[CHA 73] CHANG C.L., LEE R.C.T., *Symbolic Logic and mathematical Theorem Proving*, Computer Science Classics, Academic Press, London, 1973.

[CHE 80] CHELLAS B.F., *Modal logic: An introduction*, Cambridge University Press, Cambridge, 1980.

[CHO 10] CHOLVY L., "Evaluation of information reported: a model in the theory of evidence", *Information Processing and Management of Uncertainty(IPMU'2010)*, Dortmund, June 2010.

[CHO 11a] CHOLVY L., "How strong can an agent believe reported information?", *11th European Conference on Symbolic and Quantitative Approaches to Reasoning with Uncertainty (ECSQARU 2011)*, Belfast, 2011.

[CHO 11b] CHOLVY L., "Reasoning with information reported by imperfect agents", *First International Workshop on Uncertainty Reasoning and Multi-agent Systems for Sensor Networks (URNMASS'2011)*, Belfast, July 2011.

[CHO 12] CHOLVY L., "Collecting information reported by imperfect information sources", *Information Processing and Management of Uncertainty (IPMU'2012)*, Catania, Sicily, July 2012.

[CHO 13] CHOLVY L., "Logical representation of belief in the belief function theory", IJCAI-*Workshop on Weighted Logics for Artificial Intelligence (WL4AI)*, Beijing, China, August 2013.

[CIA 94] CIALDEA MEYER M., PIERRI F., "Propositional abduction in modal logic", *Journal of IGPL*, 1994.

[DEM 04] DEMOLOMBE R., "Reasoning about trust: a formal logical framework", *2nd International Conference iTrust*, Oxford, 2004.

[DEM 09] DEMOLOMBE R., "Graded trust", *Workshop on Trust in Agent Societies*, Budapest, 2009.

[DUB 97] DUBOIS D., PRADE H., "Valid or Complete information in databases. A possibility theory-based analysis", *8th International Conference on Database and Expert Systems Applications (DEXA'97) LNCS*, no. 1 308, Springer, Berlin, 1997.

[INO 92] INOUE K., "Linear resolution for consequence finding", *Artificial Intelligence*, vol. 56, no. 2–3, pp. 301–353, 1992.

[JAC 07] JACQUELINET J., Pertinence et cotation du renseignement, Report on internship at ENSIIE, supervised by P. Capet, Paris, 2007.

[MOR 71] MORGAN C., "Hypothesis generation by machine", *Artificial Intelligence*, vol. 2, pp. 179–187, 1971.

[NAT 03] NORTH ATLANTIC TREATY ORGANIZATION, "Standardization agreement, intelligence report", *STANAG*, no. 2 511, 2003.

[POP 73] POPLE H., "On the mechanization of abductive logic", *IJCA'73*, pp. 147–152, 1973.

[SHA 76] SHAFER G., *A mathematical Theory of Evidence*, Princeton University Press, Princeton, 1976.

Chapter 9

An Architecture for the Evolution of Trust: Definition and Impact of the Necessary Dimensions of Opinion Making

9.1. Introduction

The evaluation of algorithm performance, computational techniques and methods is full of scores of trust.[1] These scores generally rate the method rather than its output. That is to say, while it is acknowledged that automated processing yields uncertainty and imprecision, classic measurements usually characterize the way in which the information is constructed, rather than qualifying the degree of trust that should be invested in that piece of information. Although it is generally sufficient to know that an extraction algorithm is effective, say, eight times out of ten, or that its production is in line with expectations in the same proportions, once we start dealing with sensitive data, at the root of potentially tragic decisions, we may wish to measure how much to trust the information item rather than have uniform doubt about its construction. Such a measurement should vary with the contents of the information itself, instead of on the basis of the tools used to produce it. Furthermore, if the elaboration method for

---

Chapter written by Adrien REVAULT D' ALLONNES.
1 See Chapter 2 for a detailed analysis of the notion.

this trust indicator is explained, legible or even adaptable, the user can then learn to grasp the system and use its indications in the rest of his intervention. To reach such a goal, it is necessary to introduce a distinction between *rating* – the expressed degree of trust – and *evaluation* – the method used to evaluate trust.

While information evaluation, as it is usually described, often focuses on evaluating the reality of the fact to which it pertains, we propose, in this chapter, to look at how much we can trust a piece of information, independently of the truth of the fact that it reports. Indeed, because it is just as possible to believe that the *Free Resistance of Dagbas* is responsible for the attacks as to believe the contrary, we propose to study the trust which can be placed in the information. This way of looking at the issue raises the question of the construction of trust. Section 9.2 presents a perspective on trust, on the basis of which we build a model for both its establishment and evolution.

9.2. A perspective on trust

How do we form an opinion? What is the process by which we manage to be convinced of something, to make our mind up? The process is simple and more or less universal: find reliable sources, cross-reference what they say and then extract the viewpoint which most closely corresponds to your convictions, knowledge and interests. From there, new questions emerge. How are we to estimate the reliability of a source? How do we resolve eventual conflicts between reliable sources? How many confirmations do we need before being convinced? Can these certainties be revised?

With regard to information in general, many wise people tend to trust what is generally called "the media" and what, in intelligence terminology, are referred to as "open sources". On a daily basis, *compendia* of open sources are created by operators specializing in particular subjects. Journalists, representatives of the fourth power according to Tocqueville [TOC 35], offer summaries and other press reviews, addressed to the impatient rest of the world. All of them apply the same process: first find the information and then verify it [BAU 02; SIM 05]. Making certain that it comes from a reliable and competent source is the first step. Finding other people, other points of view to support it comes later, in order to reinforce the initial trust [BOR 98]. Even scientists look for high-quality references to position their own work [CHE 07].

Therefore, trust is a subject of major interest. In its broadly-accepted sense, it applies in equal measure to people ("Spontaneous or acquired belief in the moral, affective or professional value of another person, which makes it hard to imagine cheating, betrayal or incompetence on their part"), to ourselves ("assuredness that one can have in one's own resources or in one's destiny"), as it does to an object or a piece of information: "Credit, faith [...] attached to someone or something".[2] Be it the question of trust between individuals or of the conviction that a piece of information is correct, all decisions integrate it, in one way or another. The consideration of sensitive subjects and the decisions which stem from it further increase the need for a reliable, comprehensible and revisable indicator of trust.

In this chapter we propose to give an unambiguous definition of the dimensions upon which trust is built and then describe the architecture of the combination of these dimensions. Finally, we show that the flexibility of the model enables it to be adapted to suit any evaluator. The aim of the proposed model is to provide its users with a bounded and interpretable view of the constitution of trust. The reader will, of course, understand that we do not mean to impose this model as the unequivocal truth behind this central point of human reasoning.

9.3. Dimensions of information evaluation

Let us now present the dimensions we choose to perform information evaluation – an extension of our proposed system in [BES 08]. Our propositions originally stem from the existing criteria, presented in Tables 4.1 and 4.2. However, they break away from these

---

2 N.B. The definitions proposed here are drawn from the *Trésor de la Langue Française Informatisé – ATILF* (computerized treasury of the French language) – a trustworthy source if ever there were one.

existing criteria in various ways, which we shall discuss here. Among the usual criticisms made of the method for information evaluation such as it is officially defined[3], the most frequently recurring is the difficulty in interpreting and grasping the results [CHO 03; CHO 04; NIM 04]. We propose to resolve the first of these points by giving the user a unique numerical value expressing the confidence that he can have in a piece of information: its rating. Giving a value on a graded scale enables comparisons to be made between different pieces of information and sorted by level of trust: a substantial improvement on the current approach.

Our objective of readability in terms of the rating and the evaluation process is not limited to the way in which they are presented. We will, additionally, clarify the factors which we propose to use to evaluate information. In general, the quality a piece of information is measured by its conformity to a model whose quality is also guaranteed [BAT 06]. This search for quality therefore takes place in two stages. First, we produce a model capable of accurately representing all the expected information. We then check each piece of information is detailed and not redundant. Obviously, there are many other criteria which make for quality, but the expressiveness of the model and the completeness of the information are unavoidable factors in this domain. Although they are essential for the evaluation of the knowledge contained in the model and the information, these criteria are not meant to evaluate whether or not the user can believe a particular piece of information. A model of excellent quality ensures the knowledge the information describes is complete, interpretable and exploitable. A quality recording in such a model provides a maximum of knowledge. We wish to add to these guarantees of quality an estimation of trust. In order to evaluate this trust, we propose to combine different types of dimensions, some of which bear witness to the process of creation of the information rather than its content.

The factors influencing the trust that we place in a piece of information are not limited to its content. Hence, the dimensions we use for information evaluation do not necessarily pertain to the fact it

---

3 See Chapter 3 for more detail about the place of information evaluation in the military doctrinal corpus.

describes: although a piece of information is supposed to represent a real fact, it is not always possible to verify its realization. The only way in which we can have faith in its veracity is by forming an opinion with the means available, such as its context and its mode of production, its conformity with our knowledge and expectations, or validation by other sources. For instance, in order to find out whether a person is tall, we not only need to measure their height using appropriate tools, but also to have an idea of the distribution of heights in the surrounding population. Also, if that information is reported to us, the first indicators we have upon which to base our belief relate to its source.

Because there is no absolute norm for evaluating how much belief we can invest in a piece of information, we propose to consider the principles governing the elaboration of trust, as mentioned above, in order to clarify the boundaries of the factors involved in information evaluation. The essential questions – although these could doubtless be enriched by others – we propose to use to evaluate the veracity of a piece of information are presented in Table 9.1.

Who is providing it?	What does he know about it?
How likely is it?	Has it been reported elsewhere?

Table 9.1. *Crucial questions influencing the estimation of trust in a piece of information*

The two questions on the upper row relate to the source of the information. They provide the first *a priori* indications about the trust which we can afford a piece of information. Even before someone gives us a piece of information, our trust in him affects the extent to which we are prepared to believe it. Note that this *a priori* indication is related to the source but does not depend on the information, as the trust we have in the source is independent of the subject, similarly to reliability in the current doctrines. After this initialization, the second question relates to the source's qualification to express an opinion on the topic. While it still relates to the source, this capacity varies with what information is being transmitted. In an ideal universe, where the evaluation of the dimensions operates only on fact, then, unlike the previous factor, the evaluator's subjectivity should not influence the speaker's knowledge. Indeed, the trust invested in the source varies from one listener to another, on the basis of the shared history of relations between them, whereas the speaker's abilities regarding a particular subject depend only on him. Any subjective doubts about the source's capabilities should be included in the prior evaluation of trust – at least in the model proposed here.

The remaining two questions relate to the content of the information, and are no longer connected to the source. It goes without saying that the first factor to be considered is how realistic the information looks. Note that it is not a question of verifying its reality – whether the fact described actually happened – but rather of checking its compatibility with the knowledge the evaluator has of the world. Hence, this depends solely on the studied piece of information and the frame of discernment of the user, i.e. the analyst's paradigm of interpretation. The final question, on the other hand, means to verify if the same information is known anywhere else. When dealing with a piece of information which seems unusual, i.e. if the answer to the previous question is nearly negative, and supposing that we cannot easily verify the truth of the assertion, the search for concomitant cross-references or, failing that, for other individuals who believe it, is constitutive of the establishment of faith and trust.

Note that these questions separate the dimensions relating to the source from those relating to the content of the information, in the same vein as the separation between the dimensions of absolute and relative quality of information [BER 99]. The dimensions we use are naturally divided into these categories, where reliability, which is independent of the information itself, is absolute, whereas the others are relative to the piece of information in question. To this distinction, we add another one, based on whether or not the dimension takes the context into account, i.e. if its influence is stable or varies from case to case. Indeed, the separation between questions relating to the source and to the informational content can be further clarified, if we take account of the scope of each criterion. The answers to the above four questions cross the two axes of dependency on the source or on the content of the information, the *contextuality* or *generality* of the dimension. Thus, the four dimensions we propose are distributed in Table 9.2, where reliability deals with the first question, competence with the second, plausibility the third and credibility – a term used in the NATO doctrines [NAT 03] and discussed in Chapter 4 – with the last.

	General	Contextual
Source	Reliability	Competence
Content	Plausibility	Credibility

Table 9.2. *Object and scope of the dimensions of evaluation proposed hereto clarify doctrinal factors*

While we have chosen this way of dividing the dimensions, there are other possible explanations for their independence and non-redundancy. For instance, we can cite the subjectivity of the evaluator: the reliability of the source and the plausibility of the information are two subjective dimensions. Quite evidently, the degree of trust afforded to a source depends on who is consulting that source. The plausibility of the information, envisaged as a degree of compatibility with our existing knowledge of the world, also varies from one person to another. Note here that these restrictions on the subjectivity of the dimensions are questions of measure. Each of the dimensions presented here could be evaluated subjectively but, in order to clarify and standardize the use of the model, we propose to stipulate the methods to be used for their evaluation at the same time as describing their meaning.

The other two dimensions, on the other hand, should, ideally, not be subjective. If it is not known with absolute certainty, the real competence of the source does not depend on who is assessing it. Indeed, we can, for instance, circumvent our doubts about a plumber's competence in electrics by refusing to pass judgment on an unknown factor, thereby avoiding favoring or penalizing the final evaluation. Similarly, the way in which two pieces of information confirm one another does not depend on point of view, but rather on the evaluation method. These axes of separation between the proposed dimensions mean we can consider them not to be redundant, as they do not qualify the same objects and are therefore independent.

We represent the level of activation of each of these dimensions with a separate degree. In order to conform to the doctrinal line, we consider a scale with six levels, but this choice is not limiting. Obviously, these scales may contain more or fewer degrees depending on the intended application. There is no need to stick with the six degrees defined here, although it has been suggested that a scale with more than seven values loses in explicitness what it gains in precision [MIL 55].

In our discussion below, we detail these four dimensions for information evaluation, one by one. For each of them, we offer a definition and an interpretation of the discrete evaluation scale, all presented in Table 9.3. We also illustrate the meaning of each of them using the running example of this book.

A	Totally reliable
B	Usually reliable
C	Fairly reliable
D	Rarely reliable
E	Unreliable
F	Reliability cannot be estimated

Reliability

1	Expert
2	Competent
3	Partially competent
4	Insufficiently competent
5	Incompetent
6	Competence cannot be estimated

Competence

1	Certain
2	Realistic
3	Possible
4	Not very possible
5	Impossible
6	Plausibility cannot be estimated

Plausibility

1	Totally confirmed
2	Partially confirmed
3	Insufficiently confirmed
4	Partially contradicted
5	Totally contradicted
6	Credibility cannot be estimated

Credibility

Table 9.3. *Examples of degrees for the dimensions*

9.4. General evaluation of the source: reliability

The quality of the source is an intrinsic quality of the information, according to the denominations given by [WAN 96] and [BER 99]. It is a crucially-important criterion which usually serves to weight the interpretation of the information. Google's Page Rank algorithm, for one, uses the level of trust accorded to the source (the Website) to sort the responses to a query, given an equal relevance [BRI 98].

We propose to distinguish, in this quality, that which is general from that which is contextual, and here we discuss its general aspect, which we call the *reliability of the source*. This depends neither on the question at hand nor on the information already known, and applies equally to all pieces of information supplied by one source. The reliability of the source therefore qualifies only the source, independently of the information.

It should be noted that this term is frequently used for a variety of notions: it simultaneously encompasses reputation or trust, as we conceive of it, the aptitude of the source to provide the information and any doubts that he has about the information itself [DIS 01; DEP 05]. These concepts of the criterion therefore mix its general components – relating only to the source – and its contextual components – relating to other factors. In the definition we propose, reliability depends only on the source rather than on the considered piece of information. It is, however, well known that reliability depends on the observer's position and, consequently, on who that observer and evaluator is. We shall see in the examples that while the reliability does not depend on the information, it is closely connected to the user.

We propose to express reliability on a scale with five levels, as indicated in Table 9.3, representing the degrees of reliability envisaged and their interpretations. In order to preserve a link with the original scale, we represent these degrees using letters. We have supplemented this scale with a value representing the impossibility of measuring the reliability: the degree F. Indeed, it is possible that the available knowledge about the source may not be enough to estimate his reliability. This occurs, for example, when we encounter a source who has hitherto been unknown to us. The estimated reliability of this contact can therefore be distinguished from that of an interlocutor who is known but whose reliability is medium, i.e. neither weighing in his favor or against him. Such a source will be assigned a level of reliability C. Note that this additional level appears on the scales proposed for each of the criteria considered here, as detailed below.

In addition, we must stress the dynamic nature of a source's reliability, which is bound to evolve over time as the source is consulted and acquires a reputation. Thus, we may learn more about a certain source and wish to re-evaluate his reliability. This updating poses the problem of the change in the evaluation of trust in the information. Two possibilities then arise: we can recalculate that trust or we can retain the current value as an indicator of the time when it was calculated. Of course, these issues only arise for pieces of information emitted since the reliability rating changed. Consider, for instance, a source who we learn, at a date t_b, has suffered from memory problems since a date t_a (where $t_a < t_b$). All information provided between t_a and t_b is affected by this change in reliability. However, the information emitted before t_a need not be re-evaluated.

9.4.1. *Evaluation of reliability in the original scenario*

The evaluation of the respective reliability of the sources in the example running through this book can be delegated to the user, in order to take account of the subjective aspect of this task and facilitate a personalized adaptation. Usbek's intelligence agencies may, *a priori* and independently of all information, assign a maximum reliability rating (level A, completely reliable) to their infiltrated agent and a less high level (e.g. level D, usually not reliable) to the Ektimostanian blogger because of conflicting allegiances.[4]

---

4 See the example in section 4.3 – the case of *d* and *e*.

9.5. Contextual evaluation of the source: competence

Having defined the general aspect of the source, his reliability, we wish to integrate into our process an axis which is often mistaken for reliability. We have seen that, such as we understand it, a source's reliability applies in exactly the same way to all pieces of information produced by that source. However, when considering the influence the source has on the trust we invest in the information that he produces, it is often tempting to include an estimation of his knowledge of the subject area. For instance, one should always take the philosophical musings of specialized scientists *cum grano salis*.

We propose to separate this dimension, which we can say is contextual, from the former concept of reliability. Indeed, the capacity of a source to provide a piece of information depends on the information itself. It is always possible that a source will provide a piece of information outside of his particular area of expertise. Yet a piece of information such as this should not be rejected out of hand for this reason alone; however, the receiver needs to take this into account when classifying the information or evaluating the trust to invest in it.

We call this fact or the *competence of the source*, and propose to measure it with the scale given in Table 9.3. Here we see a level expressing the impossibility of evaluation. Indeed, it may be the case that we are unsure of the extent of a source's areas of expertise. For instance, it is not unheard of for certain IT specialists to have an unexpected cultural grounding in philosophy, and to be perfectly well qualified to share their philosophical knowledge. Again, we propose to distinguish these unexpected experts from those of whose cultural background we are aware.

9.5.1. *Evaluation of competence in the original scenario*

The competence of an infiltrated agent in the pay of Usbek about the situation of the rebel province should be evaluated equally by anyone who has all of the relevant information about the spy's mission. In reality, because he is supposed to keep track of internal maneuverings and shifts within Ektimostan, his observation outside of his field of expertise could justifiably be estimated as "insufficiently competent", which is a rating of 4 in terms of competence level. If the Ektimostan agencies, with the opposite objectives, had the same set of information, they would also attribute a competence of 4 to the enemy agent. An infiltrated agent who has not yet had any experience of an Ektimostanian blogger cannot evaluate that blogger's competence on the subject, so gives him a competence rating of 6.

9.6. General content evaluation: plausibility

Having taken account of the factors about the source influencing the rating, we now turn our attention to the information itself. Once more, we propose to separate the general dimension from another, more contextual one. An essential criterion for belief in a piece of information is its *plausibility*. Even before considering details or confirmations, we reject any information which seems incompatible with our perception of the world. This initial evaluation is done on the basis only of the particular piece of information in question. The search for additional intelligence and confirmation takes place later.

Thus, in the intellectual process from which we draw inspiration, we would not investigate the possible reality of a piece of information which is devoid of all plausibility. This reflex for intellectual preservation is used, for example, by detractors of creationist movements, who propose a contradiction by the absurd, with their Flying Spaghetti Monster [HOR 07].

In order to evaluate the plausibility of a fact, we refer to its compatibility with our knowledge about the world. It is not a question of determining whether or not the fact is genuine, but rather of estimating the degree to which it is possible for it to happen. An example of evaluations for this criterion is presented in Table 9.3. Because it is possible that our knowledge will be insufficient to evaluate the plausibility of a piece of information, we have again chosen to propose a level 6, representing the impossibility of measurement. The major breakthroughs in scientific paradigms have certainly been produced by geniuses who have recognized situations which are not explicable by their present knowledge of the world.

9.6.1. *Evaluation of plausibility in the original scenario*

Thus, plausibility measures the match between the information and our knowledge of the state of the world. Suppose that the analyst dealing with the information from his spy in Ektimostan also knows that the groupuscules identified by his field agent are, in reality, groups of other agents charged with influencing public opinion and that they have received no orders regarding actions to be carried out, he will deem the participation of these factions in attacks to be "impossible" and the plausibility of the information reported will be evaluated as 5. An analyst who has no knowledge of the second plan of infiltration will, in view of the powder keg that the region represents, estimate that the existence and action of such a group are "realistic" and therefore attribute the information a plausibility of 2.

9.7. Contextual content evaluation: credibility

Once we are convinced of the source's capabilities – first in general and then in respect of the information in question – and have verified that the information was not too incompatible with our own knowledge of the world, we generally proceed to verify the fact. When we learn something new, most of us seek to confirm it in order to ensure that it is credible. This phenomenon of confirmation-seeking undoubtedly partly explains the success of search engines, constructed on the basis of the most frequent requests, and possibly also certain "buzz" phenomena. This verification is a search for correlation and corroboration of the as-yet-unknown information, preferably from reliable and competent sources. What we are looking for is the *credibility* of the information.

Because of the maximum degree of veracity on the existing information evaluation grid[5], we choose to evaluate it as an indicator of confirmation by the pieces of information acquired. We must stress that the facts against which we compare the information being studied are themselves subjected to the same evaluation procedure. They are all drawn from more or less reliable, more or less competent sources,

---

5 See section 4.4.2.1.

and their plausibility is undoubtedly comparable to that of the information being examined. With each confirmation or invalidation, the combination of the *a priori* degrees of trust (i.e. the rating resulting from the previous dimensions) weights the impact of the confirmation and finally enables us to establish whether or not to believe the information. In addition, the pieces of information against which we contrast that which we are evaluating also benefit from this update. This corresponds to the quality relating to homologous data, such as described by [BER 99]. However, credibility, as an indicator of confirmation, does not depend on the *a priori* rating. This rating relies on the impact of the confirmation rather than on its measurement. The credibility will therefore be evaluated using measures of correspondence or conflict with the other pieces of information, and then integrated by combining them with their ratings.

Let us again highlight the distinction drawn between the comparisons between acquired pieces of information and their compatibility with the reasoning model. The pieces of information that we compare by evaluating the credibility are all constructed and therefore all have a changeable indicator of trust, unlike our knowledge of the world, whose level of trust is assumed to be fixed and maximal.

Table 9.3 presents the different levels on which we propose to evaluate credibility. Of particular note among these degrees of confirmation are partial confirmation and partial invalidation (levels 2 and 4). We have put forward a cumulative procedure for gaining confirmation, whereby it is not necessary to be confirmed solely by definite pieces of information in order to achieve maximum credibility [REV 07]. The accumulation of enough confirmations by less certain pieces of information yields the same result, although less quickly, as detailed in [REV 11]. However, that which is denoted by partial confirmation and invalidation relates more closely to the question of evaluation of the correlation between pieces of information. Anyone who has ever sought confirmation of a complex piece of news knows that it is rare to find complete and perfect confirmation, particularly if we insist on its coming from independent sources. It may also arise that we cannot find the link between two pieces of information although we suspect they relate to the same subject. This stems from the boundary maintained between co-occurrences, coincidences and confirmations, as anyone attempting to fix a system outside his own specialty well knows. For such cases, we again propose an inestimable, level 6: credibility.

9.7.1. *Evaluation of credibility in the original scenario*

Each of the pieces of information in the multi-source scenario therefore has an *a priori* rating. When looking for corroboration, we need to measure the degree to which two pieces of information confirm one another, e.g. the declarations of the Ektimostanian leaders, who confirm one another perfectly; those of Captain Ixil and the infiltrated field agent, which go in the same direction without absolutely echoing one another; or which contradict each other, as do those of Ixil and al-Adel.

9.8. Global expression of trust

On the basis of the four dimensions defined and described in the previous sections, our procedure outputs a degree of trust associated with the information in question: its rating. This rating expresses the combination of the above criteria, in a unique and comparable rating. We propose to express the rating as shown in Table 9.4.

1	Extremely likely
2	Likely
3	Possible
4	Doubtful
5	Unlikely
6	Confidence cannot be estimated

Table 9.4. *Final rating: degree of trust associated with a piece of information*

It would certainly be possible to integrate other dimensions into the computation of the trust to be invested in a piece of information. For instance, we have chosen not to take account of the source's conviction. Were we able to estimate this doubt, it goes without saying that it would be extremely important to include it in the evaluation.[6] However, this would raise questions about the computation of the extent of the doubt, depending on the reliability and competence of a source.

In the same vein, we could envisage a factor reflecting the influence of word of mouth on the twisting of information. Besides the difficulty in machine detection and evaluation of the impact of such a factor, we think the doubts covered by this type of techniques would also be taken into account by the proposed model. If, on the other hand, it proves possible to reconstruct the original information, or to locate those responsible for the alterations [SZ 09], the contribution to the rating would be invaluable.

9.9. Architecture of information evaluation: characteristics

We have already mentioned the process which motivates our proposals for evaluation of the rating. Thus far, we have been presenting the general principle of construction of opinion, then extracting the axes along which we propose to evaluate the rating, in the previous section. The underlying process is crucial to our propositions regarding information evaluation. It structures not only the dimensions we use to rate information, but also the way in which we combine those dimensions, from the order of integration to its resulting sequentiality. Now we give a detailed description of this model which underlies our work and its implications, and then discuss some of its consequences, in section 9.11.

We consider the rating of the information as an indicator of the trust that can be invested in it. In order to establish a graspable and interpretable process of rating, we adopt a model for evaluating that

---

6 See Chapter 7 for an example of a semi-automated information evaluation method which makes use of this dimension.

trust. It is that model which we summarized above as the four questions applied to a piece of information:

1) Who is providing it?

2) What does he know about it?

3) Is it likely?

4) Has it been reported elsewhere?

Remember that we are not seeking to evaluate the certainty of the information: we are not interested in knowing whether the information is true, but rather in determining the extent to which we are convinced by it – be it precise, vague or uncertain. In order to achieve this result, we consider the process by which we are able to form an opinion about a hitherto-unknown piece of information. Having established the definition of the factors which we integrate to the evaluation of the rating, we now turn our attention to the order in which they are taken into account, which derives from our model. In order to illustrate this process, consider what happens when we learn something new.

9.9.1. *Order of integration of the dimensions*

Whatever the information in which we are interested, the first *a priori* factor which influences our opinion is our trust in the organ presenting that information to us. In fact, when we look for a piece of information, we lend preference to sources which are certain, as indeed search engines do for us. Similarly, our opinion is already molded by the person giving us the information – in this case, we shall suppose, it is a highly trusted friend.

It is only afterwards that we look at the competence of the source on the topic of the information, aided by our knowledge of his specialties, or the intersection of our tastes. If the information deals with emerging research in number theory, we can consider that our friend – an artistic photographer with not a trace of a scientific mind – is not the best source, but this should not call into question his usual reliability.

Whether it is reported as certain or – more likely here – in a vague and imprecise manner, we then consider whether the information does or does not contradict our own knowledge. For instance, the discovery of Fermat's own original proof of his last theorem – while it may be surprising – is not inconceivable.

Finally, to consolidate our opinion, we check whether the information is given elsewhere. The search for confirmation follows a similar path, and the correlations which stem from this enable us to decide whether or not we believe the information.

Here let us insist on the process of integrating the dimensions into the rating. Our trust in our friend is independent, as already pointed out above, from what he tells us – the effect of which is projected onto everything he tells us. His competence on the topic in question, or at least our perception of that dimension, intervenes only later in the forming of our opinion. Also, the plausibility of the information transmitted and then its corroboration intervene in turn later on. From these observations about the forming of an opinion, notably borne out by the existing body of literature on intelligence [DIS 01] and on journalism [BOR 98], we deduce the ordering of the chain of information evaluation represented in Figure 9.1. It is from here as well that the notion of projection of the dimensions onto the information stems, because those dimensions are more part of our own convictions than of the information *per se*.

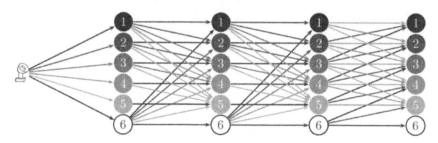

Figure 9.1. *Direction of the influence of the dimensions on trust: integration of the reliability of the source, his competence, the plausibility of the information and its credibility*

9.9.2. *Sequentiality of the information evaluation chain*

The information evaluation chain presented in Figure 9.1, which the rest of this chapter attempts to illuminate, thus formalizes the elaboration of trust. Apart from the order in which the dimensions are integrated, the chain model also presents information evaluation as a sequential process. The acceptance of our model lends itself to this conception, and this choice offers greater interpretability for the rating. The illustrative examples given below highlight the advantage to a comprehensible process of opinion construction. In addition, the constant availability of a rating reflecting the advancement in the process helps to track, understand and validate the result obtained. Sequential calculations are no more costly, and therefore do not hinder the implementation of the model, and the evolution of the rating in this presentation of the process gives clear expression to the influence of the projection of each of the dimensions.

9.10. Architecture of information evaluation: a description

The architecture we propose for the information evaluation process is therefore a formalization of the establishment of trust which we use it to represent. The information evaluation chain shown in Figure 9.1 gives an overview of its operation. This schema simultaneously represents the evaluation of the criteria and their impact on the evolution of the rating.

The sequential process of information evaluation is divided into four stages. The running rating, after integration of those dimensions which have already been evaluated, is represented by its current level: a number between 1 and 6 in a circle in different levels of gray for each stage. The complete scale is therefore present our times in Figure 9.1. The sensor represents the source, whose reliability may be activated at different levels. The arrows emanating from the sensor symbolize the impact of their level of activation on the initial estimation of the rating, to which they directly lead. Thereafter, the arrows represent the levels of activation of the particular dimension in question and indicate its influence on the rating. The intensity of activation of the criterion is symbolized by a variation in level of gray:

the darker the arrow, the more intense the evaluation of the dimension. Light-colored arrows, on the other hand, represent a minimum intensity.

9.10.1. *Reminders about the evaluation of the dimensions*

As we saw earlier on, the evaluation of each criterion, like the evaluation of the rating, operates on a different scale but one whose construction is the same – i.e. the degrees of activation of the criteria range from 1 ("high") to 5 ("low"), to which we add a degree of indecision 6 ("unquantifiable"). However, each evaluation has its own interpretation, as specified by Table 9.3.

This reminder is intended to draw the reader's attention to two points: the particular behavior when we encounter an "unquantifiable" rating, on the one hand, and the multiple arrows representing the impact of taking account of the dimensions corresponding to those levels of activation, on the other. As a consequence of the constraints imposed on the evaluation, certain arrows become indistinguishable, as explained below.

We shall now detail the usage of the process of information evaluation and present the expected constraints on the influence of the integration of each dimension. In section 9.11, we shall come back to the possibilities opened up by playing with these influences.

9.10.2. *Reliability of the source*

In the model of trust evaluation and in the information evaluation chain, we propose that the first criterion to come into play should be the reliability of the source reporting a piece of information. We therefore use the reliability of the source as an initialization of the information evaluation process.

Suppose we receive a new piece of information, which therefore has not yet been evaluated. Because this information is unknown, it is believed to the extent that we trust its source. Thus, the first step in the process attributes an unknown piece of information the level of trust

(Table 9.3, grayscale in Figure 9.1) equivalent to the reliability of its source.

9.10.3. *Competence and plausibility*

The stage of integration of competence into our process has a negative impact on the level of trust. Indeed, as the initialization of the rating takes place at the level of the trust invested in the source, we would undoubtedly have supposed that the said source "knows what he is talking about", or at least that we trust him to the level of that supposition. It is therefore natural that the only possible impact of competence is a negative one. If a completely trusted source is providing a piece of information outside of his domain of expertise, we are led to take that information with circumspection, whereas a source known for lies and manipulation will have difficulty in convincing us, even if he is talking about his specialty.

Similarly, when we take account of the plausibility of the information, it tends to lower the overall evaluation. If we believe a piece of information because of its source and if the source is competent on the subject in question, the fact that the information is possible should not reinforce our confidence, because we have begun by supposing it to be at least possible. If, on the other hand, all other things being equal, it seems improbable, we would begin to doubt it.

The arrows representing the impact of competence and plausibility therefore direct the rating downwards. The greater the level of activation of the criterion – i.e. the more competent the source or the more plausible the information – the less the rating drops by. All activation levels are considered, although there is no arrow for each one. This phenomenon is explained firstly by the implication of a total lack of knowledge and, secondly, by the fact that the constraints that we imposed are on the tendencies, rather than on the extent of the impact. We shall see, in section 9.11, that this flexibility means it is possible to adapt to each individual user.

In order to explain this phenomenon, note that we impose special treatment on an unquantifiable dimension. Because a lack of information does not enrich our knowledge, the rating does not suffer from the impossibility of evaluation one or other of the dimensions. If, for instance, the plausibility of the information "cannot be evaluated", the evaluation, after its integration, does not change, regardless of the current rating.

In addition, we can state that if it has been possible to evaluate the rating at any one stage, it will be possible to evaluate it at all following stages. Thus, no arrow points to an unquantifiable rating. Therefore, the lowest accessible level is level 5: "Improbable". Therefore, because competence and plausibility have a negative impact, a piece of information rated as 5 before one or other of these stages will not change, in spite of the activation of the dimension. The arrows for all these levels are therefore identical to the horizontal. Similarly, with the exception of a piece of information that is "extremely probable" (rated as 1), certain levels of activation become indistinguishable.

We still need to explain the particular approach for a piece of information rated as "level of trust cannot be evaluated". Such a rating is reached when none of the previous dimensions have been evaluated. In the absence of any knowledge at all, the first criterion which can be evaluated takes on the role of initialization. This explains why all trust levels are accessible for a piece of information which has not yet been evaluated, on the basis of the activation of the initialization.

9.10.4. *Credibility*

Unlike the previous steps, the last phase of corroboration of the information offers a possibility for the rating to increase. Indeed, the evolution of trust on the basis of confirmations and invalidations is a natural process. However, given that we envisage contradiction of the information, this criterion may just as easily lower the level of trust as raise it. This final step in Figure 9.1 therefore alters the rating in a unique manner.

Naturally, a piece of information rated 1, even abundantly confirmed, cannot be believed any more than it already is. On the other hand, the lowering of its level of trust is more limited than in the previous stages. Indeed, the five degrees testifying to a correlation between the pieces of information under consideration range between a positive (confirmation) and a negative influence (invalidation). Supposing that the credibility activated as "insufficient confirmation" is neutral, the negative impact is reduced to the minimum two levels. On the other hand, as it is impossible for invalidation to increase the rating, we only take account of the confirmations of a piece of information that was previously unqualifiable or whose current rating is minimal.

Finally, let us briefly return to the practical integration of corroboration into the information evaluation process. Remember that, in this stage, we compare already-evaluated pieces of information. While the trust invested in the correlated pieces of information does not enter into the evaluation of the activation of the credibility, it is sensible to take it into account in the evolution of the rating. In the same way as we lend greater credence to a column written by Andrew Wiles than to the affirmations of our friend when it comes to Fermat's theorem, the integration of invalidation or confirmation will be weighted by the *a priori* rating of the correlated pieces of information, as proposed by [BES 07].

9.11. Personalization of information evaluation: modeling levels of gullibility

The architecture we propose here has a certain subtle level of flexibility, which is precious to the user. Indeed, the arrows in Figure 9.1 represent the tendencies which we prescribe for the influence of each estimation of a criterion. However, we do not impose the strength of these influences. Given these degrees of freedom, the impact of the factors may be different depending on the importance the user attaches to each one. In addition, two users may have different configurations. These degrees of freedom therefore mean it is possible to adapt the method to the user and to represent different attitudes to levels of trust, as we describe in [REV 09].

Let us introduce the following definition:

STRATEGY.– A strategy of usage of the information evaluation chain is a set of intensities for the influence of criteria. For each dimension, the strategy gives the result of the projection of its level of activation on the current rating.

This definition leads us to what these strategies enable us to represent:

CREDULITY STANCE.– A credulity stance is an a priori choice made by the user about his expectations regarding the system's behavior. It represents the user's sensitivity to the various dimensions and his gullibility. The choice of a strategy determines the user's preferred stance.

It goes without saying that, if we are in the middle of the evaluation process, we cannot change our strategy.

In the rest of this section, we shall use examples to illustrate the notion of a stance of credulity for each of the stages, considering two extreme strategies and one neutral strategy.

9.11.1. *Reliability of the source*

Hitherto, we have presented the initialization of the chain of information evaluation as being a balance between the reliability of the source and the *a priori* opinion regarding the level of trust. However, the important point for us was less equivalence between the levels than the importance of the initial opinion. Indeed, we can imagine that a person with extreme skepticism will refuse to believe even someone in whom he has total trust, merely on say-so.

The columns in Table 9.5 show three different strategies regarding the reliability of the source. It provides the initial rating for each level of activation of the reliability of the source (from A to F, as shown by the rows). Strategy S_1 is the default strategy from Figure 9.1, with which we associate a neutral credulity stance. This associates A with 1, ... and F with 6. Note that apart from the need for equivalence between the "unquantifiable" degrees – meaning $F \equiv 6$ – any other acceptable strategy – i.e. where $A \geq B \geq C \geq D \geq E$ – can be used.

	S_1	S_2	S_3
A	1	2	1
B	2	2	1
C	3	3	2
D	4	5	3
E	5	5	4
F	6	6	6

Table 9.5. *Three strategies for integration of reliability*

We can see that strategy S_2 does not lend any more credit to a completely reliable source than it does to a source whose reliability is slightly lower. Similarly, with the lowest level of reliability (levels D and E), it retracts all trust (rating of 5). This extreme strategy represents a posture of skepticism on the part of the user. Conversely, the strategy S_3 remains open to a source whose reliability is shaky. That user begins to doubt if the source is absolutely not credible, but is prepared to believe any person who is relatively trustworthy. This strategy, which is even less common than the previous one, corresponds to a gullible user.

Consider three users (U_1, U_2 and U_3), each manifesting one of the three stances of credulity. U_1 is neutral, U_2 skeptica land U_3 gullible. Suppose that, in spite of the differences in their credulity, the three users have the same opinion about our photographer, whom they consider to be perfectly reliable. After initialization, each of them has an *a priori* stance of $c_1 = 1$ (for U_1), $c_2 = 2$ (for U_2) and $c_3 = 1$ (for U_3).

9.11.2. *Competence and plausibility*

Competence and plausibility have similar impacts on the evolution of the rating. For this reason and to make this document easier to read, Table 9.6 presents the same stances of credulity for both dimensions.

Yet this is not a constraint of the model. A user may, for instance, prefer to trust in the source's competence rather than in his personal knowledge of the subject.

	S_1	S_2	S_3
1	c	c	c
2	$\min(c + 1.5)$	$\min(c + 2.5)$	c
3	$\min(c + 2.5)$	$\min(c + 3.5)$	$\min(c + 1.5)$
4	$\min(c + 3.5)$	$\min(c + 4.5)$	$\min(c + 2.5)$
5	$\min(c + 4.5)$	$\min(c + 4.5)$	$\min(c + 3.5)$
6	c	c	c

Table 9.6. *Three strategies for integrating competence and plausibility*

This table proposes a different formulation of the strategies, as we suppose that the evaluation process has been initialized. Therefore, the influence of the evaluation of the dimension (between 1 and 6, indicated in the shaded columns) is calculated on the basis of the current level of the rating, c, and the combination is bounded by the extent of the evaluation scale, meaning that the evaluated rating must remain less than 5.

For clarity's sake, the case where $c = 6$ is not shown in the table. In that case, we would apply the initialization strategies shown in Table 9.5, with the activation levels for reliability being replaced by their equivalent for the dimension in question.

Suppose that our three users are unaware that the mentioned photographer is not well versed in mathematics and therefore suppose him to be competent, i.e. level 2. The integration of competence into their evaluation of his statements will therefore give: $c_1 = \min(c + 1, 5) = 2$, $c_2 = \min(c + 2, 5) = 4$ and $c_3 = c = 1$. We can already see a divergence of points of view depending on the users' respective stances of credulity.

All three users, in perfect harmony, also estimate that although it is surprising, the discovery of Fermat's proof is "realistic". The new update of the rating is: $c_1 = \min(c + 1, 5) = 3$, $c_2 = \min(c + 2, 5) = 5$ and $c_3 = c = 1$. The opinions range between the gullible, who believes the information, and the skeptic, who denies it. U_1, who is neutral, assumes the role of the agnostic.

Note that we can also represent a strategy by its association table for each dimension. The default strategy S_1 would, for competence and plausibility, have the association table represented in Table 9.7. We can see that as long as we do not try to represent more than one strategy, it is easy to include all combinations, particularly when $c = 6$. In addition, the development of the first column from Table 9.6 is again to be found here.

Activation of the dimension

		1	2	3	4	5	6
	1	1	2	3	4	5	1
	2	2	3	4	5	5	2
Current rating	3	3	4	5	5	5	3
	4	4	5	5	5	5	4
	5	5	5	5	5	5	5
	6	1	2	3	4	5	6

Table 9.7. *Default strategy: updating of trust, on the basis of the evaluation of the competence or plausibility*

9.11.3. *Credibility*

As previously stated, the integration of the credibility in the evaluation is a tricky business. On the one hand, this is the only dimension which can increase the trust rating. On the other, when it is projected onto the information, the *a priori* rating (the rating without the credibility) for the correlated information is taken into account. Table 9.8, once again, shows three different strategies for credibility. Again, the level of activation of the dimension indexes the rows in the table. We can see a variation in the contrast of the users, where the mistrusting stance favors invalidations over confirmations. Here again, we see the expression of the influence on the basis of the current trust rating. For the sake of legibility, we suppose that these expressions include the *a priori* rating for the correlated information. The modifications are, again, bounded so as to remain within the authorized range of levels of trust.

	S_1	S_2	S_3
1	$\max(c-2,1)$	$\max(c-1,1)$	$\max(c-2,1)$
2	$\max(c-1,1)$	c	$\max(c-2,1)$
3	c	$\min(c+1,5)$	c
4	$\min(c+1,5)$	$\min(c+2,5)$	c
5	$\min(c+2,5)$	$\min(c+3,5)$	$\min(c+1,5)$
6	c	c	c

Table 9.8. *Three strategies for integration of credibility*

Having learnt that Fermat's elegant proof has finally been discovered, the three users launch themselves – doubtless with different goals – in search of confirmations. As soon as they begin their search, they find Andrew Wiles' column, which admits the elegance of the new proof. A reliable source ($d_1 = 1$, $d_2 = 2$, $d_3 = 1$) and extremely competent ($d_1 = 1$, $d_2 = 2$, $d_3 = 1$) totally confirms a realistic fact ($d_1 = 2$, $d_2 = 4$, $d_3 = 1$), where d_i represents the rating of the new piece of information for the user U_i.

U_1 therefore is convinced ($c_1 = \max(c\text{-}2, 1) = 1$), U_2 remains doubtful ($c_2 = \max(c\text{-}1, 1) = 4$) and U_3, who has not changed at all, remains in agreement with himself ($c_3 = \max(c\text{-}2, 1) = 1$).

9.11.4. *Discussion*

This section briefly reviews the points of the proposed model whose constraints may seem significant. We also take the opportunity to suggest an avenue for potential refinement of the evaluation of the sources.

9.11.4.1. *Order and sequentiality*

The model proposed here presents information evaluation as an ordered and sequential process. This conception of the way in which trust is built may appear restrictive in the eyes of some people. Let us begin by reminding readers that there is no universally-recognized model of this phenomenon in existence. In addition, the presentation given here of the process of information evaluation is more rigid than we actually view that process as being. For us, information evaluation is not a finite process. As the dimensions can be altered during the process, the rating can also be re-evaluated. Also, although to us it seems natural and justified, the order of integration of the dimensions which we recommend is not set in stone. The presence for all the evaluations of an unquantifiable level means, in particular, that the inclusion of a certain dimension may be delayed or omitted.

9.11.4.2. *Updating*

After credibility in the evaluation process, the information in question was evaluated on the basis of the reliability of its source, his competence in the domain of definition of the information, the plausibility of that information in view of the evaluator's perception of the world and, finally, an indicator of confirmation between uncertain pieces of information. At this point, we can consider updating the reliability rating of the source, in the same vein as that proposed by [DEL 07], who updates the reliability of a source, when fusing different pieces of information, on the basis of its cumulative contradiction with other sources. This feedback of trust in the information regarding the reliability of its source is not part of the chain, but does have a very important effect. If a trusted source systematically provides unlikely pieces of information, it may be wise to review our judgment of his reliability, as shown by Figure 9.2. The rules governing the updating depend heavily on the source, and on the particular application. We see certain procedures for studying the reputation of sources of the literature as promising avenues to learn to qualify them in an automated fashion. This constitutes an important issue when handling large volumes of data, such as open sources.

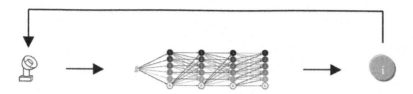

Figure 9.2. *Updating of the source's reliability rating*
following the information evaluation process

9.12. Conclusion

This entire book is dedicated to an essential task in the processing of sensitive data: information evaluation. Generally, both here and in previous literature and doctrines, information evaluation is considered to indicate the extent to which the events described by the information are accurate. Knowing whether the fact is real is, of course, of crucial importance for informed decision-making, but it may be difficult to evaluate. In such cases, most of us fall back on our own evaluation of the believability of the information, i.e. how much trust can be invested in it. Note that this evaluation is not contradictory with the previous one: before we determine whether a fact is real or not, we all have an opinion about how much trust to lend to the piece of information which alerted us to that fact.

This chapter looks at the formalization of such a process of constitution of trust, and then its evolution. Based on a simplified view of its establishment, a certain set of dimensions participating in its development are identified and described. It almost goes without saying that the selection, and definition, of the axes whereby trust evolves is debatable. However, as the objective is to propose a legible and interpretable model, each dimension needs to be interpreted in the same way by all users. Similarly, the next stage in the model, describing the influence of the dimensions on the trust, facilitates the sharing of evaluations between operators of differing levels of sensitivity.

This work opens up interesting perspectives for the study of trust. On the one hand, can humans be described by credulity stances? Are those stances constant or variable from one subject to another? How many different forms of credulity are there? The importance of the impossibility of evaluation, frequently mentioned here, also offers a whole area for future research. Must we, as we too frequently do, allow "I cannot say" to be equivalent to "whatever"? To what extent does this difference play a part in general human reasoning? Are we prepared to believe anything at all if we know nothing? The study of the evolution of trust itself brings out a variety of questions. Does the order in which pieces of information are discovered have an influence on the level of trust, if our gullibility remains the same? Finally, at the end of the chapter, we touch on the question of the source. When and how, for instance, do we change our minds about a source?

Many of the doors opened by the work discussed in this chapter correspond to essential themes in other research on information evaluation. Whatever way we conceive of it, information evaluation offers avenues for collaborations and other questions.

9.13. Bibliography

[BAT 06] BATINI C., SCANNAPIECO M., *Data Quality*, Springer, Berlin, 2006.

[BAU 02] BAUD J., *Encyclopédie du renseignement et des services secrets*, Charles Lavauzelle, Paris, 2002.

[BER 99] BERTI L., "Quality and recommendation of multi-source data for assisting technological intelligence applications", *Lecture Notes in Computer Science*, pp. 282–291, 1999.

[BES 07] BESOMBES J., CHOLVY L., "Information fusion: using an ontology to information evaluation", *International Colloquium on Information Fusion*, Xi'an, China, pp. 416–422, 2007.

[BES 08] BESOMBES J., REVAULT D'ALLONNES A., "An extension of STANAG 2022 for information scoring", *11th International Conference on Information Fusion*, pp. 1 635–1 641, Cologne, Germany, 2008.

[BOR 98] BORDEN D.L., HARVEY K., *The Electronic Grapevine: Rumor, Reputation, and Reporting in the New On-Line Environment*, Lawrence Erlbaum Associates, Mahwah, United States, 1998.

[BRI 98] BRIN S., PAGE L., "The anatomy of a large-scale hypertextual Web search engine", *Computer networks and ISDN systems*, vol. 30, no. 1–7, pp. 107–117, 1998.

[CHE 07] CHEN P., XIE H., MASLOV S., *et al.*, "Finding scientific gems with Google's Page Rank algorithm", *Journal of Informetrics*, vol. 1, no. 1, pp. 8–15, 2007.

[CHO 03] CHOLVY L., NIMIER L., "Information evaluation: discussion about STANAG 2022 recommendations", *NATO-IST Symposium on military data and information fusion*, Prague, Czech Republic, 2003.

[CHO 04] CHOLVY L., "Information evaluation in fusion: a case study", *International Conference on Processing and Management of Uncertainty in Knowledge-based Systems (IPMU 2004)*, Perugia, Italy, 2004.

[DEL 07] DELMOTTE F., "Detection of defective sources in the setting of possibility theory", *Fuzzy Sets and Systems*, vol. 158, no. 5, pp. 555–571, 2007.

[DEP 05] DEPARTMENT OF THE ARMY HEADQUARTERS, Human Intelligence Collector Operations, Field Manual, FM 2-22.3, 2005.

[DIS 01] DISS & DISC DEFENCE INTELLIGENCE AND SECURITY SCHOOL & DEFENCE INTELLIGENCE AND SECURITY CENTRE, Intelligence Wing Student Précis, 2001.

[HOR 07] HORN G. VAN, JOHNSTON L., "Evolutionary controversy and a side of pasta: the flying spaghetti monster and the subversive function of religious parody", *GOLEM: Journal of Religion and Monsters*, pp. 1–32, 2007.

[MIL 55] MILLER G.A., "The magical number seven, plus or minus two: some limits on our capacity for processing information", *Psychological Review*, vol. 101, no. 2, pp. 343–352, 1955.

[NIM 04] NIMIER V., "Information evaluation: a formalisation of operational recommendations", *Seventh International Conference on Information Fusion*, Stockholm, Sweden, pp. 1166–1171, 2004.

[REV 07] REVAULT D'ALLONNES A., AKDAG H., POIREL O., "Trust-moderated information-likelihood. A multi-valued logics approach", *Computation and Logic in the Real World*, Third Conference on Computability in Europe, Sienna, Italy, pp. 1–6, 2007.

[REV 09] REVAULT D'ALLONNES A., BESOMBES J., "Critères d'évaluation contextuelle pour le traitement automatique", *Qualité des données et des connaissances (QDC'09). Atelier des 9ᵉ Journées francophones extraction et gestion des connaissances (EGC)*, pp. A6 13–20, Strasbourg, 2009.

[REV 11] REVAULT D'ALLONNES A., Evaluation sémantique d'informations symboliques: la cotation, Doctoral thesis, Université Pierre et Marie Curie, Paris 6, 2011.

[SHA 09] SHAH D., ZAMAN T.R., "Rumors in a network: who's the culprit?", *Neural Information Processing Systems (NIPS)*, Vancouver, Canada, 2009.

[SIM 05] SIMON F., *Journaliste: dans les pas d'Hubert Beuve-Méry*, Arléa, Paris, 2005.

[TOC 35] TOCQUEVILLE A., *De la démocratie en Amérique*, Folio Histoire, Paris, 1835.

[WAN 96] WANG R.Y., STRONG D.M., "Beyond accuracy: what data quality means to data consumers", *Journal of Management Information Systems*, vol. 12, no. 4, pp. 5–33, 1996.

List of Authors

Mouhamadou El Hady BA
Cheikh Anta Diop University
Dakar
Senegal

Stéphanie BRIZARD
Invoxis
Paris
France

Philippe CAPET
EKTIMO
Cahors
France

Laurence CHOLVY
ONERA
Toulouse
France

Thomas DELAVALLADE
Thales Communications &
Security
Gennevilliers
France

Tanneguy DULONG
Invoxis
Paris
France

Bertrand DUQUEROIE
Thales Recherche & Technology
Palaiseau
France

Bénédicte GOUJON
Thales Recherche & Technology
Palaiseau
France

Alain JUILLET
Orrick Rambaud Martel
Paris
France

Christophe LABREUCHE
Thales Research & Technology
Palaiseau
France

Philippe LEMERCIER
French Department of Defense
Paris
France

Marie-Jeanne LESOT
Laboratoire d'Informatique de
Paris 6
France

Gloria ORIGGI
CNRS, Institut Jean Nicod
Paris
France

Frédéric PICHON
Laboratoire de Génie
Informatique et d'Automatique de
l'Artois
Béthune
France

Adrien REVAULT D'ALLONNES
Laboratoire d'Informatique
Avancée
University of Paris 8
Saint-Denis
France

Index

A, B

abduction, 253
abductive reasoning, 252–255
adjectives, 176, 177, 179, 180, 181, 183
adverbs, 176, 177, 179–181, 183
agent, 164, 168
aggregation operator, 189–192, 194–196, 210, 227
al-Adel, 111, 114, 115, 175, 181, 203, 205, 206, 211, 237, 238, 275
anaphora, 164, 175
answering systems, 163
antireductionism, 45, 47
argument, 168, 169, 174, 175, 180–182
asymmetrical conflict, 104
attributes, 164, 167–169, 174, 182
balldar, 111, 114, 115, 117, 118, 203, 205, 206, 211, 235, 243, 250–252, 254–256
belief, 231, 234, 237–240, 245–252, 254–256, 258

C

calibration, 221, 222
categories, 163, 166, 168, 183
certainty, 161–168, 170, 175–177
choquet integral, 131, 132, 138–141, 150, 152, 156
collection, 105
    intelligence cycle, 60, 62, 68, 73, 75, 76, 78, 84, 86, 89, 95, 99, 100
competence, 267, 271, 276–278, 281, 282, 286, 287, 289
competitive intelligence, 55, 56
complete (source), 232, 233, 237, 238, 240, 242, 245, 247, 249
confirmation, 272, 274, 278, 282, 283, 288
corpus, 162–164, 166, 168, 172, 174–176, 181–183
corroboration, 200, 205, 209
credibility, 39, 44, 49, 50, 108, 110, 112, 113, 115–117, 119, 120, 122, 123, 187, 188, 197, 233, 235, 245, 267, 273–275, 278, 283, 287–289
credulity, 284–286

D

Davidson, Donald, 5
deception, 10, 19, 20, 23, 24, 26,
    27, 30, 31
degree of confidence, 189, 190,
    197, 198, 211
Dempster–Shafer theory, 123,
    233, 234, 245, 258
dictionary, 162, 163, 172, 179–
    182
direction (intelligence cycle), 60,
    62, 95
discounting operator, 196, 208,
    223, 224
disinformation, 10, 18, 21, 23,
    26–31, 130, 149, 151
dissemination, 107, 124, 125
    intelligence cycle, 61–63, 96
dissimulation, 19–27, 30
doctrine, 103, 105, 107, 108, 110,
    112, 116, 118, 121, 125, 187,
    188
Dretske, Fred, 2, 4–6, 10–15, 17,
    31

E

Ektimostan, 24, 25, 27, 29, 111,
    113–116, 120, 129, 174, 205,
    206, 270–273, 275
Ektimostan Free Press (EFP), 251
entities (named), 162–164, 168,
    169, 173–175, 181–183
epistemology, 4
evaluation, 170, 171, 177, 181,
    183
event (extraction), 164, 168, 174,
    175, 177, 178, 180– 183
events (detected), 161
experimental
    evaluation, 189
    study, 190, 212

exploitation, 106–108, 124,
    125
    intelligence cycle, 59, 61– 63,
    65, 67, 75, 76, 78– 80, 85,
    86, 94–98, 100
extraction resources, 172, 182

F, G

factuality, 166, 167, 169, 170,
    171, 177, 179, 182
falsifier, 233, 240–245, 247–250,
    252, 254
Floridi, Luciano, 2, 5, 17–19, 21,
    23, 25, 26, 29, 31
folk psychology, 50
free resistance of dagbas (FRD),
    28, 111, 112, 116, 118, 173,
    202, 203, 212, 235, 243, 250,
    251, 252, 255, 262
fusion, 106, 118, 121–123, 125,
    200, 209–212, 217, 220, 223,
    224–227
fuzzy logic, 121
Goldman, Alvin, 38, 40, 41
grammar, 162, 163, 172, 173,
    175, 178–183
granularity, 108, 112, 115, 118,
    122
Grice, Paul, 2, 4–10, 14, 15, 17,
    31

I

immaterial field, 15, 16
influence, 16, 27–29, 266, 271,
    276, 278–280, 283, 284, 286,
    288, 290, 291
information capitalization, 63, 76,
    79, 84, 85, 89, 95
    retrieval, 85, 95
    valorization, 84, 85, 100

information and communication
  technology (ICT), 16
  evaluation, 17, 31, 103–109,
    111, 112, 119–125, 180,
    187, 188, 190, 191, 194,
    197, 198, 200, 209, 218,
    221, 226, 227, 234, 236, 255
  extraction module, 172, 175
  mining, 152
  society, 1, 3
  source, 129, 132, 133, 141, 143,
    147, 156
  warfare, 10, 16, 19, 25, 26, 30
informativeness, 221, 222
intelligence, 104–107, 109–114,
    121, 122, 124, 125, 163, 165,
    234, 30
  elaboration, 62, 65, 79, 80, 82,
    85, 87, 94, 96–99
  knowledge, 93, 94, 100
  understanding, 93, 94, 100
intoxication, 30, 31
Ixil, 111, 114–117, 175, 203, 205,
    206, 208, 209, 212, 275

K, L

knowledge, 35, 36, 38–40, 42, 44,
    45, 47, 51
  model, 79, 80, 82, 94, 96
linguistic, 161, 163, 164, 168,
    172–174, 176, 181–183
logic, 233, 234, 236–238, 240,
    245, 253, 256, 257

M, N, O

machine learning, 163, 164
manually-annotated, 166, 181
marker, 161, 162, 164, 178, 182,
    183

material field, 15
mathematical theory of
  communication (MTC), 3, 11,
    12
meaning, 179
message understanding
  conference (MUC), 162, 164,
    168
misinformation, 21
misinformer, 233, 240–250, 252,
    254
modalities, 164, 179
monotonicity, 132
multiple criteria aggregation, 131,
    132
  decision support, 133
  model, 148–150, 156
multi-valued logic, 120
naturalized epistemology, 5, 41
ontologies, 162, 168, 172–174,
    182
operation of discounting, 129,
    141

P

plausibility, 267, 272–274, 278,
    281, 282, 285–287, 289
possibility distribution, 190, 193,
    194, 196–198, 205–209, 211,
    213–216, 221–223
predicate, 168, 169, 174, 175
predicative noun, 175
Press Ektimo-Agency, 181, 235,
    243, 250
processing, 105, 106, 108, 125
  intelligence cycle, 60, 62, 63,
    67, 72, 75, 76, 78, 84, 89
propaganda, 30, 31

R

rating, 66, 69, 70–72, 76, 108,
  110, 112–121, 131, 141, 146,
  148, 152, 262, 264, 270, 272,
  274–290
receiver, 109, 113, 231, 232, 237,
  239, 245, 251
reductionism, 45
relations
  dynamic, 168
  static, 168
reliability, 32, 36, 41, 44, 46–48,
  108–110, 112–115, 117, 120–
  124, 129–132, 136, 140–150,
  152–154, 156, 161, 177, 179,
  187, 189, 196, 197, 199, 200,
  204, 205, 207, 208, 213–218,
  262, 265–267, 269–271, 276–
  281, 284–286, 289
reported speech, 164, 167, 170
resources, 162, 168, 172–176,
  181–183

S

semantic traits, 169, 179
semantico-logical model, 174
Shannon, Claude, 3, 4, 11, 12
similarity, 198, 203, 221–224
simulation, 19–26, 30, 213–215,
  218, 219
  in military context, 27
sincerity, 50
social epistemology, 35, 36,
  38–42
social network, 142, 145, 148,
  156

source, 63, 64, 66–74, 78, 84–86,
  95
  primary source, 66, 68–72, 170,
    171
  secondary source, 68, 71, 72
strategies, 138
strategy, 284–288
supergrammar, 180, 181
syntactic category, 179

T

tense, 170, 177–179
thesaurus, 162, 168, 182
transmitter, 18, 21, 25, 26, 113,
  239
trust, 35, 36, 38, 39, 42, 44–46,
  49–51, 112, 113, 119, 121, 123,
  130, 161, 179, 188, 189, 199,
  210,
  epistemic, 43
twitter, 130, 132, 140, 142–150,
  152, 153, 156

U, V, W

uncertainty, 132, 153, 161, 162,
  164, 168–170, 176–178, 180,
  181, 183, 190–193, 197, 202,
  207, 212–217, 221, 222, 226
Usbek, 111, 113–117, 122, 270,
  271
valid (source), 232, 237, 240, 242,
  243, 245–247, 249, 250
veracity, 18, 130, 149, 265, 273
verbs, 176, 177, 181
W3C, 172

CPSIA information can be obtained at www.ICGtesting.com
Printed in the USA
BVOW08*1843260115

385031BV00004B/34/P